Cambridge International Examinations

Skills Award

Information Technology

Standard Level

CAMBRIDGE International Examinations

Skills Award

Information Technology

Standard Level

P. K. McBride

CAMBRIDGE
UNIVERSITY PRESS

PUBLISHED BY THE PRESS SYNDICATE OF THE UNIVERSITY OF CAMBRIDGE
The Pitt Building, Trumpington Street, Cambridge, United Kingdom

CAMBRIDGE UNIVERSITY PRESS
The Edinburgh Building, Cambridge CB2 2RU, UK
40 West 20th Street, New York, NY 10011-4211, USA
477 Williamstown Road, Port Melbourne, VIC 3207, Australia
Ruiz de Alarcón 13, 28014 Madrid, Spain
Dock House, The Waterfront, Cape Town 8001, South Africa

http://www.cambridge.org

© Cambridge University Press 2003

This book is in copyright. Subject to statutory exception and to the
provisions of relevant collective licensing agreements, no reproduction
of any part may take place without the written permission of
Cambridge University Press.

First published 2003

🐾 Designed and typeset by P. K. McBride, Southampton
Printed in the United Kingdom at the University Press, Cambridge

Typeface AGaramond, FFDax, Century Gothic *System* PageMaker®

A catalogue record for this book is available from the British Library

ISBN 0 521 52528 4 paperback

TRADEMARKS/REGISTERED TRADEMARKS
Computer hardware and software brand names mentioned in this book
are protected by their respective trademarks and are acknowledged. The
content in screenshots of Web pages is copyright of the pages' authors.
Every effort has been made to reach copyright holders. The publishers
would be pleased to hear from anyone whose rights they have unwittingly
infringed.

The publisher has used its best endeavours to ensure that the URLs for
external websites referred to in this book are correct and active at the time
of going to press. However, the publisher has no responsibility for the
websites and can make no guarantee that a site will remain live or that the
content will remain appropriate.

Contents

How to use this book ix

Introduction to the award x

Conventions xi

1 Using the computer and managing files............1

Managing files... 2

Paths to folders 3

Managing folders 4

Skills builder 1: 5

Properties and attributes 6

Viewing files 7

Finding files 8

Skills builder 2: Files and folders 10

2 Word processing 11

Word controls and tools.. 12

Editing and formatting 13

Skills builder 3: Word processing basics 15

Bulleted lists 16

Indents 17

Tabs 18

Headers and footers 19

Templates 20

Page Setup 22

Skills builder 4: Layout 24

Pictures from files 25

Clip Art (Office 97) 26

Clip Art (Office 2000) 27

Formatting pictures 28

Tables 29

Formatting tables 31

Modifying tables 32

Worksheets in Word... 33

Skills builder 5: Images and tables 35

Mail merge 36

Skills builder 6: Mail merge 40

3 Spreadsheets 41

Excel screen and tools 42

Data and formulae 43

Skills builder 7: Basic spreadsheet skills 44

References and formulae 45

Using functions 46

Multiple worksheets 48

Logical formulae 50

Skills builder 8: Formulae and functions 51

AutoFormats 52

Inserting images 53

Creating charts 54

Formatting charts 57

Skills builder 9: Excel charts 58

Page Setup 59

Headers and footers 60

The Print area 61

Print Preview 62

Skills builder 10: Sorting and printing 63

4 Databases 65

The Access screen 66

Modifying databases 67

Skills builder 11: Modifying a table 68

Relational databases 69

Making relationships 70

Skills builder 12: Relationships 72

Queries using operators 73

Multi-table queries 74

Sorting the dynaset 75

Skills builder 13: Further queries 76

Forms 77

Modifying a form 79

Reports 80

Report structure 82

Modifying a report 83

Skills builder 14: Forms and reports 84

5 Electronic communications 85

Internet Explorer 86

Internet options 87

Show pictures 88

URLs, sites and pages 89

Searching from IE 90
Data from Web pages 92
Printing Web pages 94
Favorites 95
Skills builder 15: Data from the Web 96
Outlook Express 97
Outlook Express options 98
Sending e-mail 99
Reply and forward 100
Copying between messages 101
Copying from messages 101
Attaching files 102
Detaching files 103
The Address Book 104
Skills builder 16: Using e-mail 106

6   Presentations 107

The PowerPoint screen 108
Master Slides 109
Modifying slides 110
Drawing lines or arrows 112
Rectangles and ovals 114
Skills builder 17: The drawing tools 115
Objects on slides 116
Charts 118
Organization charts 120
Clip Art 122
Borders 123
Skills builder 18: Objects on slides 124
Animation 125
Transitions 126
Notes Page view 127
Notes and handouts 128
Custom shows 129
Skills builder 19: Printing and slide shows 130

Index 131

How to use this book

This book is intended for students on courses leading towards the Cambridge Skills Award, IT Skills at Standard level. It can be used in conjunction with the additional resources that are available on *Information Technology: CD-ROM for Foundation and Standard Level*. These include teacher guidelines and sample files, plus student checklists and pre-test exercises, supplied as Word documents ready to be printed as needed.

It is assumed that students have reached Foundation level competence, but there are revision pages at the start of most sections, covering the key features of the screens and the main tools. The first skills builder exercise in each section is designed to reinforce Foundation level skills.

Chapter 1, *Using the computer and managing files*, looks at how files are stored in folders, the attributes of files and folders, and how to find 'lost' files.

Chapters 2, 3, 4, and 6 cover the main applications in the Microsoft Office suite – Word, Excel, Access and PowerPoint – building on the core skills introduced at Foundation level. These chapters can be tackled in any order, though it would be best to start with *2, Word processing*, as some of the skills acquired there will be useful when you turn to the other applications.

Chapter 5, *Electronic Communications*, covers exploring the World Wide Web with Internet Explorer and the use of e-mail using Outlook Express. This chapter can be dealt with at any time.

The skills builders

In each chapter you will find two or more skills builder exercises. Each has been designed to reinforce and test your understanding of the skills and concepts covered in the preceding pages. Before tackling any skills builder, make sure that you have fully understood the material leading up to it. Several of the exercises require the use of sample files which are not included in this book. They can be accessed on Cambridge International Examination's website (www.cie.org.uk) and are incorporated in the Cambridge Skills and Careers Award pages of the Qualifications and Awards section. The sample files are also included on the supporting CD-ROM, *Skills Award in Information Technology: CD-ROM for Foundation and Standard Level*. After successfully completing all the skills builders in each chapter, you should be ready to attempt the Cambridge Skills Award assessment.

Introduction to the award

The IT Skills Award is a certificate of competency in using computer applications accredited by Cambridge International Examinations. It is based on two syllabuses designed to test skills at Foundation and Standard levels. This book is intended to assist candidates to develop and practise skills at Standard level.

The IT Skills Award syllabus is composed of six modules each of which can be tested at any time and in any order. Successful completion of any combination of five modules will result in the issue of the Cambridge IT Skills Award at the appropriate level.

The modules are:

Using the computer and managing files

Word processing

Databases

Spreadsheets

Electronic communications

Presentations

Word processing, *Databases*, *Spreadsheets* and *Presentations* are all tested in either Microsoft Office 97 or 2000 versions. *Electronic communication* is tested by practical exercises and some multiple choice questions and *Using the computer* is a practical test of managing files, using Windows Explorer.

When a candidate is ready to be tested in an application, the IT Skills testing software is used to check their work as they progress and to give immediate feedback on success, or, in case of failure to meet the required degree of accuracy, to provide detailed feedback on specific assessment objectives. The testing software provides automated and objective testing of a candidate's skills in the various modules. The software works in all versions of Microsoft Windows from 95 to 2000, and specifically with Microsoft Office 97 or 2000.

Testing in the Microsoft Office applications allows the candidate the full range of functionality of the software and tracks their progress through the activities of three-part tests delivered in random combinations. A time allocation of 45 minutes per test is allowed and timed by the software. As each part of the test is completed so it is marked and at the end of the test immediate feedback of results is given to the candidate.

The IT Skills testing software can be obtained by a centre from Cambridge International Examinations. Tests can be purchased and allocated to candidates by a centre administrator. The tests can be taken by the candidate at any time agreed by the centre. Immediate feedback of result is given to the candidate. The centre sends results to Cambridge at regular intervals, and, when a candidate is recorded as achieving the requisite number of module passes, a full IT Skills Award certificate is automatically issued.

Conventions

Menu items, labels on buttons, headings and other key words on the screen are shown in **bold**, e.g. the **File** menu, the **OK** button.

Filenames are shown in *italics*, e.g. the *tes.doc* file.

Anything which you are asked to type is shown in single quotes, e.g. enter the formula 'A1 + B2'.

Keys are identified by [brackets], e.g. [**Insert**]. Where two or more keys must be pressed, they are linked by a + sign, e.g. [**Alt**] + [**F**] means hold down the [**Alt**] key and press [**F**].

Menu commands may be presented in a short form, with > indicating the steps through the menu, e.g. 'open the **File** menu and select **Print**' may be written as 'use **File** > **Print**'.

Which Windows? Which Office?

There are currently six versions of Microsoft Windows and three versions of Microsoft Office in general use. This book has been written around Windows 98 and Office 2000. The screen displays, toolbars and menu systems shown here can be found either unchanged or with very slight variations in Windows 95, Me, NT and 2000, and in Office 97. Where the differences may be enough to cause any confusion, they are pointed out.

At the time of writing, the CIE software works on Windows 95, 98, Me, NT and 2000, and tests are available for Office 97 and 2000.

1 Using the computer and managing files

You should know how to:

- Start and close an application
- Use the keyboard and the mouse
- Select, copy, move and delete files
- Create folders
- Use Notepad to create a text file
- Save and print files from Notepad
- Make backup copies

You will learn how to:

- Manage files and folders
- Read and set file and folder attributes
- View hidden files
- Find lost files

Additional resources:

- Checklist 1: Using the computer
- Sample files and folders in the *Cambridge* folder

Managing files

You can move, copy or delete files one at a time, or in sets.

To select a block:

❶ Click on the file at one end of the block.

❷ Hold [**Shift**] and click on the file at the far end – you may need to scroll the window to bring the other end into view.

To select scattered files:

❸ Hold [**Control**] and click on each of the files in turn – click a second time if you pick one by mistake.

To select all the files:

❹ Open the **Edit** menu and choose **Select All**.

Move and copy files

To move or copy files use Cut or Copy and Paste.

To move:

❶ Select the files.

❷ Open the **Edit** menu and select **Cut**. The files will be removed from the folder.

❸ Go to the target folder.

❹ Open the **Edit** menu and select **Paste**. The files will be moved into the folder.

To copy:

Follow the steps for moving, but at ❷ use **Edit > Copy**.

Tip!

This is a revision page. Moving, copying and other basic file management tasks are covered in the Foundation level book.

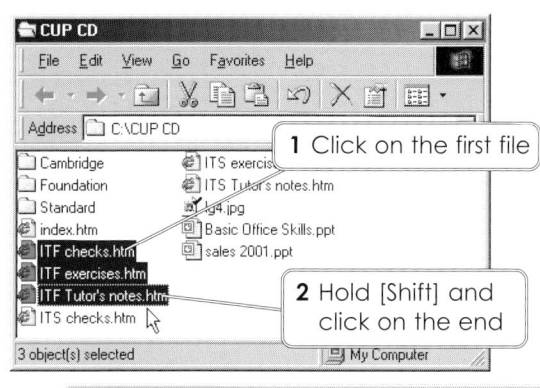

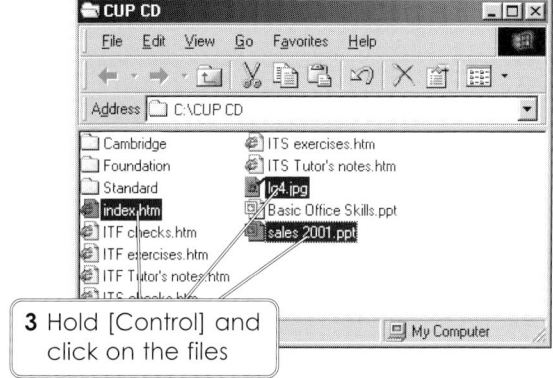

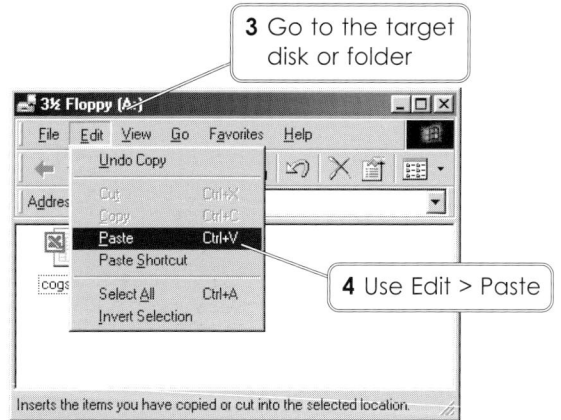

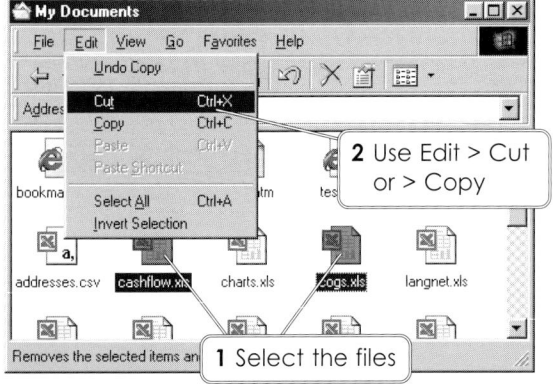

Paths to folders

The path describes the location of a file on a PC. It consists of the drive letter, followed by the names of the folders and subfolders in their logical order – i.e. the order in which you have to open them to reach the file.

The path to the current folder is shown in the **Address** box of My Computer or Windows Explorer, e.g. in the screenshots below the path to the folder is:

C:\Cambridge\Users\Archie\Job

The path to the selected file has the file name attached to the end, e.g.:

C:\Cambridge\Users\Archie\Job\CV.doc

Notice these features of paths:

➤ The drive letter is followed by a colon(:), e.g. *C:*

➤ A backslash (\) is used to separate the folder and file names.

➤ There may be spaces within a folder name, e.g. '*My Documents*', but there are no spaces between the names in the path.

When you are asked for the location of a file, you can type in the path, though it is usually easier to browse through a folder display.

> ## Tip!
> File and folder names are not case sensitive – 'cambridge', Cambridge' and 'CAMBRIDGE' are all the same to the PC.

The Address shows the path to the current folder

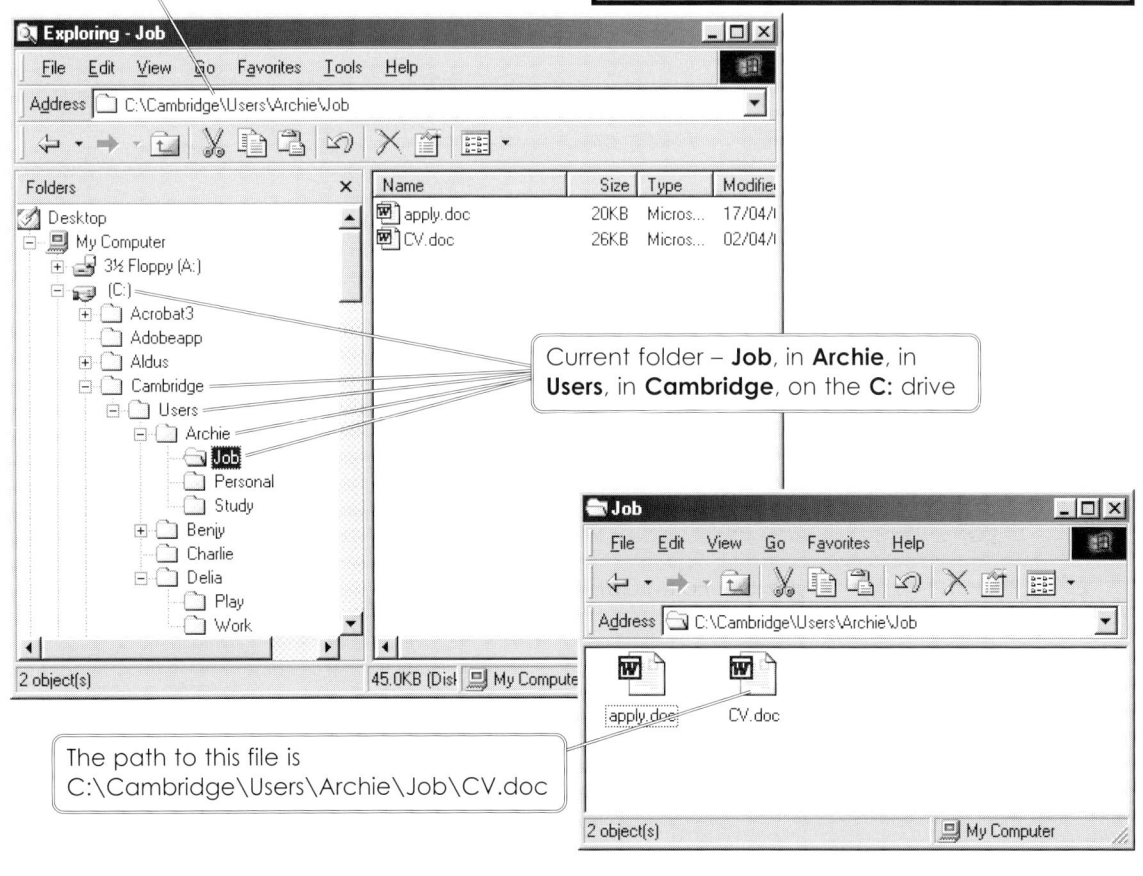

Current folder – **Job**, in **Archie**, in **Users**, in **Cambridge**, on the **C:** drive

The path to this file is
C:\Cambridge\Users\Archie\Job\CV.doc

Word processing

Spreadsheets

Databases

Electronic communications

Presentations

3

Managing folders

Folders can be managed using almost the same techniques as for files. The main difference is that you can only select one folder at a time, though this may contain subfolders.

Copying and moving

Key points when copying or moving folders:

➤ If you drag and drop a folder within a drive, it will normally be moved.

➤ To copy a folder within a drive, hold the right mouse button down while you drag and drop, then select **Copy Here**.

➤ If you drag and drop a folder from one drive to another, it will normally be copied.

➤ To move a folder to another drive, hold the right mouse button down while you drag and drop, then select **Move Here**.

➤ If you copy a folder within the same folder, it will be renamed 'Copy of …', otherwise the name remains the same.

Deleting folders

When you delete a folder, you will be prompted to confirm that you really want to move it *and its contents* to the Recycle Bin.

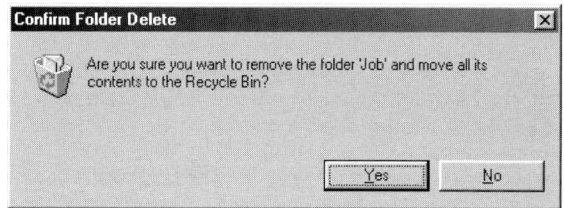

If you want to restore a single file from a deleted folder, you must restore the whole folder – you cannot open the folder in the Recycle Bin and select individual files.

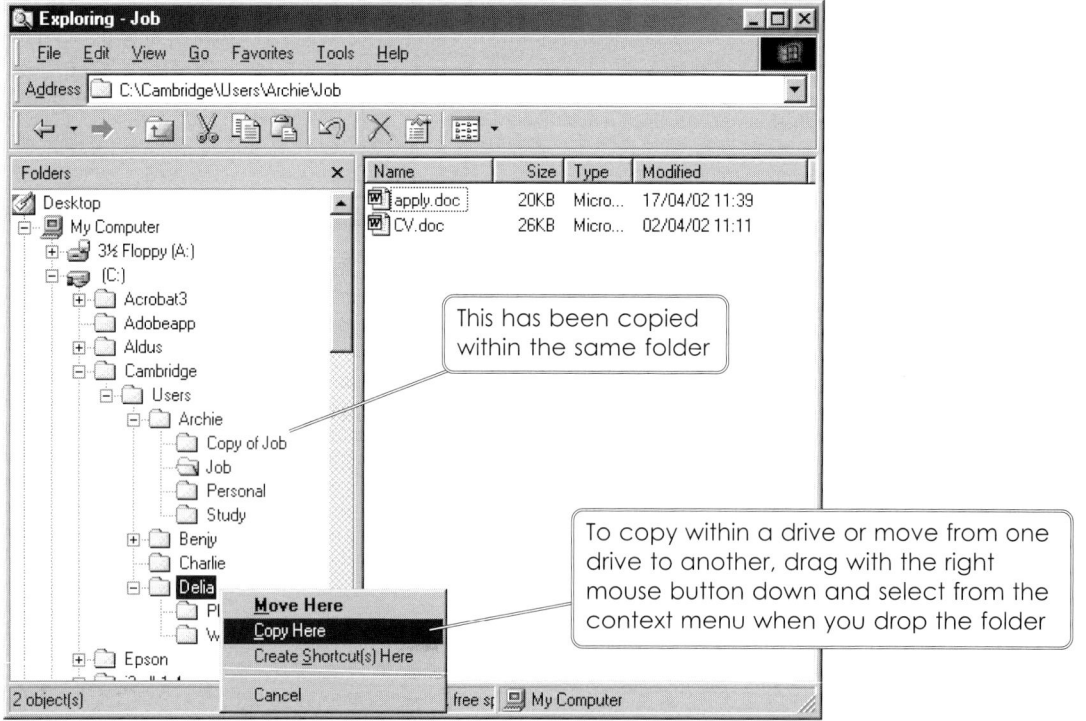

This has been copied within the same folder

To copy within a drive or move from one drive to another, drag with the right mouse button down and select from the context menu when you drop the folder

Skills builder 1:
File management basics

This exercise is designed to practise working with folders and to reinforce skills covered in the Foundation level course. If you have any difficulties, go back to the Foundation level book, and reread Chapter 2, *Using the computer and managing files*.

❶ Run My Computer and display **Folders** in the Explorer bar.

❷ Open the *CUP CD* folder and within it locate the *Accounts* folder. Copy it into your IT Skills folder.

❸ Locate the file *cashflow00.xls* in the *2000* folder. Right-click on the icon and select **Properties**. At the dialog box find out how large it is and when it was last modified.

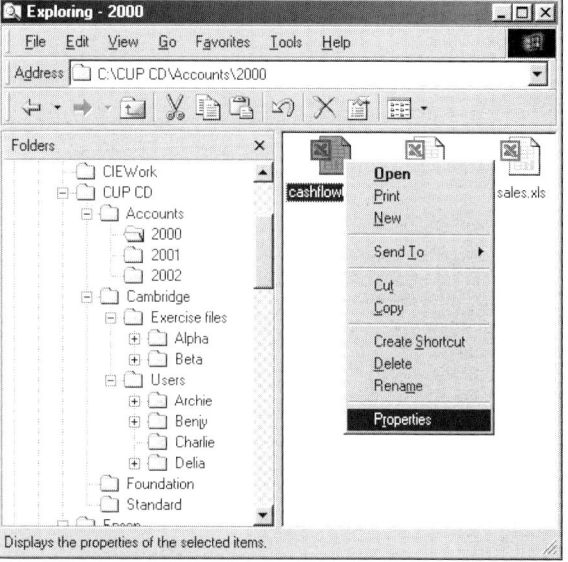

❹ The file *cashflow01.xls* has been stored in the wrong folder. Move it from *2002* to *2001*.

❺ Copy the file *invoice.xls* from the *2000* folder into the *2001* folder.

❻ In the *2000* folder, rename the file *sales.xls* to become *sales 2000.xls*.

❼ In the *2001* folder, delete the file *sales.xls*.

❽ Create a new folder, within *Accounts*, and call it *2003*. Copy into the new folder the following files:

   invoice.xls from *2000*

   cashflow01.xls from *2001*

❾ Use Notepad to create a file listing the skills you should already have, i.e. those under 'You should know how to' on the opening page of this chapter. Save the file as *preskills.txt* and print it.

Using the computer

Word processing

Spreadsheets

Databases

Electronic communications

Presentations

Properties and attributes

All files and folders have properties, which can be viewed through the **Properties** dialog box. Properties include their names, types, locations, dates of creation and last use, and their *attributes*.

The attributes control how the files and folders can be viewed and managed. There are three which can be turned on or off.

➤ **Read-only**, if on, allows a file to be opened for viewing or reading, but prevents it from being deleted or saved after editing.

➤ **Hidden**, if on, means that the file or folder may not be listed in My Computer or Windows Explorer. This depends upon the **View** settings – see the next page.

➤ **Archive**, if on, can be used by some backup software for managing automatic backups.

A fourth attribute, **System**, may be turned on by Windows to indicate that the file is essential for the operating system. Never delete a System file.

An attribute is on if its checkbox is ticked. If you select multiple files and look at their properties, the checkboxes may be ticked but shaded. This shows that the attribute is turned on for only some of the selected files.

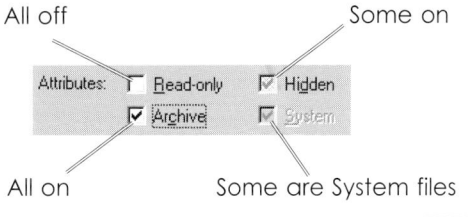

All off   Some on

All on   Some are System files

Setting attributes

❶ Select the file or files.

❷ Right-click to open the context menu.

❸ Select **Properties**.

❹ If necessary, switch to the **General** tab – Office files open with the **Summary** tab at the front.

❺ Click on an attribute checkbox to turn it on or off as required.

❻ Click **OK** to save the changes and close.

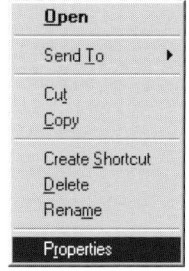

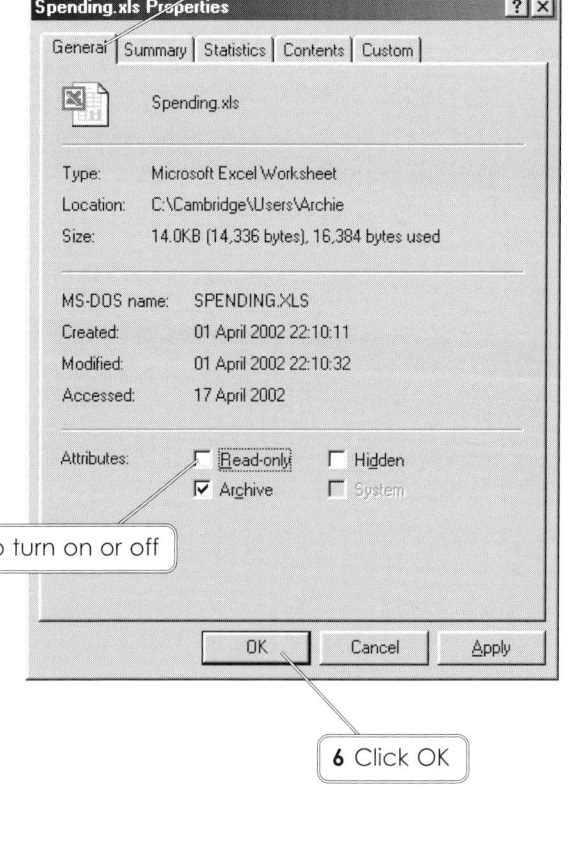

4 Open the General tab

5 Click to turn on or off

6 Click OK

Tip!

Read-only is the only attribute that you are likely to want to change. Turn it on to protect a file. Files copied from CDs have this turned on because you can't change a file on a CD. So you need to turn it off before you can work on the files.

Viewing files

My Computer and Windows Explorer offer many ways of displaying the contents of your disks. For example, hidden and system files can be displayed or not displated as you prefer.

If these these files are not displayed, they cannot be moved or deleted accidentally, but it is useful to be able to see hidden files when doing 'house-keeping' jobs.

You can choose to keep the files hidden in some folders, such as *Windows*, but visible in others, e.g. *My Documents* or other folders where you keep your own files.

❶ In My Computer or Windows Explorer, open the **View** menu and select **Folder Options**… (In Windows Me, the command is **Tools > Folder Options…**)

❷ Switch to the View tab.

❸ In the **Hidden files** area, select whether or not to show hidden and system files.

❹ If you want to apply the setting to all folders, click **Like Current Folder**.

❺ Click **OK**.

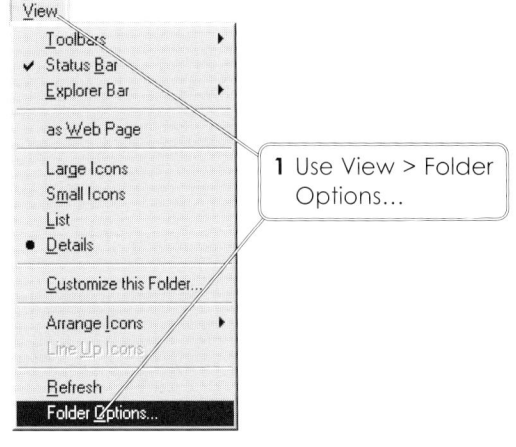

1 Use View > Folder Options…

2 Open the View tab

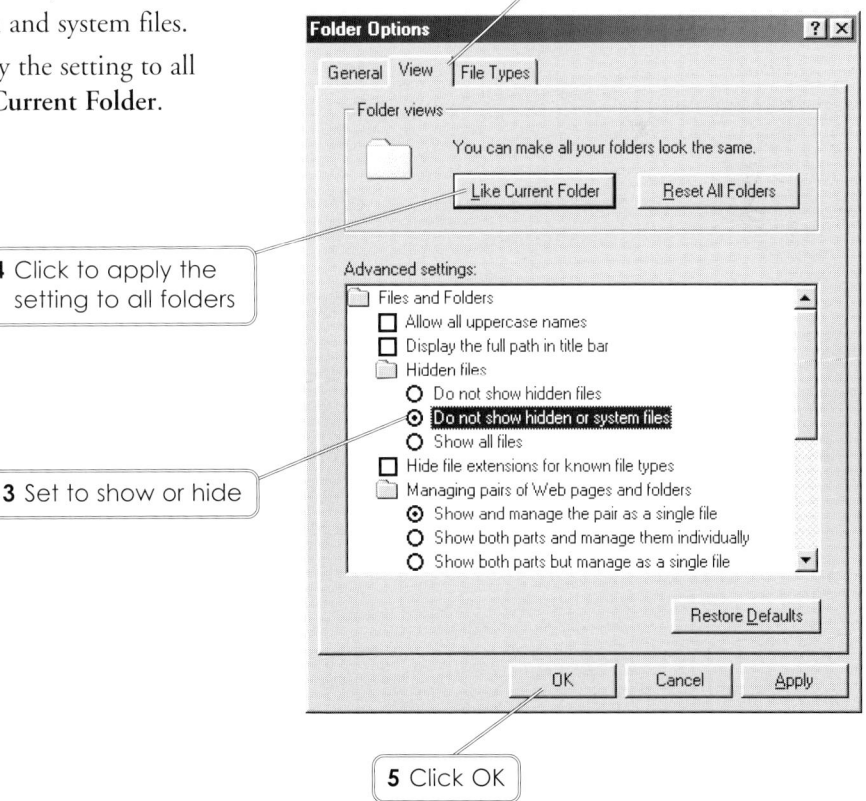

4 Click to apply the setting to all folders

3 Set to show or hide

5 Click OK

Word processing

Spreadsheets

Databases

Electronic communications

Presentations

Finding files

If you can remember the name of a file and in which folder you stored it, finding it again is easy. But sometimes you forget, or sometimes a file will be stored in the wrong folder by mistake – and without you realising it. A hard drive can hold hundreds of thousands of files, making it almost impossible to find a lost one. Fortunately, there is a Find utility, which can track down lost files, hunting for them by name, location, contents, date, type and/or size.

❶ In My Computer or Windows Explorer, open the **Tools** menu, point to **Find** and select **Files or Folders...**

Or click **Start**, point to **Find** and select it there.

The **Find: Files** panel has three tabs. Details of the lost file can be entered into any of these.

❷ Use the **Name & Location** tab if you can remember the filename, or any part of it. **Find** will look for any file (or folder) that contains the **Named** characters.

For example, if **Named** contains '*bill*', it would find files such as 'gas*bill*.xls', '*bill*s and beaks.doc' and the folder '*bill*s stuff'.

❸ If you know in which drive or folder the file will be, select it from the **Look in** list.

❹ Click **Find Now**.

Tip!

Remember that if you use Details View, you can list files in order of name, size, type or date. As long as you know the folder to look in, one or other of these orders will usually help you to locate a lost file.

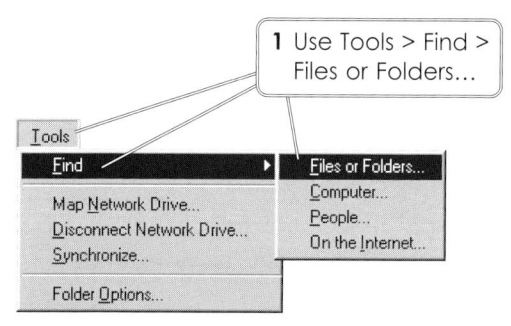

1 Use Tools > Find > Files or Folders...

4 Click Find Now

2 Enter all or part of the name

3 Tell it where to look?

Matching files will be listed in the lower pane

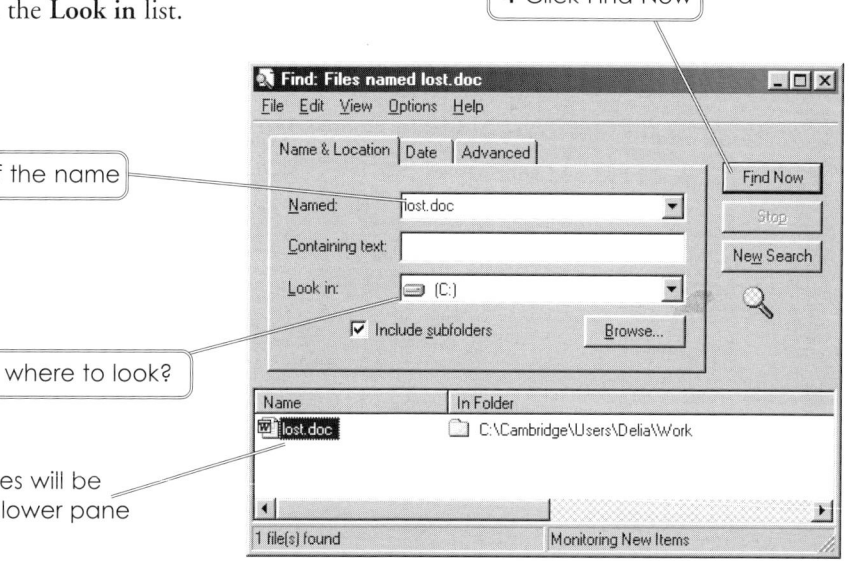

Advanced searches

If you cannot remember enough of the filename to identify the file, you may still be able to find it.

Containing text

This option is on the **Name & Location** tab. It is useful if the file contains some distinctive text, e.g. the name of a person, place, project or a significantly different expression.

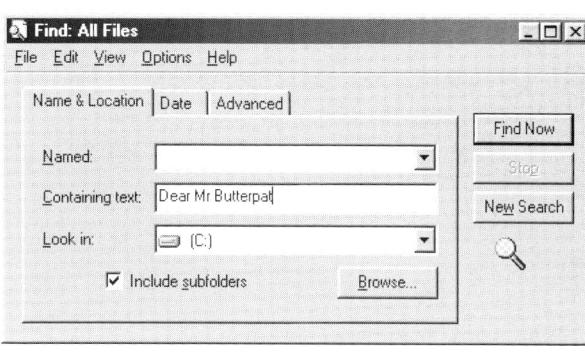

Date

Windows keeps track of when a file is created, modified and last opened. If you know when you were working on a file, you can set limits on the **Date** tab.

❶ Either select **All files**, or specify **Created**, **Modified** or **Last Accessed**.

❷ Set the **between** limits – the drop-down calendar provides an easy way to set dates!

Or

❸ Set the number of **previous months** or **days**.

1 All files, or those created, modified or accessed?

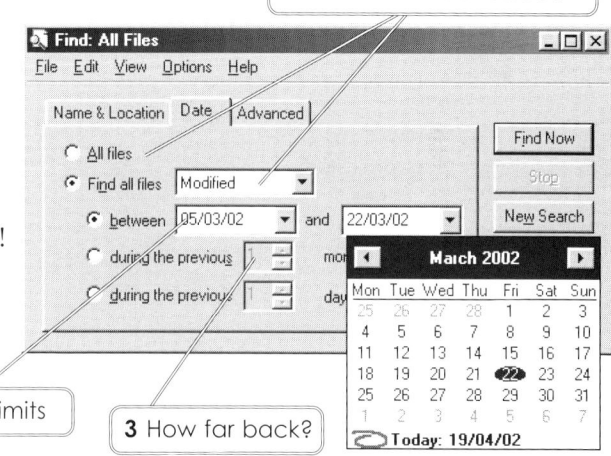

2 Set the limits

3 How far back?

Advanced

This is probably the least useful tab. You can select the type of file from the drop-down list, and/or set the minimum or maximum file size.

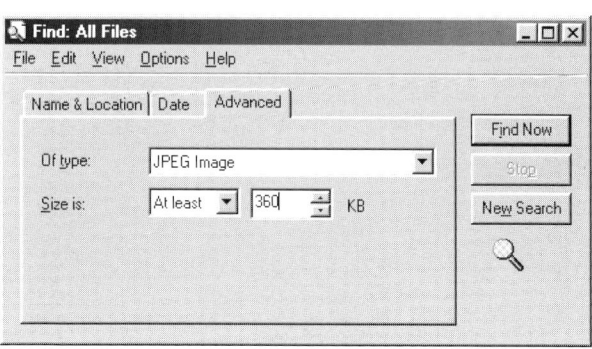

Tip!

In Windows Me, Find has been renamed **Search**, and looks different but is used in the same way. It runs in the Explorer Bar of My Computer, with the Date and Advanced facilities tucked into a drop-down area labelled **Search Options**.

Word processing

Spreadsheets

Databases

Electronic communications

Presentations

Skills builder 2:
Files and folders

❶ Somewhere in the *Cambridge* folder is a file holding the text shown on page 4. It is a Word document and probably has 'path' as part of its filename. Locate the file and write down its full name and path.

❷ Somewhere in the *Cambridge* folder is a letter to Mr Lee. The only thing that you know for sure about it is that it will contain the phrase 'Dear Mr Lee'. Find the file and rename it *Letter to Lee.doc*.

❸ Go to your IT Skills folder.

❹ Open *Accounts*, and copy the folder *2000* and its contents. Create a new copy within *Accounts* and name it *2004*.

❺ Sorry, we do not need that folder after all. Delete *Cambridge\Accounts\2004*.

❻ Locate the file *cashflow00.xls* in the *2000* folder and turn off its **Read-only** attribute.

Are you ready?

Get your tutor to check your work.

If you have successfully completed the skills builder exercises in this section, and are confident in using those skills, you are ready for the *Using the computer and managing files* CIE test.

If you need a little more practice before taking the test, ask your tutor for the *Using the computer and managing files* pre-test exercise.

2 Word processing

You should know how to:

- Open and close documents
- Create, edit and format text
- Use the spell checker and the Help system
- Save and print documents

You will learn how to:

- Use bulleted lists and indents
- Use and set tabs
- Use headers and footers
- Create documents from templates, and make new templates
- Import objects and images
- Create simple tables
- Create worksheets from within Word
- Use the mail merge facility

Additional resources:

- Checklist 2: Word processing
- Sample documents in the *Cambridge* folder

Word controls and tools

The controls and tools that you should know already, or which will be introduced in this chapter are labelled on the screenshots here (those covered in this chapter are shown in bold).

Tip!

These first three pages provide a quick summary of key word processing skills.

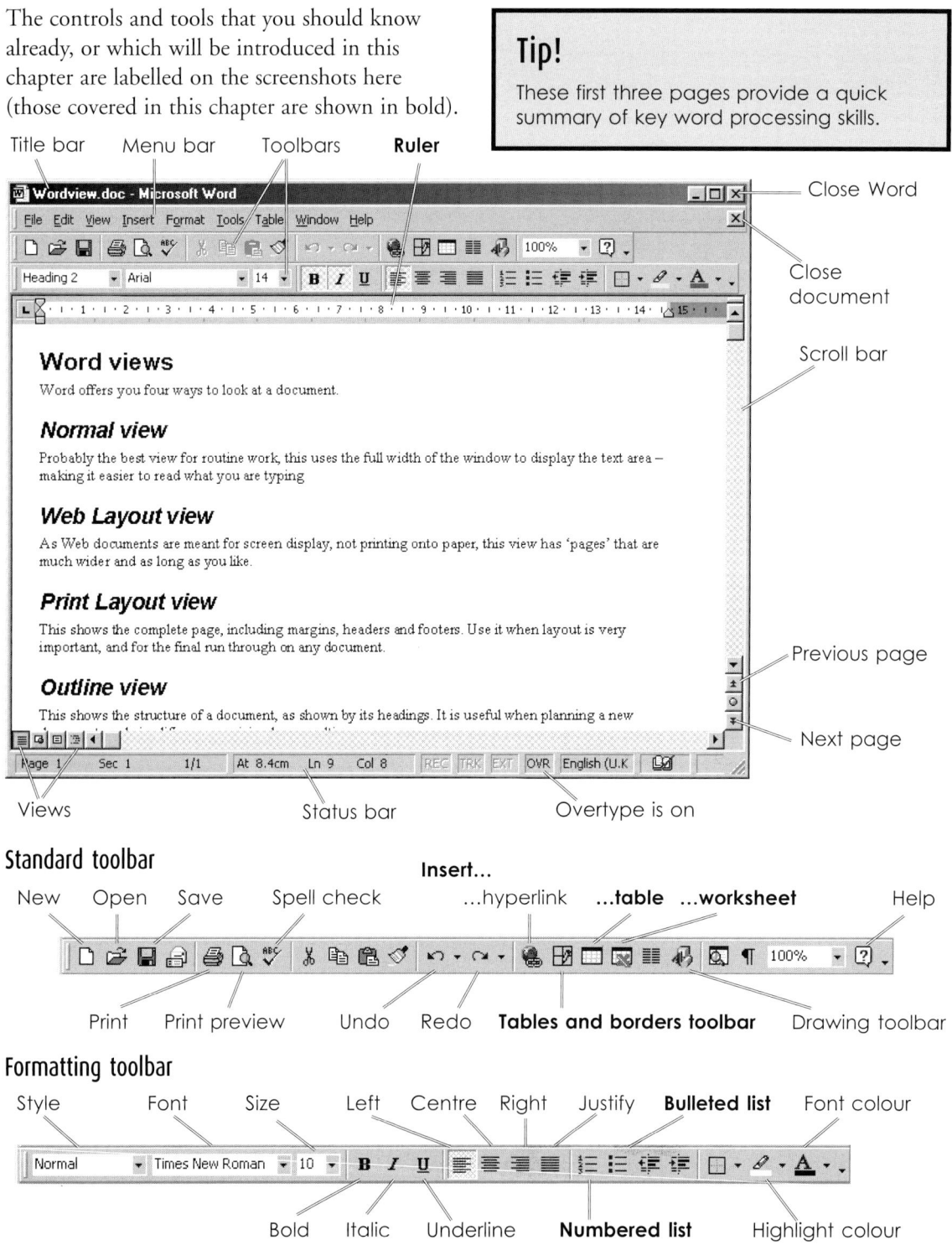

Title bar Menu bar Toolbars **Ruler**

Close Word

Close document

Scroll bar

Previous page

Next page

Views Status bar Overtype is on

Standard toolbar

New Open Save Spell check Insert... ...hyperlink **...table ...worksheet** Help

Print Print preview Undo Redo **Tables and borders toolbar** Drawing toolbar

Formatting toolbar

Style Font Size Left Centre Right Justify **Bulleted list** Font colour

Bold Italic Underline **Numbered list** Highlight colour

Editing and formatting

Selecting text

To select:

A word – double-click anywhere in the word.

A line – click in the margin to the left of the line.

A paragraph – triple-click inside the paragraph.

Any other text – drag from the start to the end.

Any size block – click at the start of the text, hold down [**Shift**] and move to the end using…

[**Arrows**] – one character left or right, one line up or down; one word left or right if [**Ctrl**] is held down;

[**Home**] – start of line; start of text with [**Ctrl**];

[**End**] – end of line; end of text with [**Ctrl**];

PgUp – one screenful up;

PgDn – one screenful down.

Text formatting

You can set the font, size, style and colour of any amount of text, from a single character to the whole document.

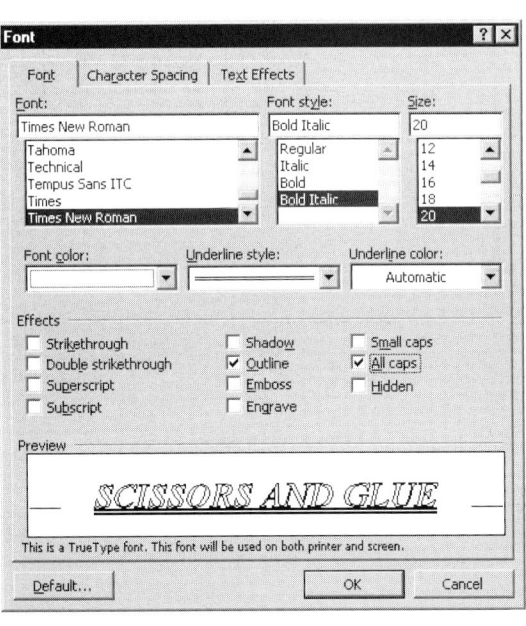

Most formatting can be set using the buttons and drop-down lists in the **Formatting** toolbar.

➤ Click a button to turn a format option on or off again.

Or

➤ Click ▾ to the right of the setting to drop down the list, then select an option.

If you want to set several font options at the same time, or you want to set one of the less-used options, you can do it through the Font dialog box.

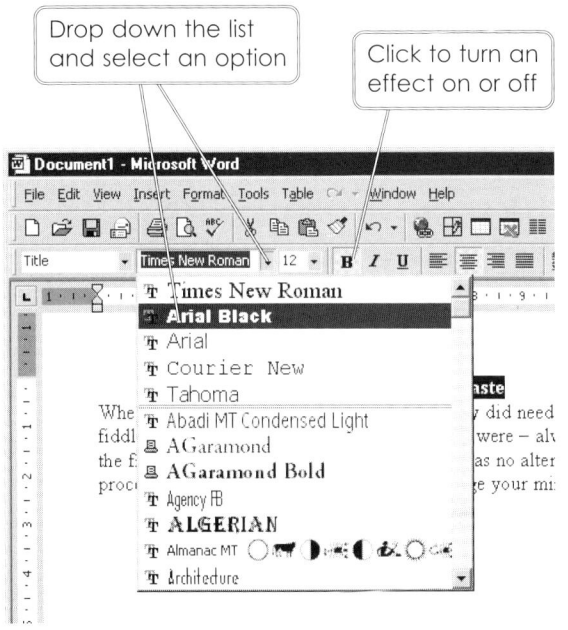

Use **Format > Font** to open the **Font** dialog box. The main options are on the **Font** tab. As well as the font, style, size and colour, you can also set the underline style and colour and some special effects.

The options on the **Character Spacing** and **Text Effects** tabs are rarely used.

Using the computer

Word processing

Spreadsheets

Databases

Electronic communications

Presentations

Paragraph formatting

Some formatting options can only be applied to whole paragraphs.

Alignment

Alignment determines how the text fits within the margins. Use the toolbar buttons to set the alignment.

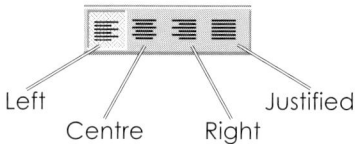

Left   Justified

Centre   Right

Line spacing

Line spacing refers to the amount of vertical space between lines of text. This can only be set through the **Paragraph** dialog box, using the options on the **Indents and Spacing** tab.

❶ Select the paragraph(s).

❷ Open the **Format** menu and select **Paragraph…**

❸ On the **Indents and Spacing** tab, drop down the **Line spacing:** list and select the level. Use **Double** spacing if you want to leave room for people to write notes on the printout.

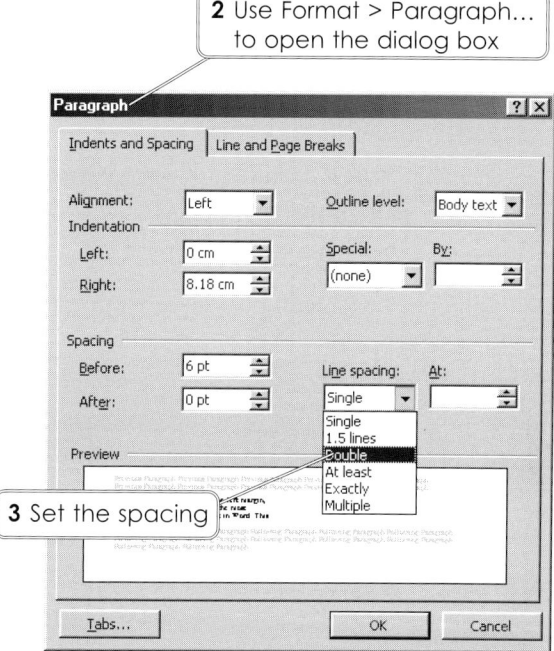

2 Use Format > Paragraph… to open the dialog box

3 Set the spacing

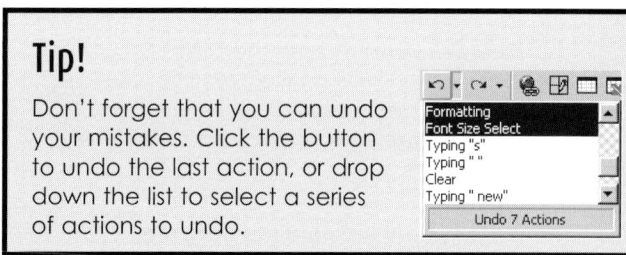

Tip!

Don't forget that you can undo your mistakes. Click the button to undo the last action, or drop down the list to select a series of actions to undo.

Skills builder 3: Word processing basics

This exercise is designed to reinforce skills covered in the Foundation level course. If you have any difficulties, go back to the Foundation level book, and read Chapter 3, *Word processing.*

❶ Starting from within Word, open the file *help.doc* in the *Exercise files* folder.

❷ Swap instructions 3 and 4, changing their numbers to suit.

Edit the new instruction 4 so that it reads:

'4 Click the Search button.'

The last line, starting 'You will be offered…' should be numbered '5'.

❸ Change the font of the title, 'Getting Help', to Arial, 14 point, bold, italic, and the sub-title 'The Office Assistant' to Arial, 12 point, bold. The rest of the text should be set as Times New Roman, 11 point.

❹ Run a spell check, correcting any errors.

❺ Print one copy of the corrected document.

❻ Save the edited file as *newhelp.doc* in your IT Skills folder.

❼ Use Word's Help system to find out what graphics file types Word can use.

❽ Copy the Help pages on Windows metafiles and bitmaps and paste them into a new document.

❾ Print the document to file, saving it as *graphics.prn* in your IT Skills folder.

Using the computer

Word processing

Spreadsheets

Databases

Electronic communications

Presentations

Bulleted lists

Bulleted (or numbered) lists can be created very easily, and in either of two ways.

You can:

➤ Turn on the bullets at the start, type your bullet points, then turn them off.

➤ Or create your lines of text first, and then add bullets to them.

Either way, the bullet points can be formatted afterwards as required.

Creating a bulleted (or numbered) list:

❶ Click the **Bullets** 📋 or **Numbering** 📋 button to start the list. A bullet/number will be put at the start of the line.

❷ Type the points, pressing [**Enter**] after each. A bullet will appear ready for each point.

❸ After the last point, press [←] to delete the unwanted bullet.

To add/remove bullets or numbers:

❹ Select the points, then…

❺ Click the **Bullets** button to turn bullets on or off.

❻ Click the **Numbering** button to add/remove numbers.

❼ To change the style, open the **Format** menu and select **Bullets and Numbering…**

❽ Go to the **Bulleted** or **Numbered** tab and select a style.

❾ Click **OK**.

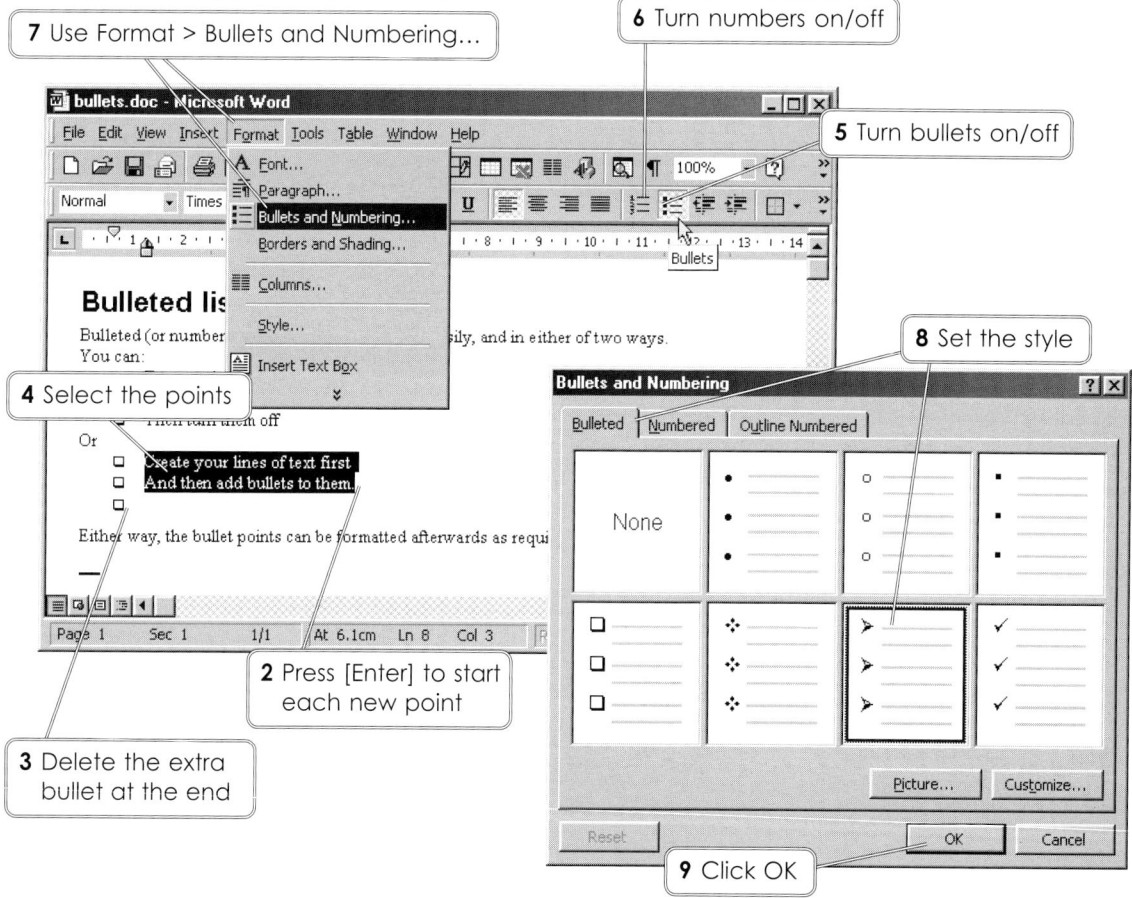

7 Use Format > Bullets and Numbering…

6 Turn numbers on/off

5 Turn bullets on/off

8 Set the style

4 Select the points

2 Press [Enter] to start each new point

3 Delete the extra bullet at the end

9 Click OK

Indents

The width of lines of text can be controlled by both margins and indents.

➤ *Margins* are printer settings and are defined in the **Page Setup** (see page 22).

➤ *Indents* position the text further from the margins, and are mainly used to pick out paragraphs for emphasis.

> Left and Right indents set the distance of all the lines from the margins. This paragraph has a left indent of 1.5 cm and a right indent of 1 cm.

First line indent sets the difference between the first and later lines. It can be negative – left of the left indent – to create a hanging indent, as here.

Indents can be set most accurately by typing values into the **Indents and Spacing** tab of the **Paragraph** dialog box, but it is simpler to use the indent markers on the ruler.

❶ If the ruler is not visible, open the **View** menu and click on **Ruler**.

❷ **To set the right indent**, point anywhere on the right triangle and drag it into position.

❸ **To set the left indent**, drag on the lower left triangle.

❹ **To set the first line indent**, drag on the upper left triangle.

❺ **To move the left and first line indents together**, drag on the square beneath the left indent triangle.

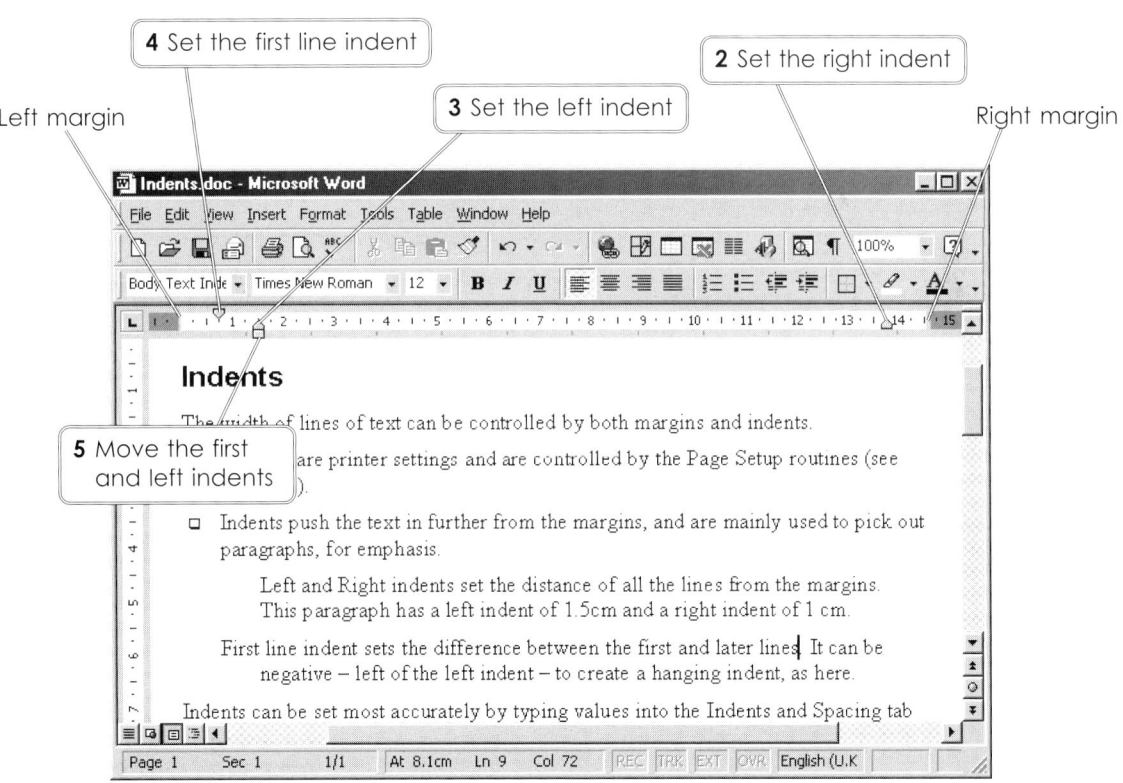

4 Set the first line indent

2 Set the right indent

3 Set the left indent

Left margin

Right margin

5 Move the first and left indents

Using the computer

Word processing

Spreadsheets

Databases

Electronic communications

Presentations

Tabs

If you are writing a price list, CV or similar document where text or figures need to be in accurate columns, you should use tabs.

By default, the tabs are at ½ inch (1.2 cm) intervals and left aligned. The position and the style of the tabs can be easily changed.

When you press the [Tab] key, the insertion point moves to the next tab position, moving any existing text across with it.

Tab styles

- **Left** edge of the text aligns with the tab.
- Text **centres** on the tab.
- **Right** edge of the text aligns with the tab.
- **Decimal** points align with the tab
- **Bar** tab draws a vertical line at the tab point.

Setting tabs

❶ If the ruler is not present, open the **View** menu and tick **Ruler**.

❷ Select the text for which you want to set tabs.

❸ The current tab style is shown at the left of the ruler. To change the style, keep clicking the icon until you see the style you want.

❹ Click on the ruler to place the tab. The default ½ inch interval tabs to its left will be removed.

❺ To move a tab, click on it and drag it into its new place.

❻ Repeat steps ❸ to ❺ to set any other tabs for the selected block of text.

❼ Click anywhere in the working area to clear the highlight from the text.

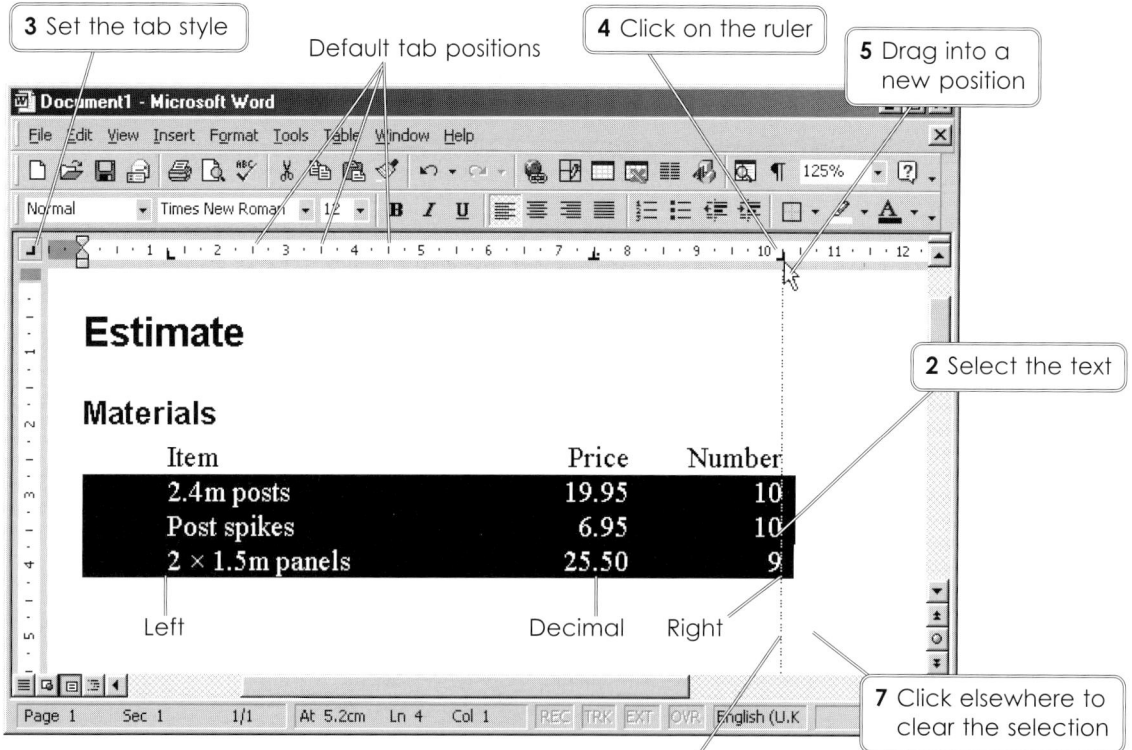

3 Set the tab style

Default tab positions

4 Click on the ruler

5 Drag into a new position

2 Select the text

7 Click elsewhere to clear the selection

Left   Decimal   Right

When you click on a tab, a dotted line shows its position in the text

Headers and footers

Headers and footers appear at the top and bottom of every page. They can display the page number, date and time, filename, author and similar file details, or any typed text.

The page number, date, etc. can be produced by field codes. These are replaced by the appropriate information when the page is printed. For example, {PAGE} tells Word to display the number of the current page.

The header and footer have tabs in place so that items can go on the left, centre or right.

To define a header or footer:

❶ Open the **View** menu and select **Header and Footer**. The header always appears first. If you want to start in the footer, click 🔲 on the **Header and Footer** toolbar.

❷ Type your text.

Or

❸ Select a field code from the **Header and Footer** toolbar.

❹ Press [**Tab**] to move to the centre or right and repeat step ❷ or ❸ if required.

❺ Click **Close** to go to the normal page view.

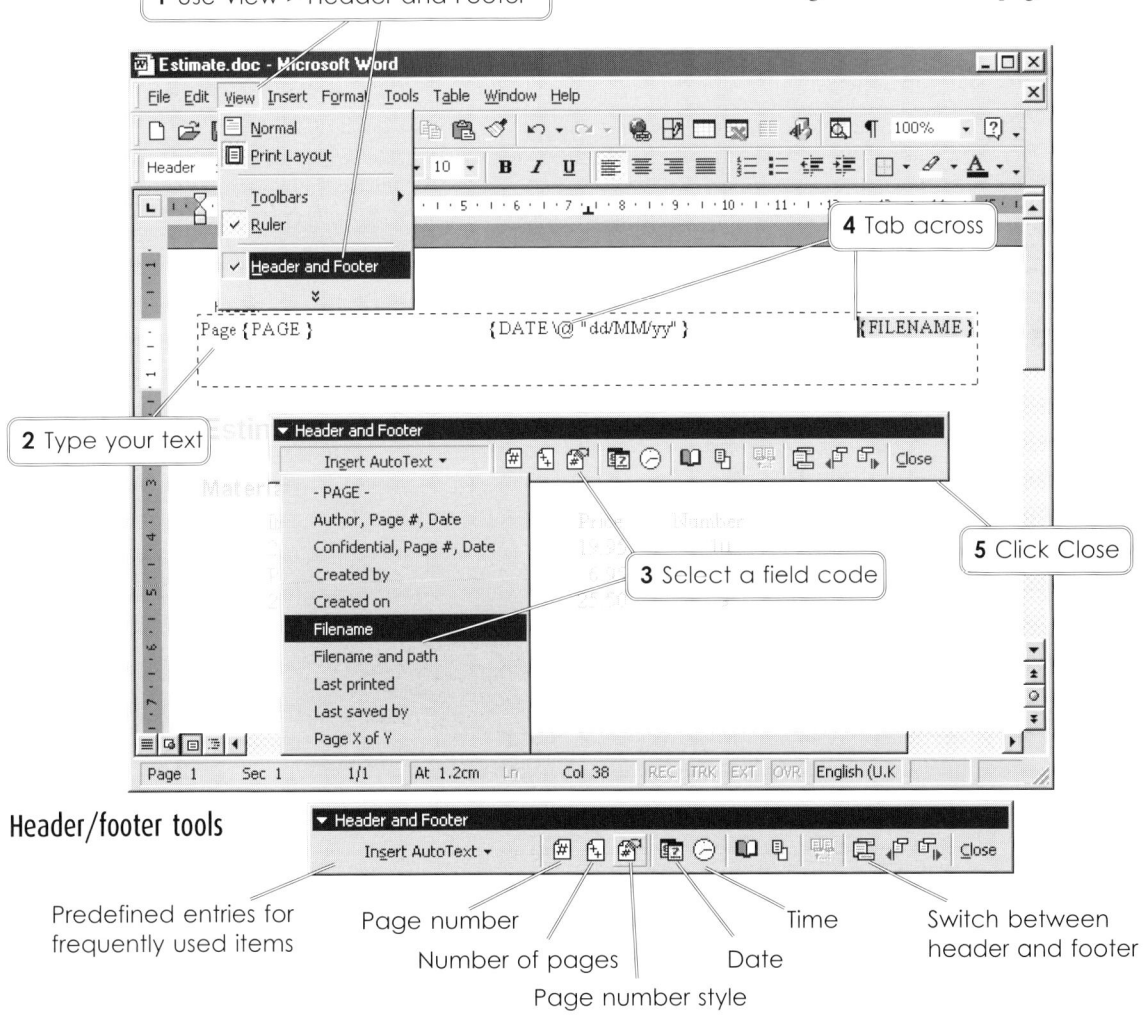

1 Use View > Header and Footer

4 Tab across

2 Type your text

3 Select a field code

5 Click Close

Header/footer tools

Predefined entries for frequently used items

Page number

Number of pages

Page number style

Date

Time

Switch between header and footer

Using the computer

Word processing

Spreadsheets

Databases

Electronic communications

Presentations

Templates

All documents start from some kind of template which sets up the basic design. Even the 'blank document' is a template, though this simply sets the page size and the fonts for the normal and heading text. Other templates may have more elaborate design features and suggestions for content and layout of the items to include in the new document.

❶ Open the **File** menu and select **New**.

❷ At the **New** dialog box, click on a tab to bring its set of templates to the front.

❸ Click on a template to see its preview.

❹ When you find a suitable template, click **OK**.

❺ Click into the prompts and replace them with your own details and other text.

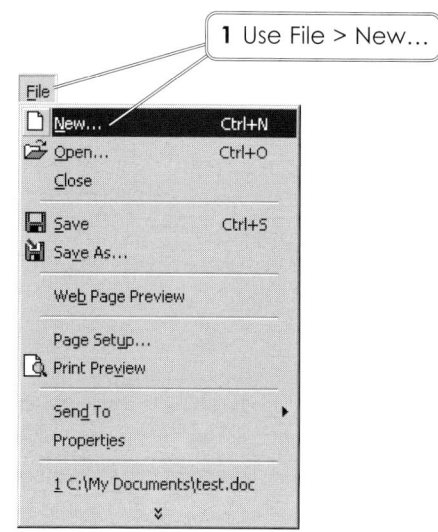

1 Use File > New...

If you had an earlier version of Office, its templates will also be available

2 Select a tab

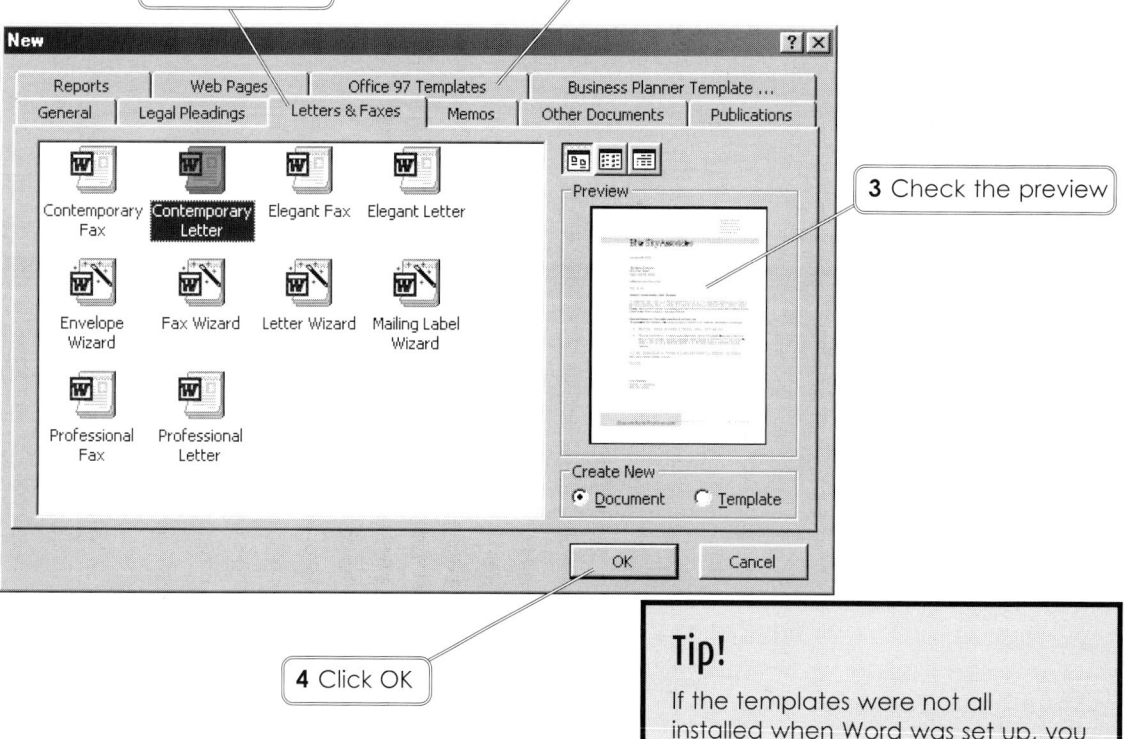

3 Check the preview

4 Click OK

> ## Tip!
>
> If the templates were not all installed when Word was set up, you may need to put the Office 2000 CD into the CD-drive to use them.

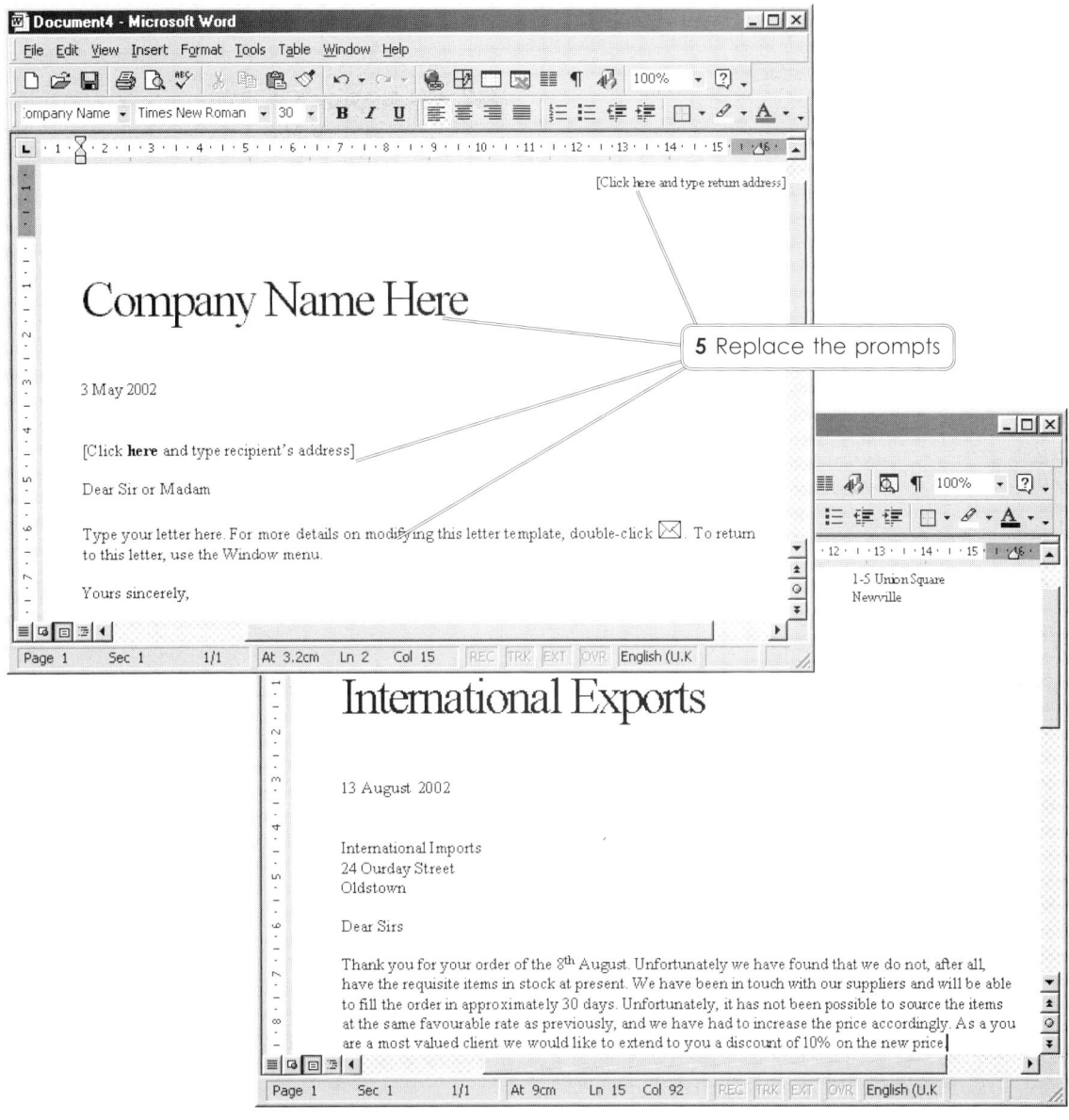

Making your own templates

You can create your own templates for everything from headed notepaper to draft contracts. Set up a document with a suitable design and layout and all the fixed information, but leave out any specific details – the name of the person, the quote for the job, the text of the letter, and so on – then save it as a template.

❶ Starting from a template or blank document, enter the fixed text and other items.

❷ Open the **File** menu and select **Save As…**

❸ From the **Save as type** drop-down list select *Document template*.

❹ Enter a filename.

❺ Click **Save**.

Using the computer

Word processing

Spreadsheets

Databases

Electronic communications

Presentations

Page Setup

The settings in the **Page Setup** dialog box control the overall size and layout of the page. The two most important aspects are on the **Paper Size** and **Margins** tabs.

Paper Size

Check this when you first use Word and make sure that it is set up for the paper that is loaded into your printer.

If the default size is correct, you only need to come to this tab if you are printing envelopes or unusual-sized paper, or if you want to print landscape (sideways) instead of Portrait.

❶ Open the **File** menu and select **Page Setup…**

❷ Go to the **Paper Size** tab.

❸ Check the **Paper size** and select a new size from the drop-down list if necessary.

❹ If you want to print with the paper sideways, set the **Orientation** to *Landscape*.

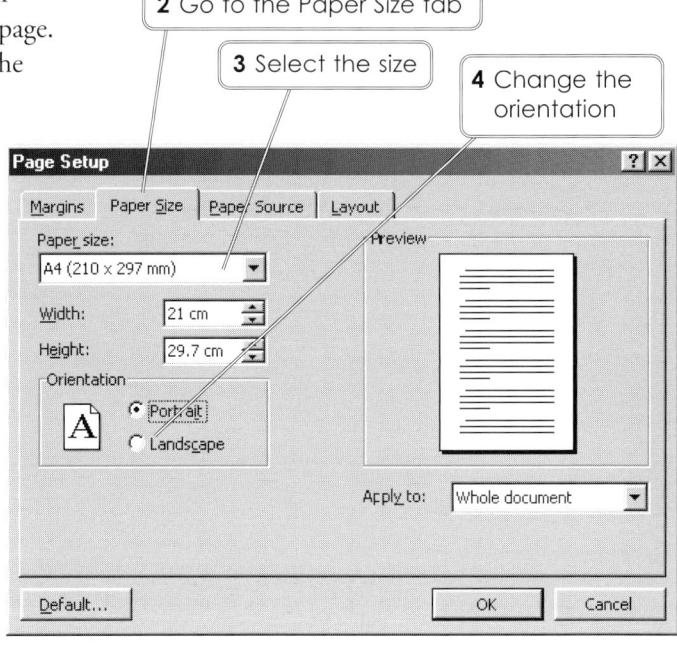

Margins

The margins are the areas around the edge of the page where text cannot be typed (except for headers and footers – see page 19). They are normally the same for the whole document.

The main settings are the distances from the page edges. The defaults are 1 inch (2.54 cm) for the top and bottom, and 1¼ inches (3.17 cm) on the left and right. You must always have some margins. The minimum depends upon the printer, but is typically 1 cm all round.

The default settings assume that the sheets will be printed on one side only.

If the sheets are to be stapled or bound, an extra margin – the **gutter** – can be added on either the left or top of the page.

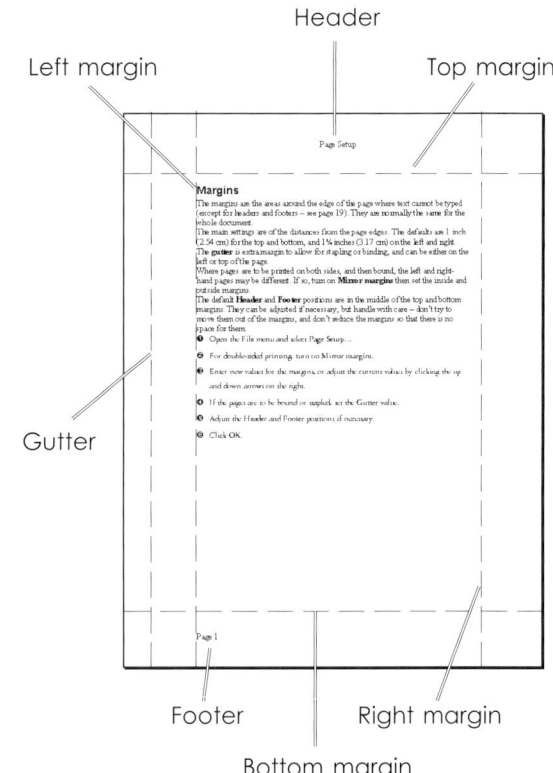

Where pages are to be printed on both sides, and then bound, the left- and right-hand pages may be different. If so, turn on **Mirror margins** – so that the settings on one side are a mirror image of the other – then set the inside and outside margins.

The default **Header** and **Footer** positions are in the middle of the top and bottom margins. They can be adjusted if necessary, but be careful – don't try to move them out of the margins, and don't reduce the margins so that there is no space for them.

❶ Open the **File** menu and select **Page Setup…**

❷ Go to the **Margins** tab.

❸ For double-sided printing, turn on **Mirror margins**.

❹ Enter new values for the margins, or adjust the current values by clicking the up and down arrows on the right.

❺ If the pages are to be bound or stapled, set the **Gutter** value.

❻ Adjust the **Header** and **Footer** positions if necessary.

❼ Click **OK**.

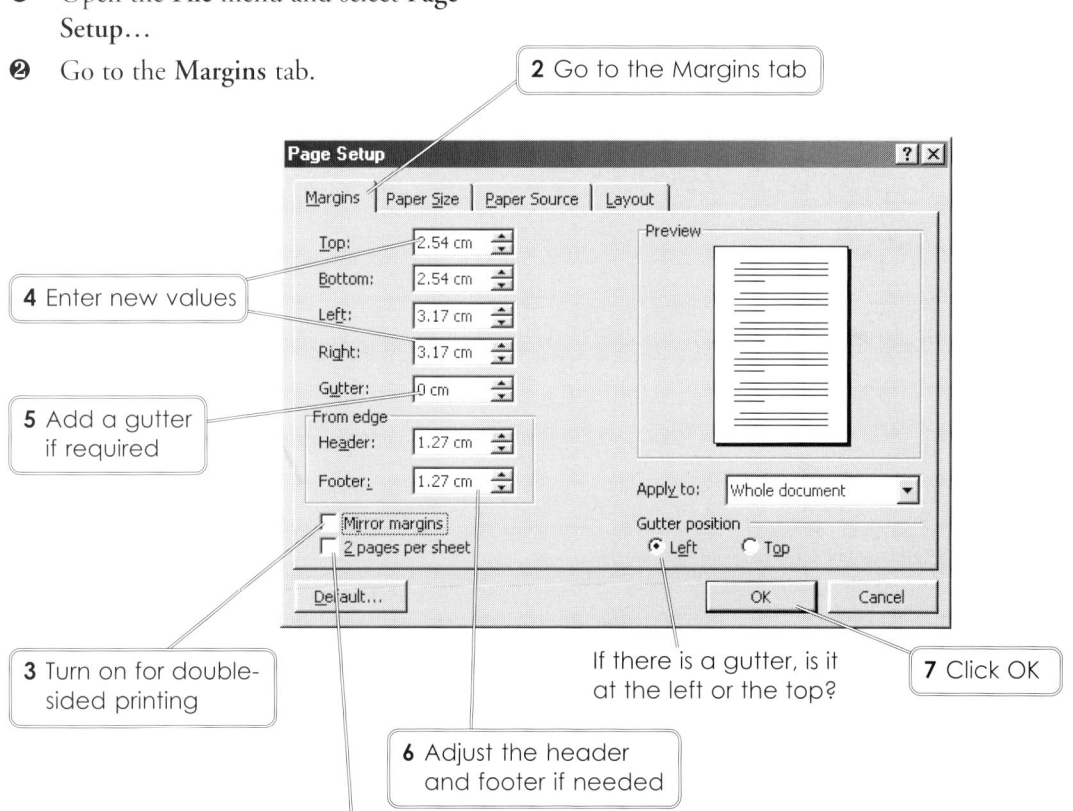

2 Go to the Margins tab

4 Enter new values

5 Add a gutter if required

3 Turn on for double-sided printing

6 Adjust the header and footer if needed

If there is a gutter, is it at the left or the top?

7 Click OK

Could be used to produce small flyers – the sheets would need to be cut after printing

Using the computer

Word processing

Spreadsheets

Databases

Electronic communications

Presentations

Skills builder 4: Layout

❶ Start a new Word file.

❷ Set the margins as follows:

Top	2.5 cm
Bottom	4.0 cm
Left	3.0 cm
Right	3.0 cm
Header	1.5 cm
Footer	2.0 cm

The page size should be A4.

❸ Type in a contents list for this chapter up to here, as shown below, putting a single tab between the pages' headings and their numbers.

❹ Set the heading in Arial, bold, 14 point.

❺ Use the ruler to set the indents and tabs for the contents display.

Set the left indent at 1 cm.

Set a right tab at 11 cm.

❻ In the header, write the text 'IT Skills: Standard Level'.

❼ In the footer, display the page number and the current date.

❽ Save the document as a template, with the name *IT contents*.

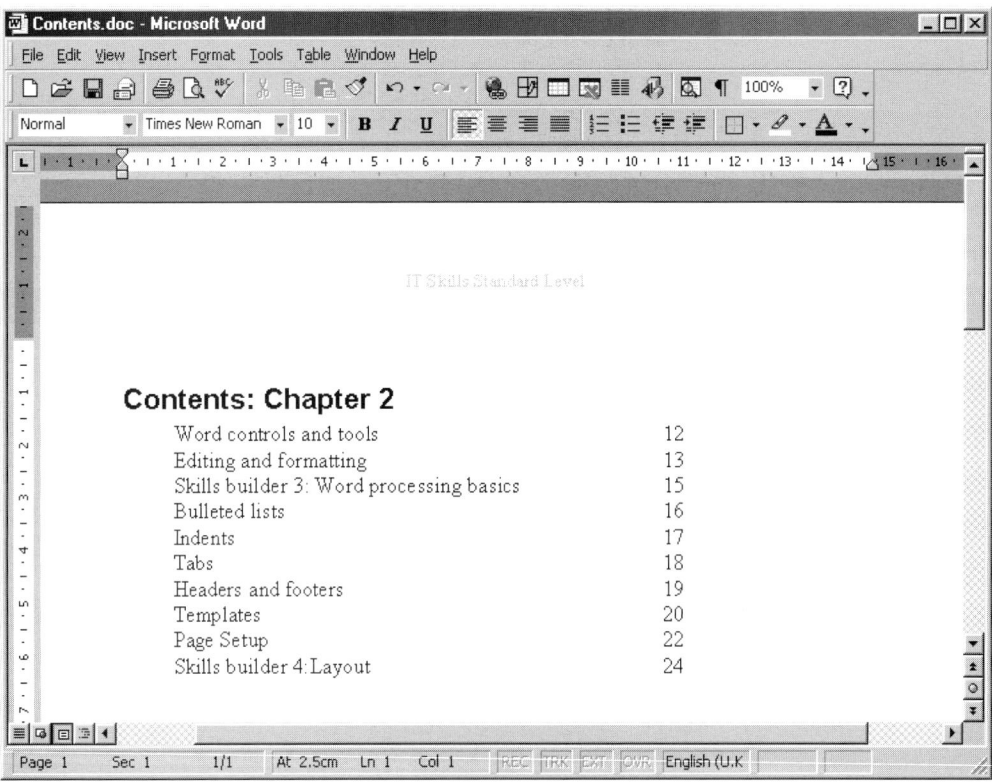

Inside the screenshot:

Contents: Chapter 2

Word controls and tools	12
Editing and formatting	13
Skills builder 3: Word processing basics	15
Bulleted lists	16
Indents	17
Tabs	18
Headers and footers	19
Templates	20
Page Setup	22
Skills builder 4: Layout	24

Pictures from files

Word can handle graphics files in many formats including BMP, JPG, GIF, Photo CD and possibly many more, depending upon which graphic converter routines have been installed. The pictures may have been captured by a scanner or digitial camera, downloaded from the Web, or drawn in a graphics program.

To insert a picture:

❶ Open the **Insert** menu, point to **Picture**, then select **From File...**

Or

❷ Click [img] on the **Picture** toolbar.

❸ Go to the picture's folder in the **Look in** box.

❹ If there are a lot of pictures, use the **Files of type** box to filter out the right type.

❺ Select a picture, checking its preview.

❻ Click **Insert**.

Using the computer

Word processing

Spreadsheets

Databases

Electronic communications

Presentations

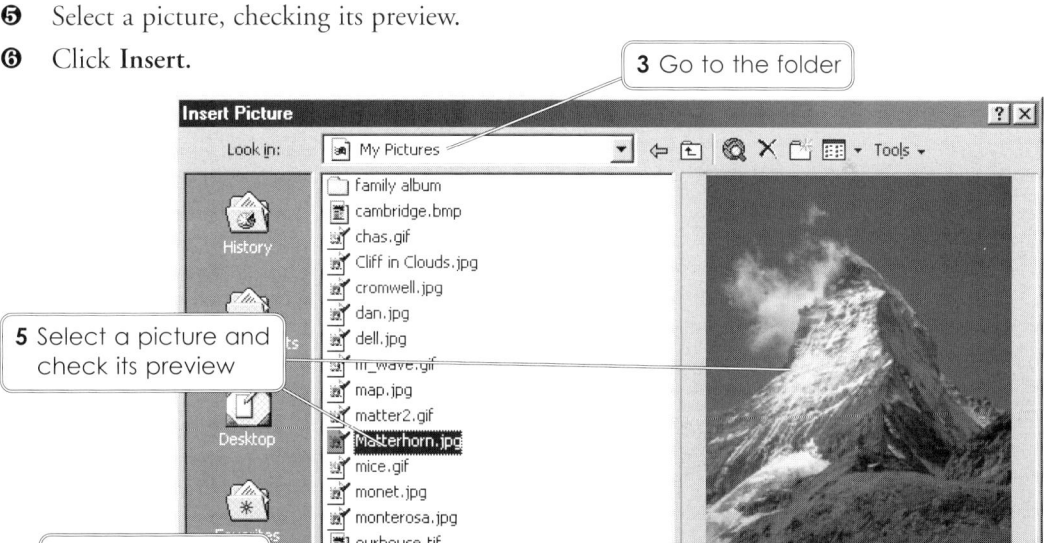

1 Use Insert > Picture > From File...

3 Go to the folder

5 Select a picture and check its preview

4 Set the File type

6 Click Insert

Clip Art (Office 97)

Clip Art pictures from the Clip Gallery can be inserted into any application – but don't add too many. There is so much Clip Art available that you must use it selectively to have any impact.

The Clip Gallery is one of the few aspects of Microsoft Office that has changed between 97 and 2000. Here is how it works in Office 97.

❶ Use **Insert** > **Picture** > **Clip Art.**

Or

❷ Open the **Insert** menu and select **Object.**

❸ At the **Object** dialog box, select **Clip Gallery.**

❹ Select the **Clip Art** tab.

❺ Choose a **Category.**

❻ Scroll through and select a picture.

❼ Click **Insert.**

These are video clips

3 Select Clip Gallery

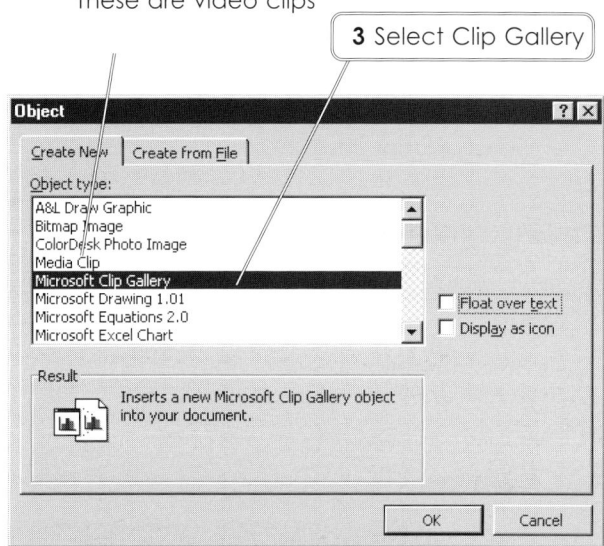

4 Go to Clip Art

6 Select a picture

7 Click Insert

5 Choose a Category

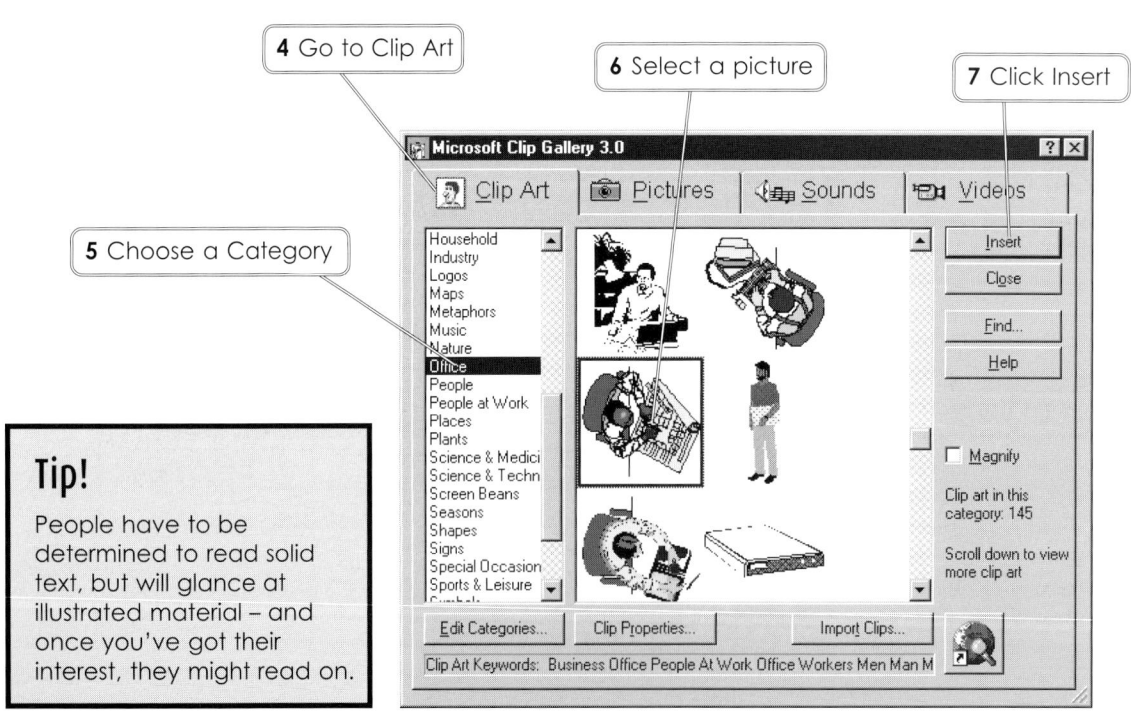

Tip!

People have to be determined to read solid text, but will glance at illustrated material – and once you've got their interest, they might read on.

Clip Art (Office 2000)

In Office 2000, Clip Art and pictures are stored together in the Gallery, and there are many more of both! The layout has been redesigned to give more space for the images, but this is used in almost exactly the same way as the old Gallery.

❶ Use **Insert > Picture > Clip Art…**

❷ On the **Pictures** tab choose a **Category**.

Or

❸ Type a **Search** word and press [**Enter**].

❹ Click on a picture.

❺ Click:

     to insert it;

     to preview it;

     to add it to your Favorites;

     to find similar clips.

❻ Close the Gallery.

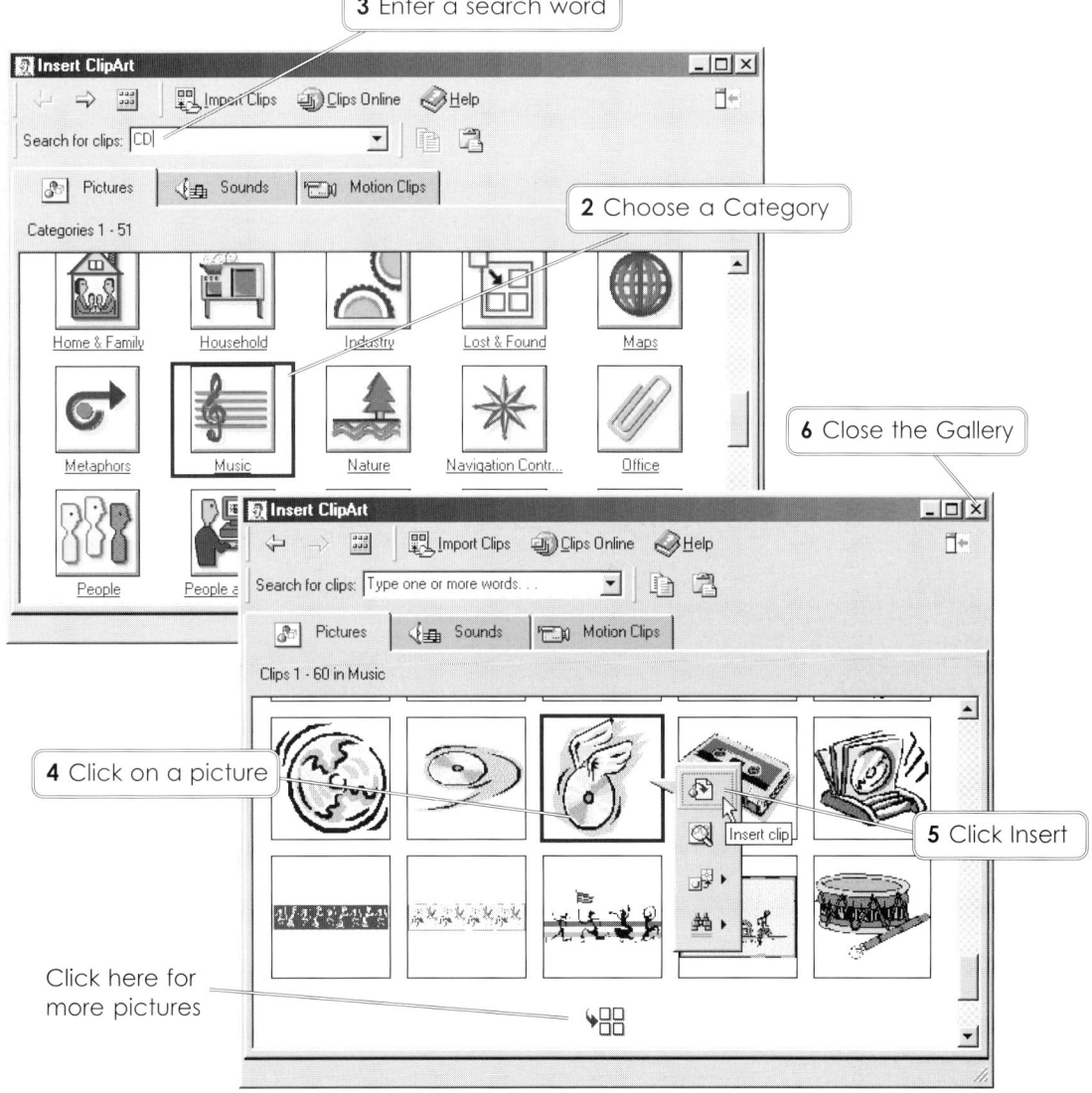

3 Enter a search word

2 Choose a Category

6 Close the Gallery

4 Click on a picture

5 Click Insert

Click here for more pictures

Using the computer

Word processing

Spreadsheets

Databases

Electronic communications

Presentations

Formatting pictures

The final appearance of any picture – file or clip art – can be adjusted at any point. Use the mouse to change the size, shape or position, or use the Picture toolbar or the right-click context menu to add a border or caption, crop it, adjust the colours, or set how the text wraps around it.

❶ Select the picture.

❷ Drag a handle to adjust the size.

❸ Drag anywhere within the area to move.

❹ Use the **Picture** tools to adjust the settings.

❺ Right-click for the context menu and use its options to add a border or caption.

The Picture toolbar

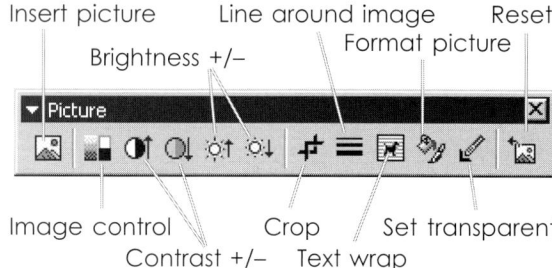

Insert picture — Line around image — Reset
Brightness +/– — Format picture
Image control — Crop — Set transparent
Contrast +/– — Text wrap

Image control options:

Automatic – in its normal colours;
Grayscale – for output to black-only printers;
Black & White – for high-contrast printing, use with line drawings or for special effects;
Watermark – ultra-pale, for use as background.

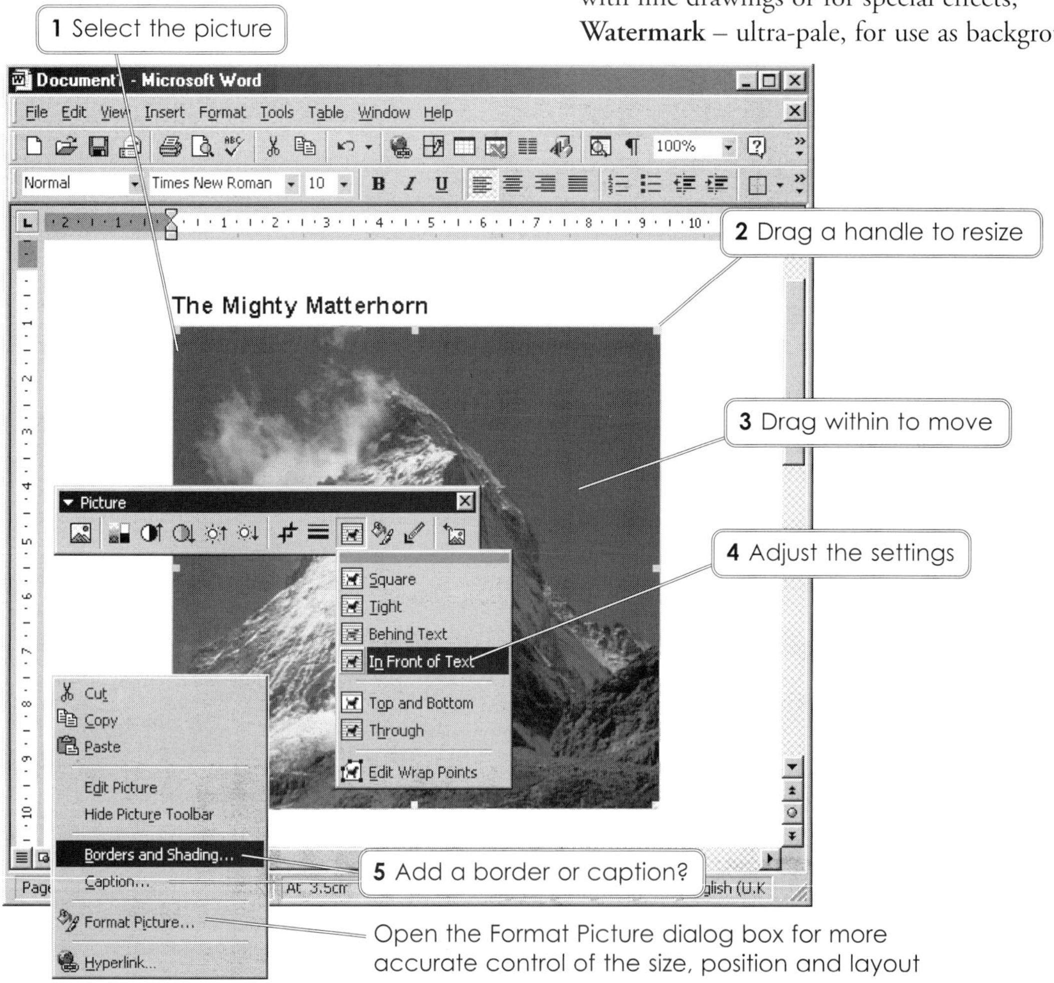

1 Select the picture

2 Drag a handle to resize

The Mighty Matterhorn

3 Drag within to move

4 Adjust the settings

Square
Tight
Behind Text
In Front of Text
Top and Bottom
Through
Edit Wrap Points

Cut
Copy
Paste

Edit Picture
Hide Picture Toolbar

Borders and Shading...

5 Add a border or caption?

Caption...

Format Picture...

Hyperlink...

Open the Format Picture dialog box for more accurate control of the size, position and layout

Tables

If you need to lay out data in neat columns and rows, the simplest way to do it is with a table.

If you want to create a simple regular table, use the ☐ button on the Standard toolbar or the **Table > Insert > Table** command. The size you set at the start can be changed – rows and columns can be added or deleted later.

In Office 2000, if you start from the **Insert Table** command, you can specify the AutoFit behaviour and apply an AutoFormat at the same time.

The **AutoFit behaviour** sets how the table fits around its contents and within the 'window'.

➤ *Fixed column width* – the widths stay the same unless you change them.

➤ *AutoFit to contents* – the columns shrink or stretch so that they match the contents.

➤ *AutoFit to window* – the table adjusts to fit the width of the page or screen (useful if you are using Word to create a Web page).

AutoFit is not available in Office 97.

AutoFormats are ready-made border/shading designs.

To create a table:

❶ Place the cursor where the table is to go.

❷ Click ☐ and drag the highlight across the grid to set the size, and go to ❽.

Or

❸ Use the **Table > Insert > Table…** command.

❹ At the Insert Table dialog box set the number of columns and rows.

❺ Choose an **AutoFit** behaviour.

❻ Click **AutoFormat…**

❼ Select a design from the dialog box if you want to apply a ready-made format (see next page).

❽ Enter the data into the cells, formatting the text if required.

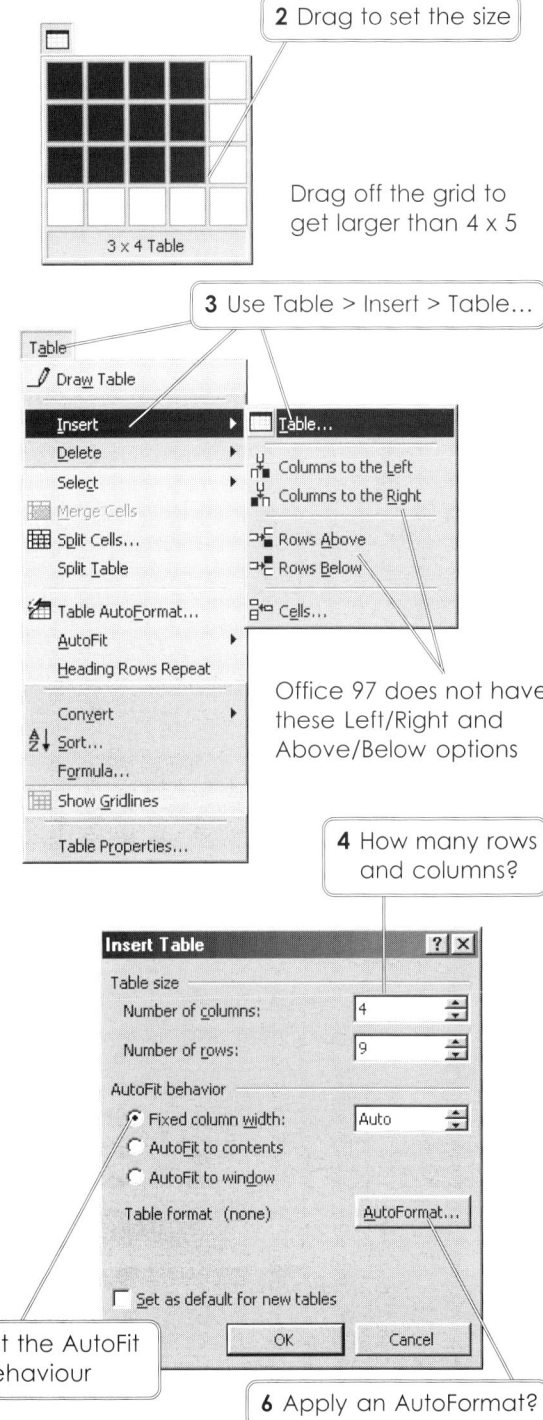

2 Drag to set the size

Drag off the grid to get larger than 4 x 5

3 x 4 Table

3 Use Table > Insert > Table…

Office 97 does not have these Left/Right and Above/Below options

4 How many rows and columns?

5 Set the AutoFit behaviour

6 Apply an AutoFormat?

Using the computer

Word processing

Spreadsheets

Databases

Electronic communications

Presentations

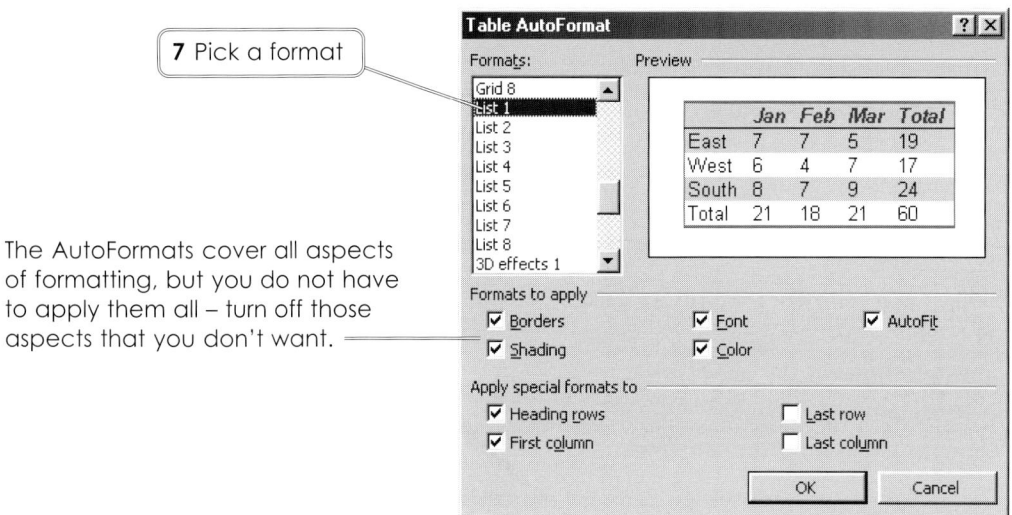

7 Pick a format

The AutoFormats cover all aspects of formatting, but you do not have to apply them all – turn off those aspects that you don't want.

To change the width of a column, drag a dividing line or the column marker in the Ruler

8 Enter the data

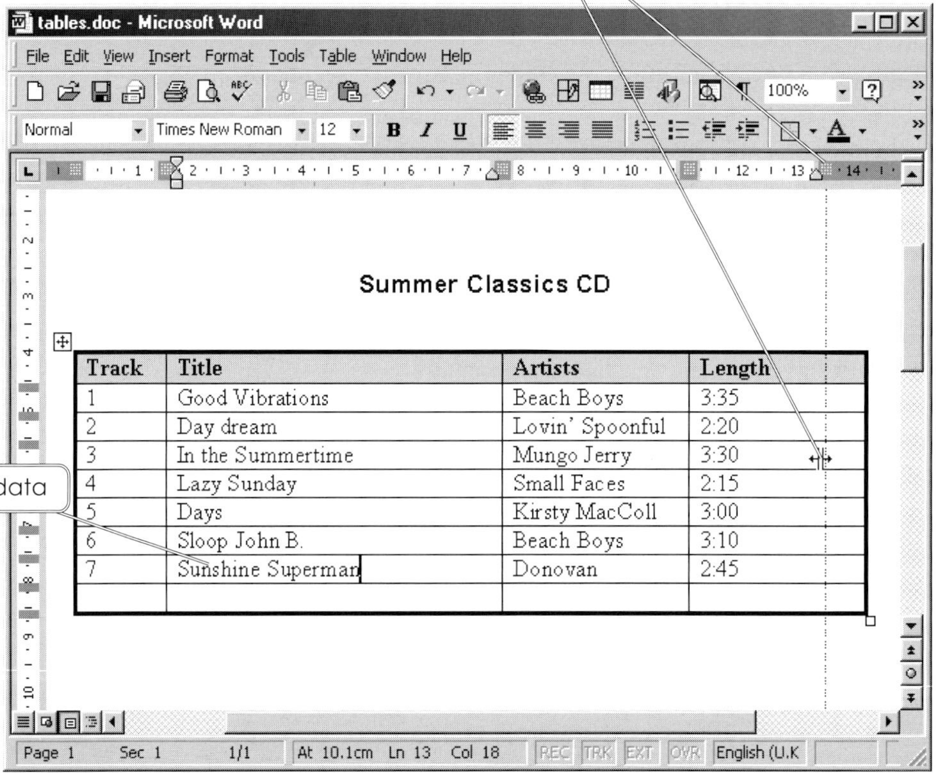

Track	Title	Artists	Length
1	Good Vibrations	Beach Boys	3:35
2	Day dream	Lovin' Spoonful	2:20
3	In the Summertime	Mungo Jerry	3:30
4	Lazy Sunday	Small Faces	2:15
5	Days	Kirsty MacColl	3:00
6	Sloop John B.	Beach Boys	3:10
7	Sunshine Superman	Donovan	2:45

Formatting tables

Text in cells can be formatted as normal. You can also:

➤ Set the vertical and horizontal alignment of cell contents;

➤ Format the borders and the lines within the table – this is slightly complicated (see below);

➤ Change the background colour.

Setting borders

❶ Open the **View** menu, point to **Toolbars** and turn on the **Tables and Borders** toolbar.

❷ Select the cells.

❸ Set the line style, width and colour.

❹ Click the **Border** tool and select the lines to be styled.

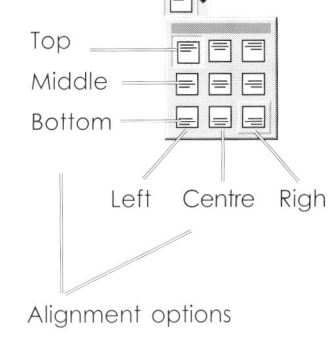

Top
Middle
Bottom

Left   Centre   Right

Alignment options

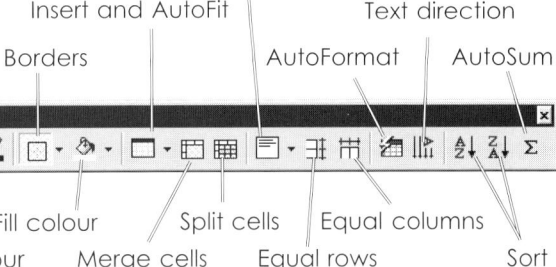

Insert and AutoFit
Borders
AutoFormat
Text direction
AutoSum

Draw
Eraser
Line width
Fill colour
Split cells
Equal columns
Sort
Line style
Line colour
Merge cells
Equal rows

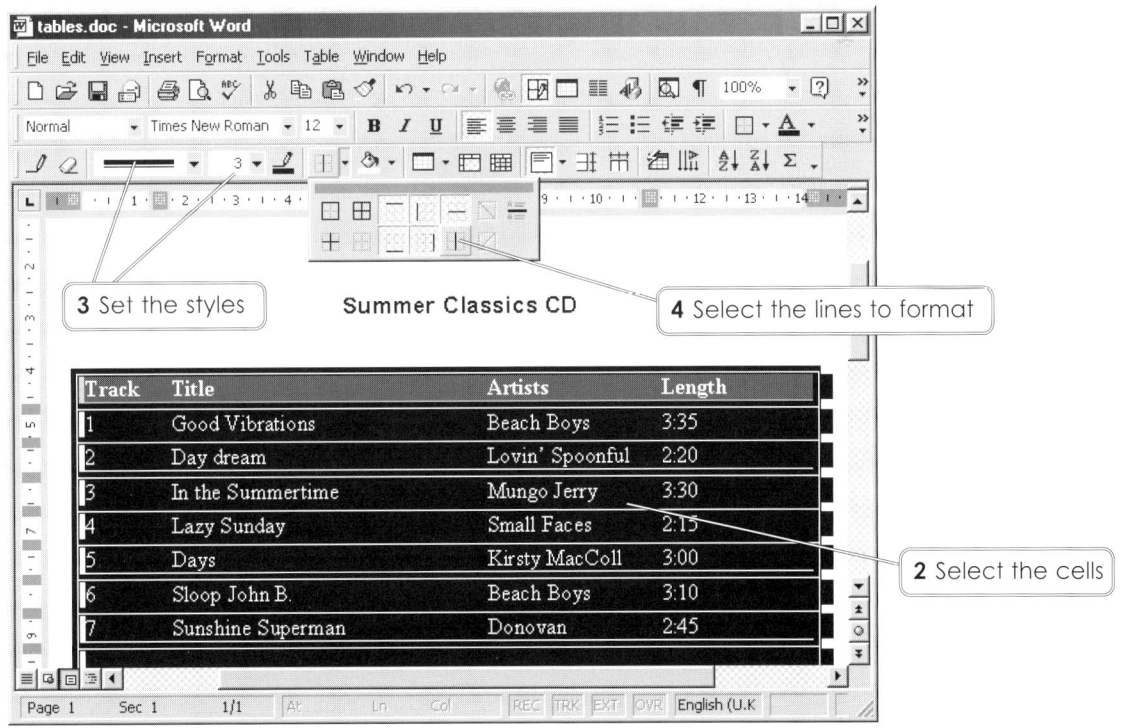

3 Set the styles

Summer Classics CD

4 Select the lines to format

2 Select the cells

Track	Title	Artists	Length
1	Good Vibrations	Beach Boys	3:35
2	Day dream	Lovin' Spoonful	2:20
3	In the Summertime	Mungo Jerry	3:30
4	Lazy Sunday	Small Faces	2:15
5	Days	Kirsty MacColl	3:00
6	Sloop John B.	Beach Boys	3:10
7	Sunshine Superman	Donovan	2:45

Using the computer

Word processing

Spreadsheets

Databases

Electronic communications

Presentations

Modifying tables

A table's size, shape and layout can be changed at any time – even after data has been entered. You can:

➤ Insert or delete rows or columns;

➤ Change the width of columns;

➤ Change the overall size of the table.

To insert rows or columns:

❶ Click into a cell in the row or column adjacent to where the new one will go.

❷ Select an **Insert** option from the **Table** menu.

To delete rows or columns:

❸ Click into a cell in the row or column, or drag across (or down) the table to select two or more rows or columns.

❹ Select a **Delete** option from the **Table** menu.

To change the column width:

❺ Point to the dividing line on the right of a column to get the double-headed arrow then drag the line left or right to set the width.

Or

❻ Drag on the column marker on the ruler. (See screenshot on page 30.)

To change the table size:

❼ Point to a corner so the cursor becomes the resize arrow, then drag the table outline to the required size.

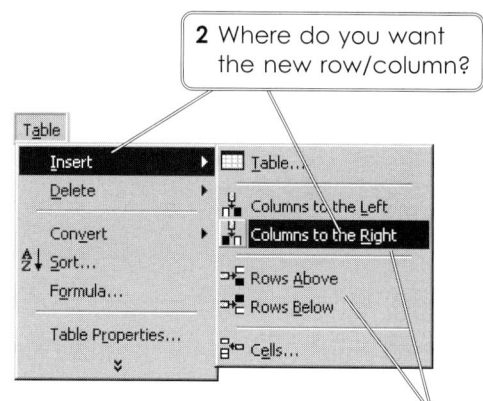

2 Where do you want the new row/column?

In Office 97, columns are always inserted to the left of the selected column and rows inserted above the selected row

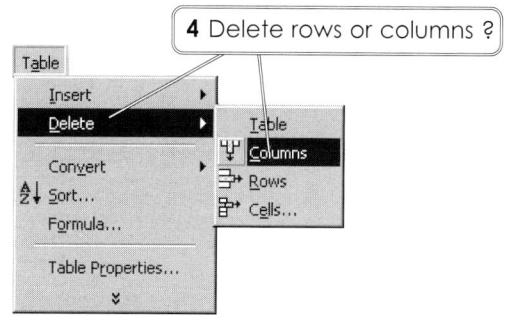

4 Delete rows or columns ?

Worksheets in Word

A Word table will let you lay out and format data neatly, and you can even perform calculations on numbers in it – though the formulae are limited.

If you want to have calculations in a Word document, it is usually easier to insert an Excel worksheet. This gives you the full range of Excel functions, formulae and formatting facilities.

The worksheet can be created from new, or you can insert an existing sheet.

To insert a new worksheet:

❶ Place the insertion point where you want the worksheet to go.

❷ Click 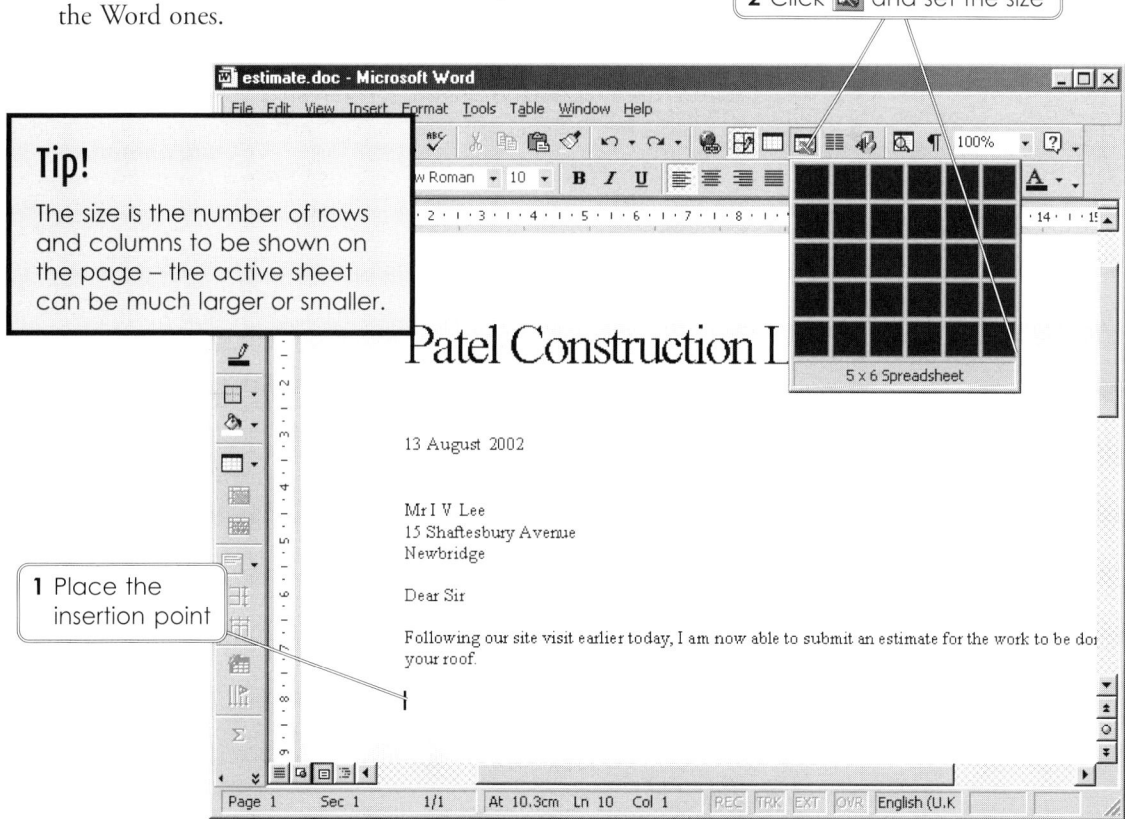, the **Insert worksheet** tool, and drag the highlight across to set the size. Set any convenient size – it can be adjusted at ❺.

An Excel worksheet will open in your document and the Excel toolbars will replace the Word ones.

❸ Enter the data and formulae as if you were working in Excel (see next page).

❹ Format the cells as required, by selecting them and setting options on the toolbar.

❺ When you have finished, adjust the size of the worksheet so that it shows those rows and columns that you want to display in the document – this will probably just be the active cells.

❻ Click on the document, away from the worksheet. The Excel display will be replaced by a simpler table.

❼ If you need to edit the sheet in any way – whether to change the data or adjust the formatting – double-click on the sheet to take it back into Excel.

Tip!
The size is the number of rows and columns to be shown on the page – the active sheet can be much larger or smaller.

2 Click and set the size

1 Place the insertion point

Using the computer

Word processing

Spreadsheets

Databases

Electronic communications

Presentations

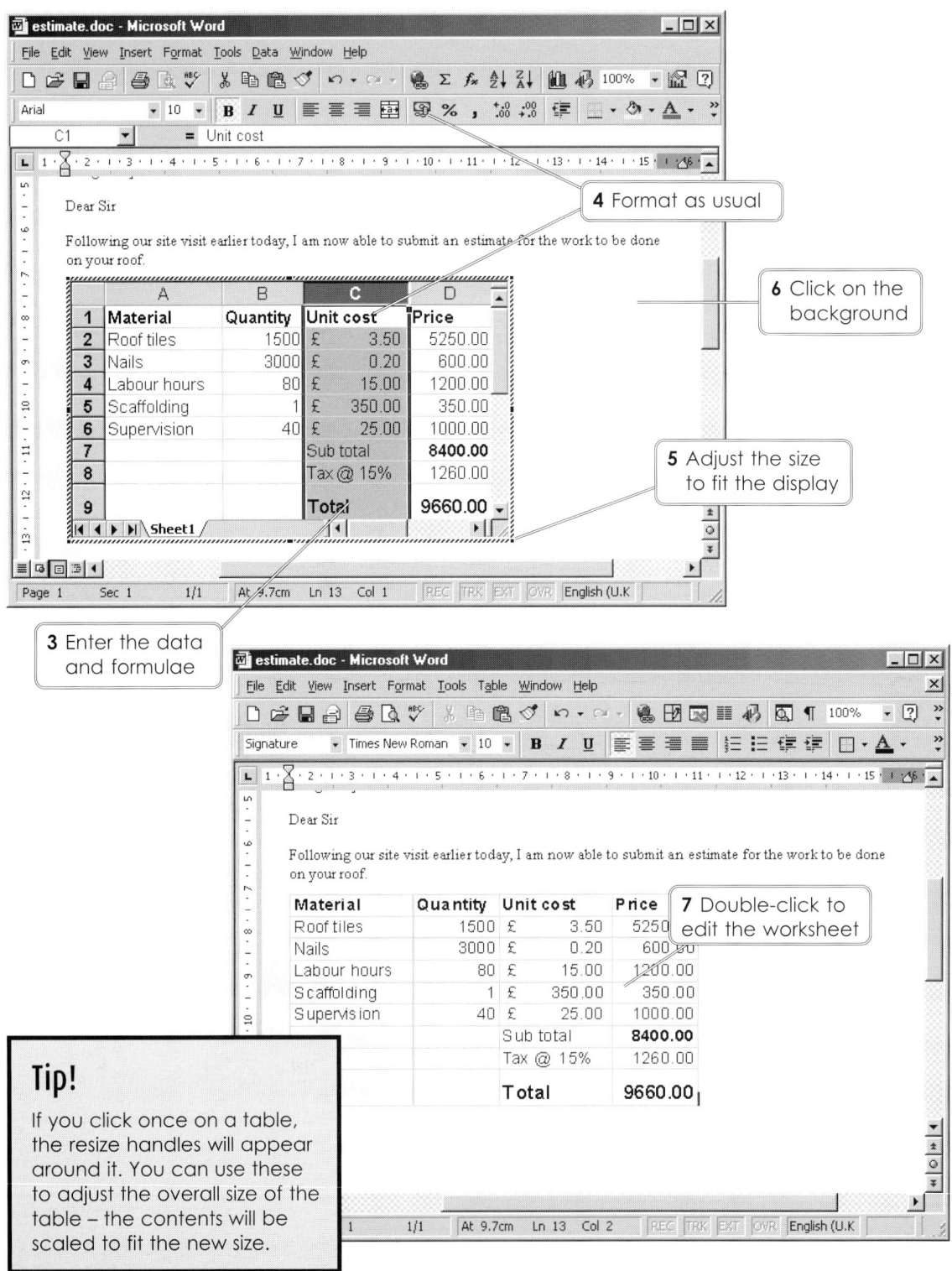

4 Format as usual

6 Click on the background

5 Adjust the size to fit the display

3 Enter the data and formulae

7 Double-click to edit the worksheet

Tip!

If you click once on a table, the resize handles will appear around it. You can use these to adjust the overall size of the table – the contents will be scaled to fit the new size.

Skills builder 5:
Images and tables

❶ You are going to create a document to be used as an invoice. Start a new Word file.

❷ Type a name and address for the firm, setting it centrally at the top of the page.

❸ Insert a picture, either from file or from the Clip Gallery, to act as a logo for the firm.

❹ Set the Text wrap to 'In front of text'. Resize the picture to around 4 cm across, and move it to the top right of the page.

❺ Below the name and address, type 'Invoice'. Below that, on the left, type the headings 'Date:' and on the next line, 'To:', and leave three lines blank for the customer's details.

❻ Insert a worksheet, 4 columns by 10 rows.

❼ Type the column headings, 'Item', 'Unit price', 'Quantity' and 'Cost'. Increase the width of the Item column until it is about as big as the other three combined.

❽ Type in some sample items, prices and quantities. Write a formula to work out the cost and copy it down 8 rows of Cost cells.

❾ Create a Sum formula to add up the costs, and type the heading 'Total' to its left.

❿ Save and print the document.

Your invoice should look something like this

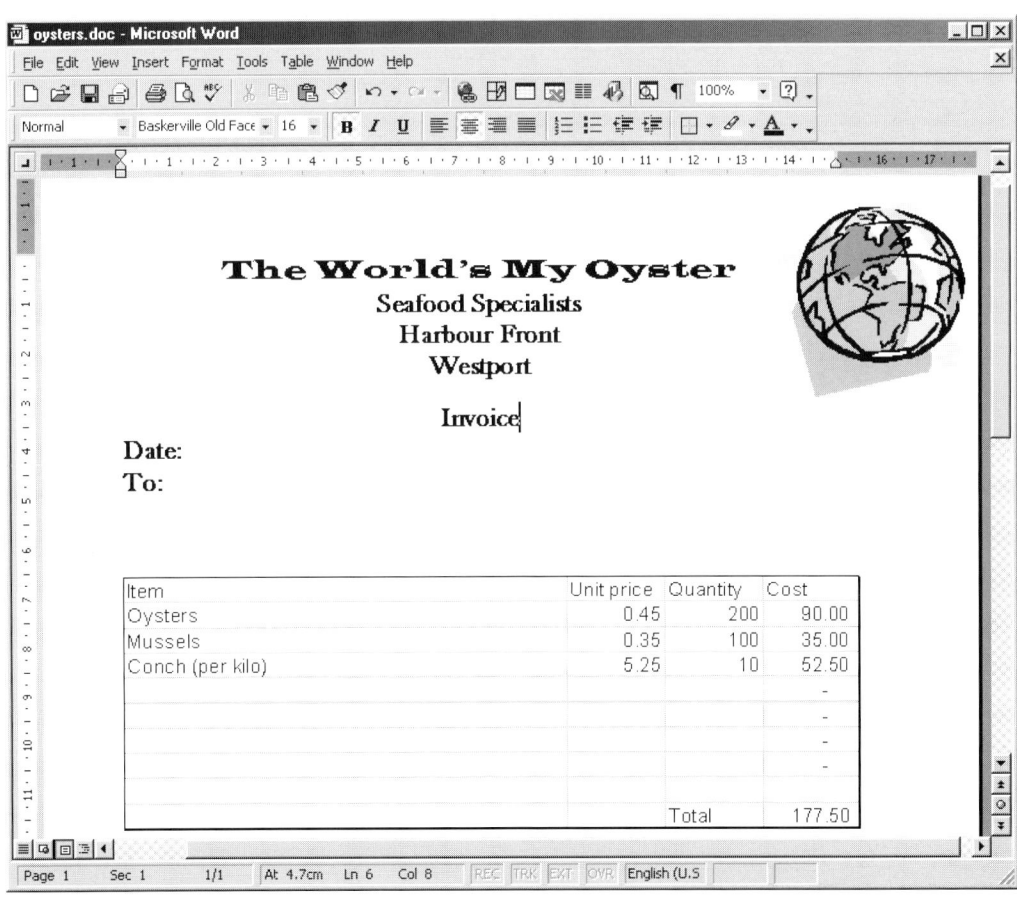

Mail merge

In a mail merge, a standard letter is combined with names and addresses from a data file to produce personalized letters or mailing labels. The data file can come from Excel, Access or another database, or be created within Word. Its data is drawn into the Word document through *merge fields*, which link to fields in the data file.

Setting up a mail merge is easy, and is made even easier by the Mail Merge Helper, which guides you through the process.

There are three stages:

1   Create the main document – typically a standard letter or circular.

2   Create the data source – which may mean typing the data into a new file, or locating an existing file.

3   Merge the data into the document. There are three aspects to this:

➤   Inserting the merge fields into the document;

➤   Selecting the records to include from the data file;

➤   Outputting the merged letters.

The main document

This will have all its text, apart from the name and address, and perhaps other details of its recipients. It will be formatted and have its page setup and other options set, so that it is ready to run once the data has been added.

❶   When the document is ready, save it, then open the **Tools** menu and select **Mail Merge…**

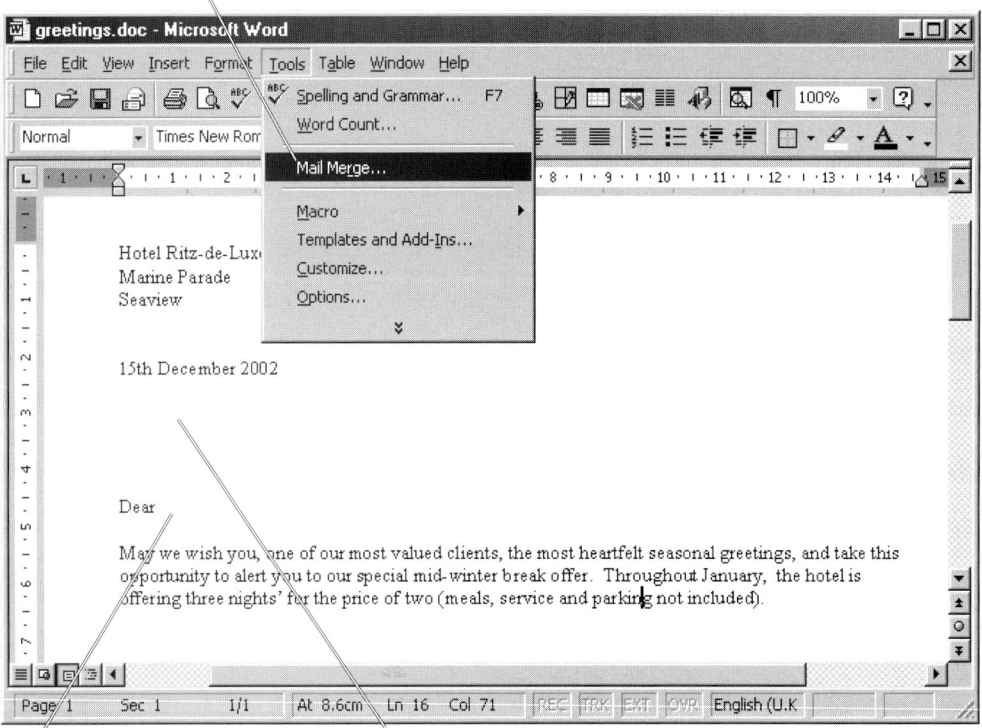

1 Use Tools > Mail Merge…

The name and address will go here

The salutation, e.g. 'Mr Smith', will go here

❷ In the **Main document** area, click **Create** and select **Form Letters…**

❸ You will be asked if you want to use the current document or to create a new main document. Choose **Active Window**.

> **2** Click Create and select Form Letters…

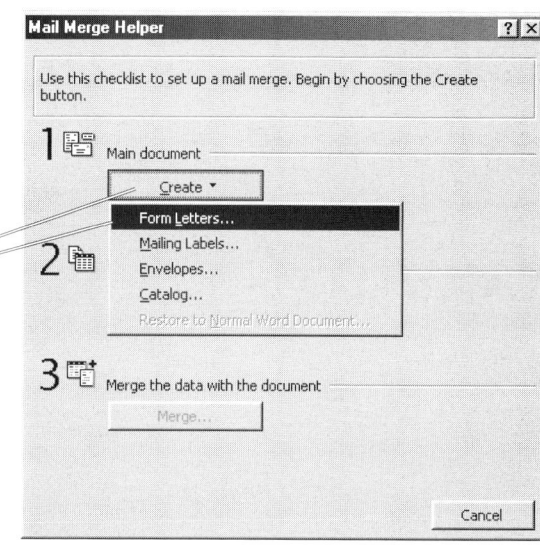

The data source

❶ If the Mail Merge Helper is not visible, use **Tools > Mail Merge…** to reopen it. Click **Get Data** and select **Create Data Source…**

If you were using an existing data file, it would be opened now. The Address Book, which holds the e-mail addresses and other details of your contacts, could also be used.

❷ You will be offered a list of field names that are typically used in contacts data files. To remove an unwanted field, select it and click **Remove Field Name**.

❸ If you need other field names, type them into **Field Name** and click **Add Field Name**.

❹ Click **OK** when you are done. You will be taken to the **Save As** dialog box. Give a filename and select a folder to hold the file.

continued…

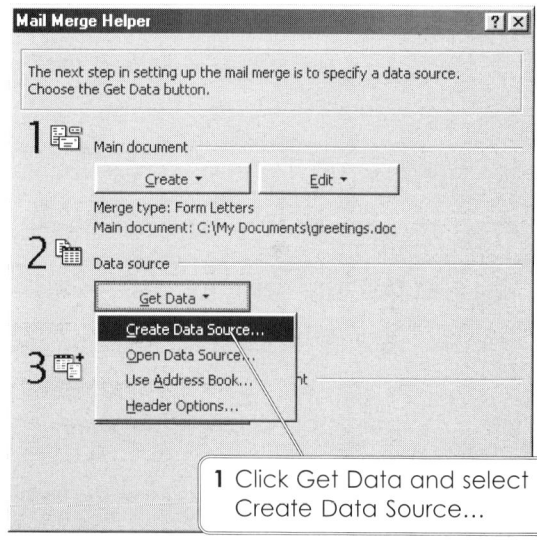

> **1** Click Get Data and select Create Data Source…

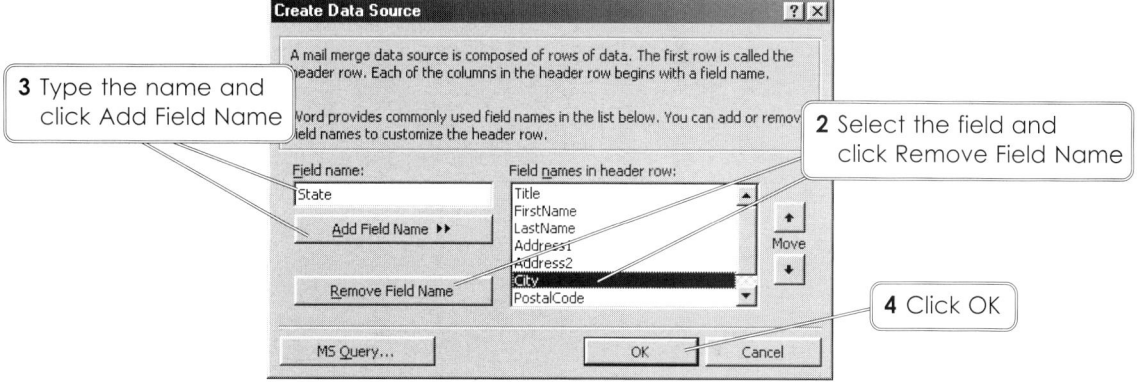

> **3** Type the name and click Add Field Name

> **2** Select the field and click Remove Field Name

> **4** Click OK

Using the computer

Word processing

Spreadsheets

Databases

Electronic communications

Presentations

❺ At this point, there is only the file structure and no data. You will be asked if you want to create some data records or edit the main document. Choose **Edit Data Source**.

❻ The **Data Form** will open. Enter the names and other details, one record at a time, clicking **Add New** after each.

❼ Click **OK**.

The merge

The Mail Merge toolbar will have been opened. Note the tools indicated on the screenshot below.

❶ Place the insertion point where you want the first field to be written.

❷ Click **Insert Merge Field** and select the field from the list.

❸ Type in a space, comma, or press [**Enter**] to move to the next line, as required, then repeat for the other fields.

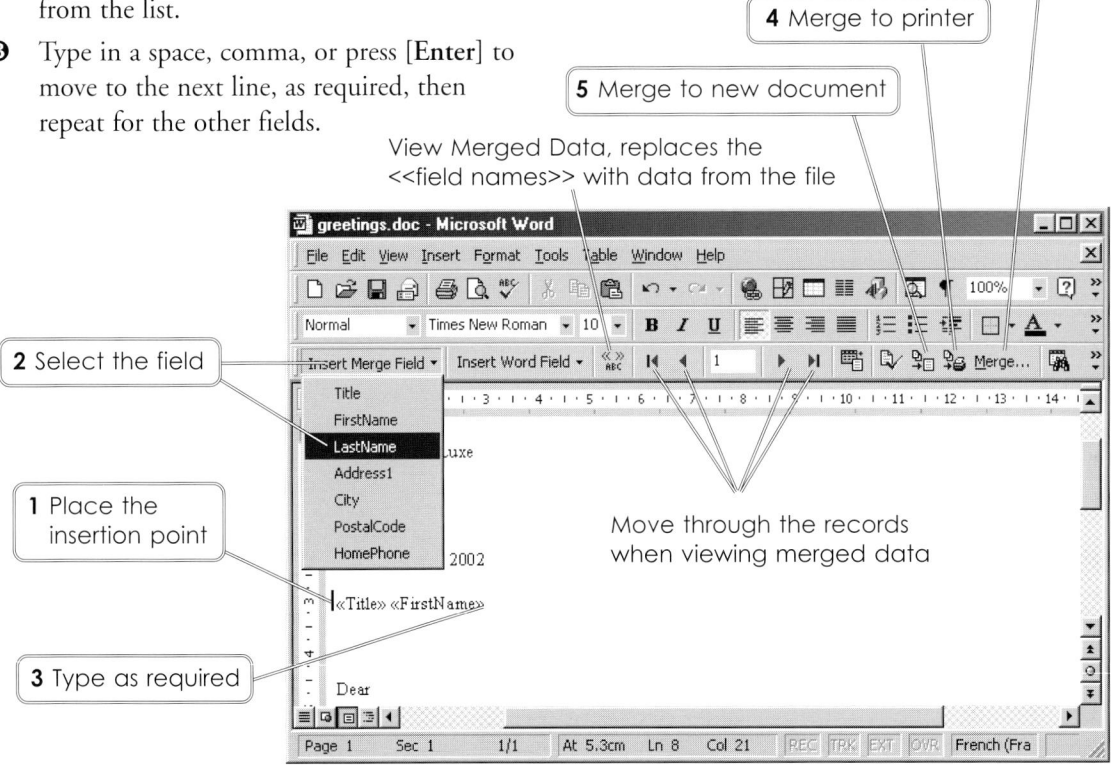

6 Enter the data and click Add New

7 Click OK

Open Merge dialog box to set options before merging

4 Merge to printer

5 Merge to new document

View Merged Data, replaces the <<field names>> with data from the file

2 Select the field

1 Place the insertion point

3 Type as required

Move through the records when viewing merged data

❹ For a simple mail merge, press ▣. This will merge in the selected fields and print a copy of the document for every record in the file.

❺ If you want to be able to edit before printing, press ▣. This will create a new document containing one merged copy of the standard letter for every record.

❻ If you only want to include selected records in the merge, click Merge... . First set the **Merge to:** option – **Printer** or **New document** – then select the records.

❼ You can pick a range by giving the **From** and **To** numbers, or click **Query Options...** to define a query. This is done in the same way as in Access – but this is not tested in the IT Skills award.

❽ Click **Merge** to run the merge.

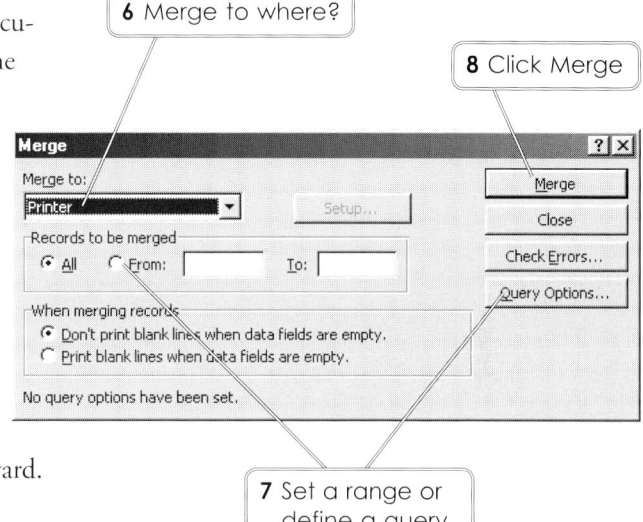

6 Merge to where?

8 Click Merge

7 Set a range or define a query

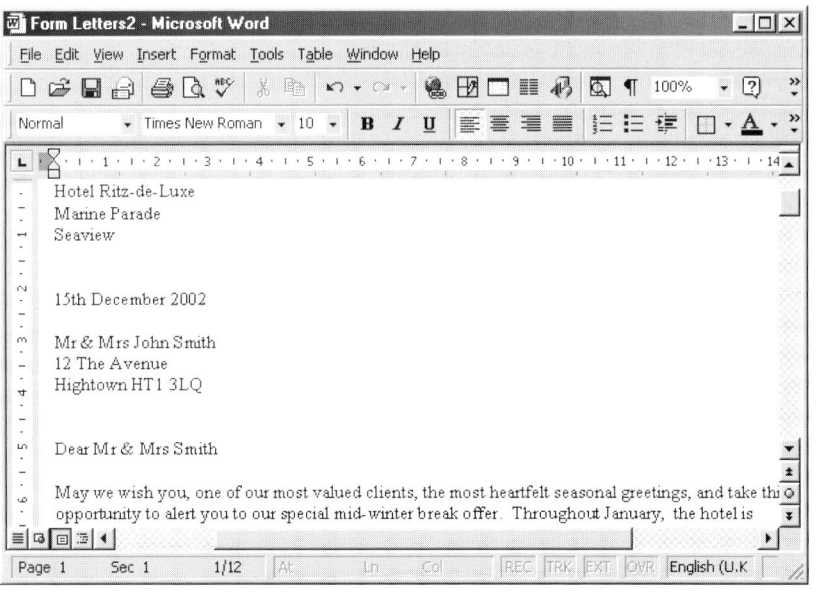

The merge to new document option gives you the chance to add special personal touches to letters, or to remove any that you do not want – it can be simpler to select records this way than through the Query option.

Skills builder 6: Mail merge

In this exercise, we use mail merge to produce a set of letters to friends, informing them of a change of address.

❶ Start a new blank document and type in the basic letter. It should be something similar to the one shown below, but without any <<field codes>>. Save it as *moving.doc*.

❷ Display the Mail Merge Helper and choose Form Letter using the document in the active window.

❸ Create a new data source. You will only need the name and address fields.

❹ Enter the details of two or three friends – enough to test the merge. Save the file as '*friends.doc*'.

❺ Edit the main document to insert the merge fields. You will need a name and address block at the top left, plus the *First name* or the *Title* and *Last name* after 'Dear'.

❻ Merge the main document and data source to a new document. Check for errors. If you find any mistakes, edit the main document or the data source as required.

❼ Save the merged document as '*mymove.doc*'.

Are you ready?

Get your tutor to check your work.

If you have successfully completed the skills builder exercises in this section, and are confident in using those skills, you are ready for the *Word processing* test.

If you need a little more practice before taking the test, ask your tutor for the *Word processing* pre-test exercise.

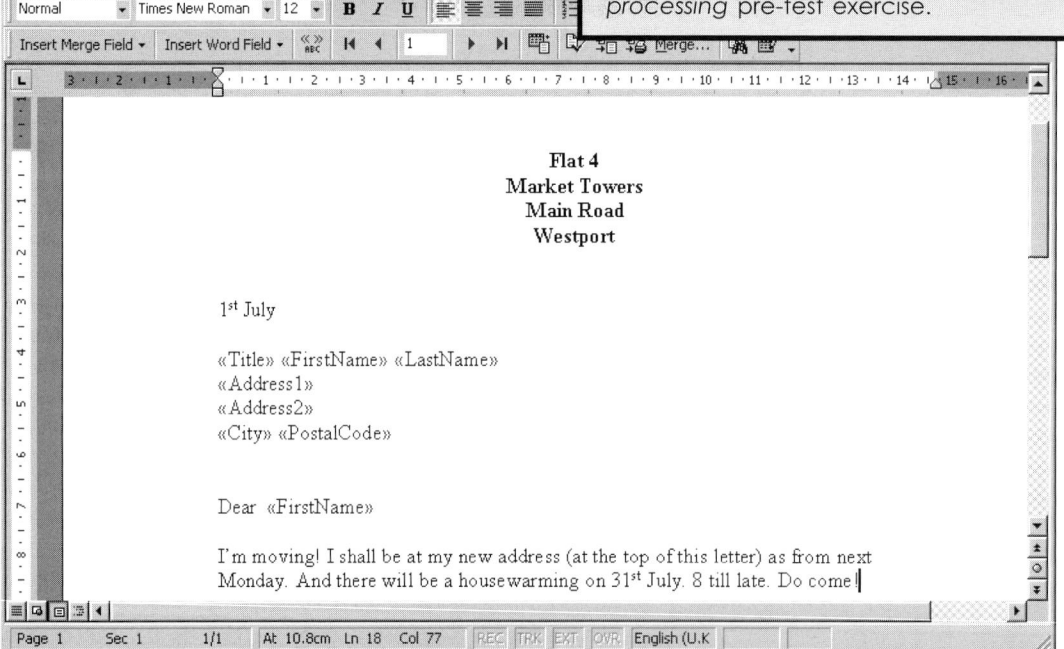

The main document, with the merge fields in place

3 Spreadsheets

You should know how to:

- Enter and edit data
- Use simple formulae
- Adjust the sheet layout
- Format text and numbers
- Sort data
- Print a worksheet

You will learn how to:

- Use relative and absolute references
- Use functions in formulae
- Copy data between worksheets
- Apply AutoFormats
- Insert images
- Create and format charts
- Define headers and footers
- Use key print options

Additional resources:

- Checklist 3: Spreadsheets
- Sample files in the *Cambridge* folder

Excel screen and tools

The controls and tools that you should know already, or which will be introduced in this section are labelled on the screenshots here (those covered in this chapter are shown in bold).

Tip!

These first three pages provide a quick summary of key spreadsheet skills.

Formula line displays contents of current cell – you can edit here or directly in the cell

Column letters

Address of current cell

Wide text will flow into empty cells, but ...

... be cropped short if the next cell is not empty

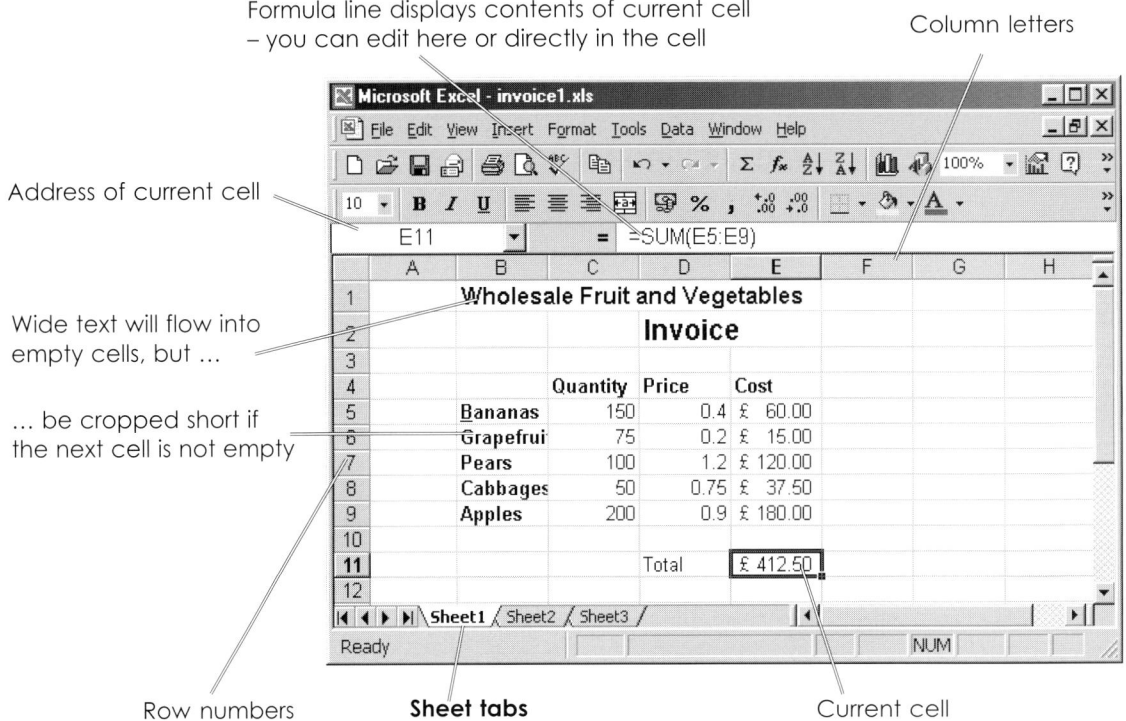

Row numbers

Sheet tabs

Current cell

Standard toolbar

Sort Ascending

Functions

Sort Descending

Autosum

Chart Wizard

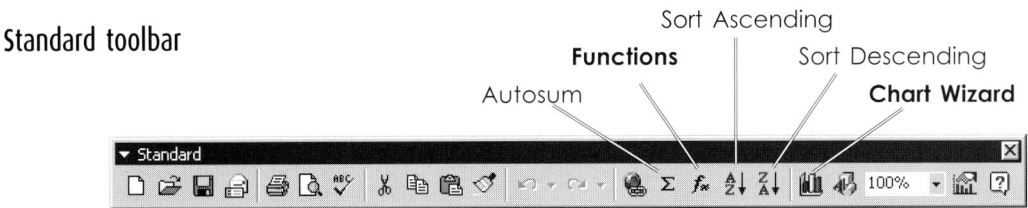

Formatting toolbar

Font formatting

Underline

Alignment

Centre

Currency

Number formatting

Increase decimals

Size

Italic

Left

Right

Percentage

Decrease decimals

Font

Bold

Comma

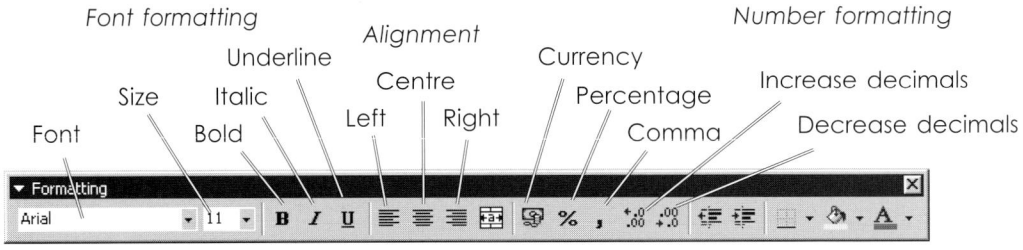

42

Data and formulae

Text and numbers

To enter text or numbers, simply type them in. Excel will recognise the data as text or numbers and treat it accordingly. The only exception is when you want to use figures as text, e.g. for a telephone number. In this case, type a single quote at the start of the entry:

'0101 555 123456

Formulae

You can write formulae to process either text or numbers. Formulae can contain a mixture of cell references, numbers, text and functions, joined by operators. You must type an = sign at the start of a formula, otherwise Excel will treat it as text.

Cell references can be typed into the formula or pulled in by selecting the cells.

➤ To identify a single cell, give the column letter followed by the row number, e.g. A4.

➤ To identify a range of cells, give the references of the top left and bottom right cells, separated by a colon, e.g. E5:G9.

A range can be a single line of cells in a row or column, or a rectangular block.

Arithmetic operators

These operators can be used to calculate values:

+ Addition

− Subtraction

* Multiplication

/ Division

( ) Brackets

Where there are several operators in a formula, multiplication and division are calculated first, then addition and subtraction. If an operation is in brackets, it gets priority, e.g.

$$4 * 3 + 2 = 14$$

but $\quad 4 * (3 + 2) = 20.$

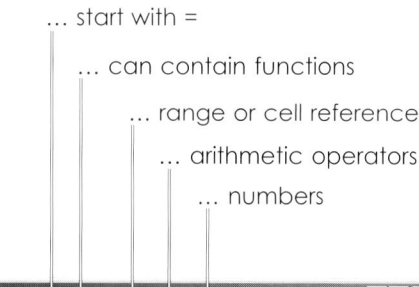

Formulae...

... start with =

... can contain functions

... range or cell references

... arithmetic operators

... numbers

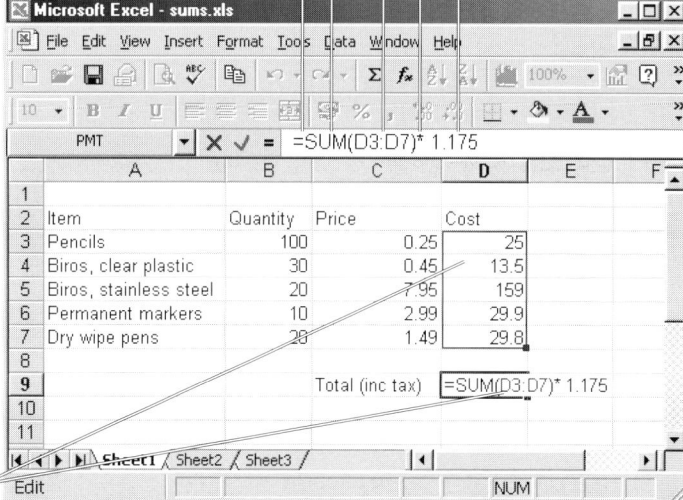

When Excel expects a reference, clicking on a cell or selecting a range writes the reference into the formula

Using the computer

Word processing

Spreadsheets

Databases

Electronic communications

Presentations

Skills builder 7:
Basic spreadsheet skills

This exercise is designed to reinforce skills covered in the Foundation level course. If you have any difficulties, go back to the Foundation level book and read Chapter 4, *Spreadsheets*.

❶ Start Excel, then open the file *budget.xls* in the *Cambridge\Exercise files* folder.

❷ Enter suitable values in the *Clothes*, *Fun* and *Other* rows.

❸ In cell B12, create a formula to calculate the sum of the values in cells B4 to B10.

❹ Copy the formula from B12 into cells C12 to G12.

❺ In cell B14, create a formula to work out the difference between the income and total spending. Copy the formula across to G14.

❻ Format the headings in row 1 and column A to make them bold.

❼ Adjust the width of column A so that the headings are fully visible.

❽ Apply the Currency format to the numbers in cells B2 to G14, then reduce the decimal places to 0.

❾ Print to file one copy of the sheet, saving it as *budget.prn* in your IT Skills folder.

❿ Save the edited file as *mybudget.xls* in your IT Skills folder.

References and formulae

Relative references

Cell references in formulae are normally relative. This means that when you copy a formula, its references are adjusted so that they refer to the same cells in relation to the formula.

For example, the first Cost formula, in D5 is:

= C5 * B5

which means, 'multiply the value in the cell to the left in the same row, with the value in the cell two columns to the left in the same row'.

We could copy this formula down into the other Cost cells. The version in D8 reads:

= C8 * B8

which means, as before, 'multiply the value in the cell to the left in the same row, with the value in the cell two columns to the left in the same row'.

Try it. Type in the headings and data shown on the right. In D5, write the formula:

= C5 * B5

Copy this and paste it into cells D6 to D8.

Absolute references

Sometimes you need to keep a reference fixed when you copy a formula, so that it continues to refer to the same cell. This might hold the tax rate, or a discount or sales markup percentage.

To make a reference absolute, you must add $ signs before the column letter and row number. You can do this by typing them in, or by pressing the [F4] key when you select the cell. Try it.

❶ In D2, type 'Tax rate'.

❷ In E2, type 15% or 0.15, then format it with the **%** button.

❸ In E5, create the formula =D5 * E2, by clicking on the cells and immediately after selecting E2, press [F4]. The reference will change to read = D5 * $E$2.

❹ Copy the formula into cells E6 to E8, and view the resulting formulae.

	A	B	C	D
1				
2				
3				
4	Item	Price per kilo	Quantity	Cost
5	Apples	3.49	10	=B5*C5
6	Apricots	7.25	6	
7	Aubergines	1.99	20	
8	Avocados	8.49	15	
9				

The formula refers to the two cells to the left

	A	B	C	D
1				
2				
3				
4	Item	Price per kilo	Quantity	Cost
5	Apples	3.49	10	34.9
6	Apricots	7.25	6	43.5
7	Aubergines	1.99	20	39.8
8	Avocados	8.49	15	=B8*C8

The formula refers to the same relative cells

2 Type the fixed value up here

	A	B	C	D	E
1					
2				Tax rate	15%
3					
4	Item	Price per kilo	Quantity	Cost	Tax
5	Apples	3.49	10	34.9	=D5*$E$2
6	Apricots	7.25	6	43.5	
7	Aubergines	1.99	20	39.8	
8	Avocados	8.49	15	127.35	

3 Press [F4] to make a reference absolute

	A	B	C	D	E
1					
2				Tax rate	15%
3					
4	Item	Price per kilo	Quantity	Cost	Tax
5	Apples	3.49	10	34.9	5.235
6	Apricots	7.25	6	43.5	6.525
7	Aubergines	1.99	20	39.8	5.97
8	Avocados	8.49	15	127.35	=D8*$E$2

4 The absolute reference is unchanged when copied

Using the computer

Word processing

Spreadsheets

Databases

Electronic communications

Presentations

Using functions

You should already know the SUM function that can be called up from the **Autosum** button ∑. This is only one of Excel's many ready-made functions. The rest are almost as easy to access and many are just as easy to use.

In this example, we will use the AVERAGE function, to calculate the mean of a set of figures.

❶ Open a new spreadsheet and enter the data shown here, in cells A1:D9, or a similar set of names and marks.

❷ Go to E4 and start to write a formula by typing =

❸ Click the down arrow by the Function list.

❹ If AVERAGE is listed, select it.

❺ If it is not listed, click **More Functions…** and select it from the **Paste Function** dialog box. You will find it in the Statistical set.

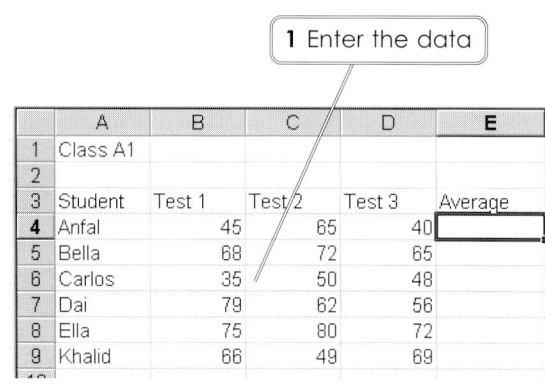

1 Enter the data

	A	B	C	D	E
1	Class A1				
2					
3	Student	Test 1	Test 2	Test 3	Average
4	Anfal	45	65	40	
5	Bella	68	72	65	
6	Carlos	35	50	48	
7	Dai	79	62	56	
8	Ella	75	80	72	
9	Khalid	66	49	69	

3 Open the Function list

This also opens the Function list

2 Start a formula

4 Select AVERAGE

5 Open the Paste Function dialog box and select AVERAGE

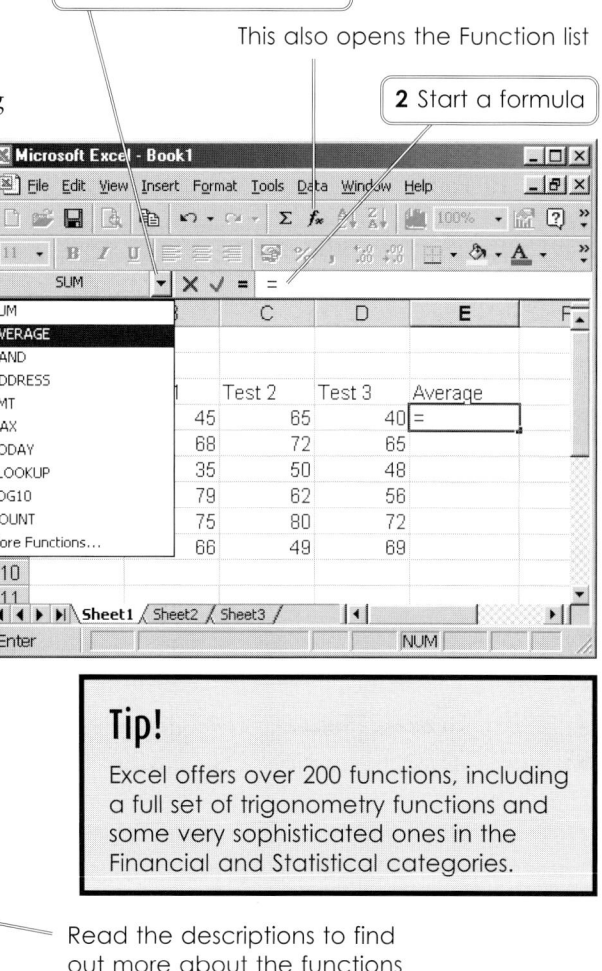

Tip!

Excel offers over 200 functions, including a full set of trigonometry functions and some very sophisticated ones in the Financial and Statistical categories.

Read the descriptions to find out more about the functions

46

Using the computer

Word processing

Spreadsheets

Databases

Electronic communications

Presentations

⑥ The **Formula Palette** will open, showing the function. Excel will guess which cells you want it to apply to. Check the range.

⑦ If the range is not correct, click 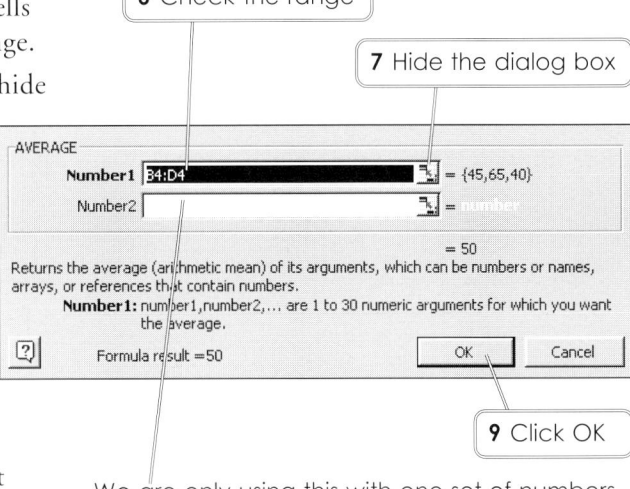 to hide the **Formula Palette**.

⑧ Select the range and click ▣.

⑨ Click **OK**.

⑩ The formula can now be copied down to find the average marks for the other students. Format the cells to show the results as whole numbers – use the **Format Cells** dialog box or keep clicking ▦.

Save the file as you will need it later. Name it *marks.xls*.

6 Check the range

7 Hide the dialog box

9 Click OK

We are only using this with one set of numbers, but you could give the references for up to 30 ranges or single cells – ignore the options and complexities that you do not need!

10 Format the cells

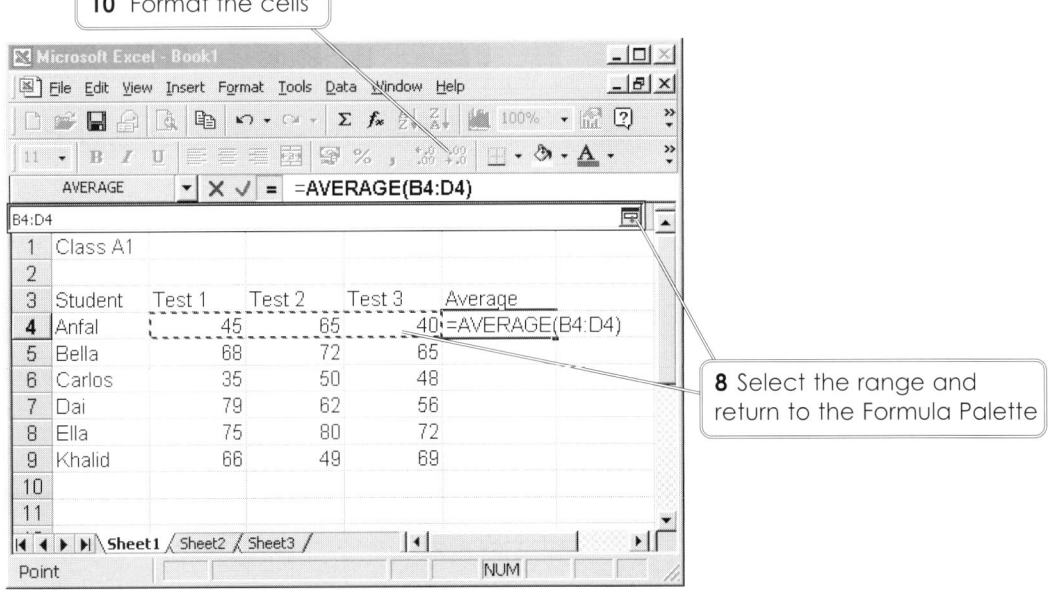

8 Select the range and return to the Formula Palette

Tip!

Save this file when you have finished – it will be useful in the next examples.

47

Multiple worksheets

An Excel file, or workbook, can contain any number of worksheets. Using multiple worksheets, you can keep different sets of data in their own distinct places, while being able to move easily between the sets and to draw values from one set for use in another. For example, a lecturer might use multiple worksheets to store students' marks. Each class could have its own sheet, with a further sheet used for summaries.

The following exercise sets up such a workbook. You will need to have open the students' marks spreadsheet, created in the previous exercise.

❶ First, give Sheet1 a new and more meaning-ful name. Open the **Format** menu, point to **Sheet** and select **Rename**.

❷ The name will be highlighted on the tab. Delete it, type 'Class A1' and press [**Enter**].

❸ Click the tab to move to Sheet 2, then rename that sheet as 'Class A2'.

❹ The two sheets will have a similar structure. You can copy headings and formulae from one to the other. Select the headings from sheet Class A1 and copy them. Click the tab to move to sheet Class A2, and paste the headings in the same place on this sheet.

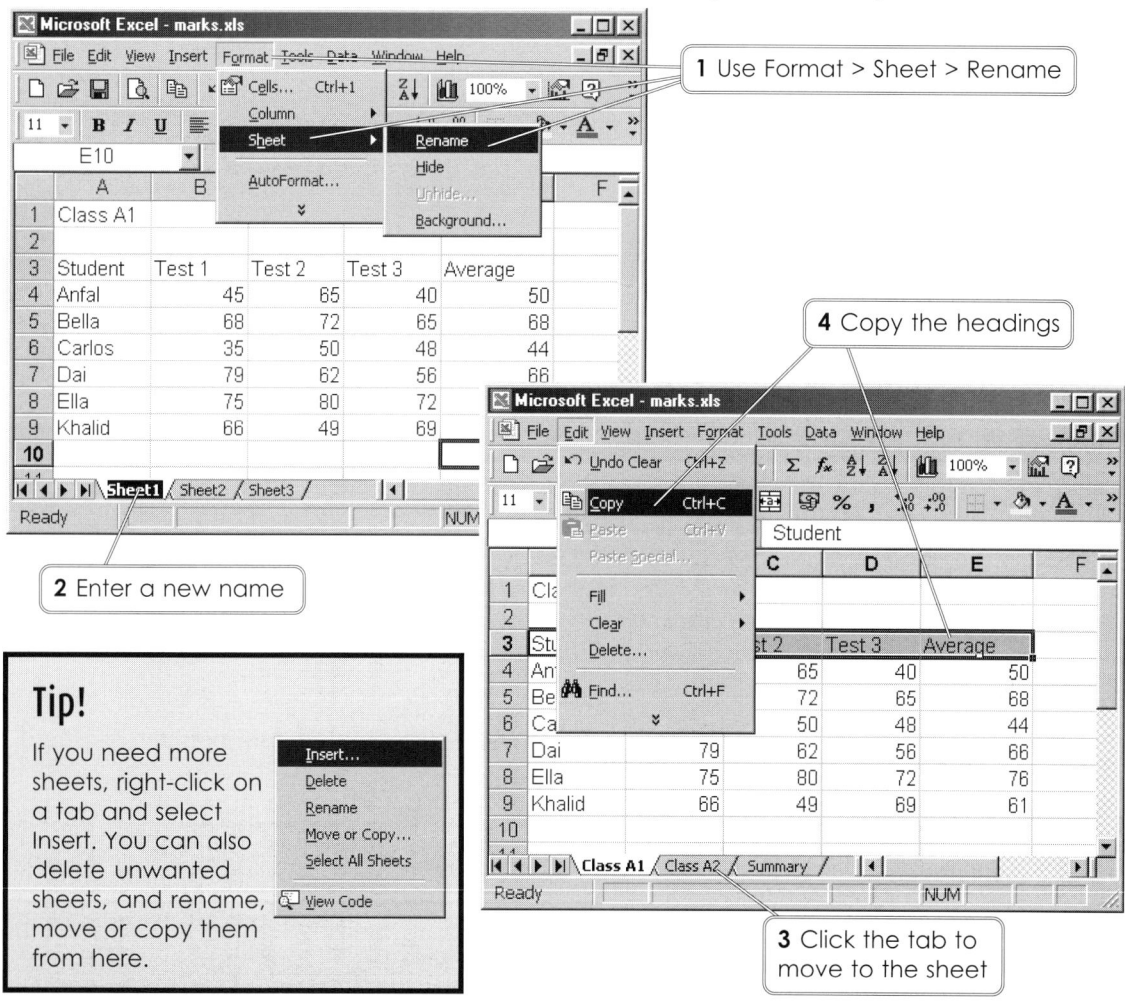

1 Use Format > Sheet > Rename

2 Enter a new name

4 Copy the headings

3 Click the tab to move to the sheet

Tip!

If you need more sheets, right-click on a tab and select Insert. You can also delete unwanted sheets, and rename, move or copy them from here.

⑤ Add the data for Class A2.

⑥ Copy the Average formula from Class A1 to Class A2.

⑦ Go to Sheet 3, and rename this 'Summary'. Copy the student names from the Class sheets into a single column, A4:A15.

⑧ We need to copy the Averages results – not the formulae – from the Class sheets to the Summary. Go to sheet Class A1, select and copy cells E4:E9.

⑨ Select the block where the values are to go (B4:B9), then open the **Edit** menu and select **Paste Special…**

⑩ In the **Paste** area, select **Values** and click **OK**. The values will be pasted in. They will need formatting to hide the excess decimals.

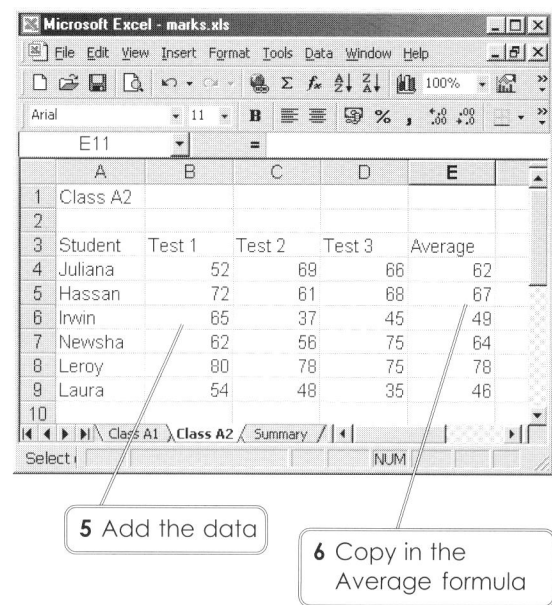

5 Add the data

6 Copy in the Average formula

Tip!
Save the finished file – you will need it in Skills builder 10.

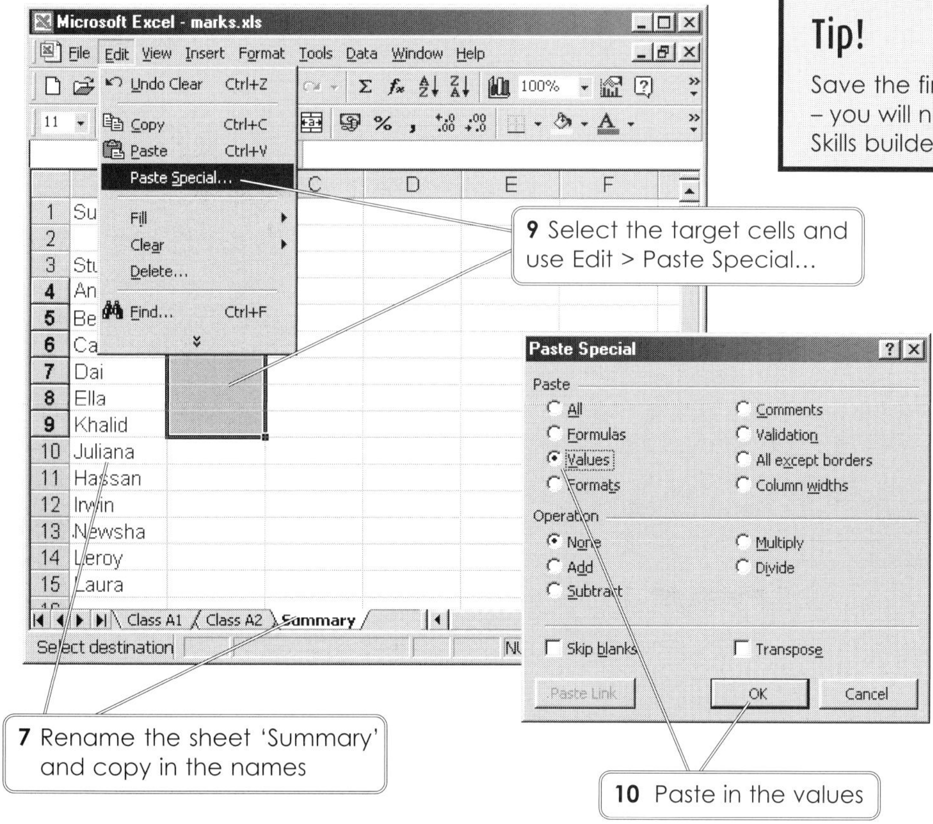

9 Select the target cells and use Edit > Paste Special…

7 Rename the sheet 'Summary' and copy in the names

10 Paste in the values

Using the computer

Word processing

Spreadsheets

Databases

Electronic communications

Presentations

Logical formulae

Excel has a set of 'logical' functions which you can use to compare values. The result of a logical formula then depends upon the comparison.

The simplest, and most important, of the logical functions is IF. It has this shape:

= IF (test, result-if-true, result-if-false)

Note the three parts are separated by commas. 'result-if-true' and 'result-if-false' can be numbers, text, functions or other calculations – we'll keep ours simple!

For example, a business may give customers a discount if an invoice is over a certain amount. This could be handled by an IF function in an invoicing worksheet. In the fragment on the right, the formula in C11 reads:

= IF(C10>1000, C10*0.1, 0)

which means:

If the value in C10 is more than 1000, then the discount is 10% of C10, otherwise it is 0.

We can use IF tests on our students' marks Summary sheet to show if they have passed.

The shape of the test is:

If the average is more than or equal to the pass mark, it is a pass, otherwise it is a fail.

That translates to this formula in C4:

=IF(B4>=$D$1, "Pass", "Fail")

NB: any text must be written in double quotes.

This compares the first student's average (B4) with the pass mark (D1), and displays "Pass" if the average is high enough, or "Fail" if not.

What is the advantage in giving the pass mark as a cell reference rather than a simple value?

Why is the reference $D$1 and not D1?

❶ Type the words 'Pass mark' in C1, and the value in D1.

❷ Write the formula in C4, pressing [**F4**] to give the absolute reference $D$1.

❸ Copy the formula down from C5 to C15.

If the total is more than 1000, there is a discount of 10%

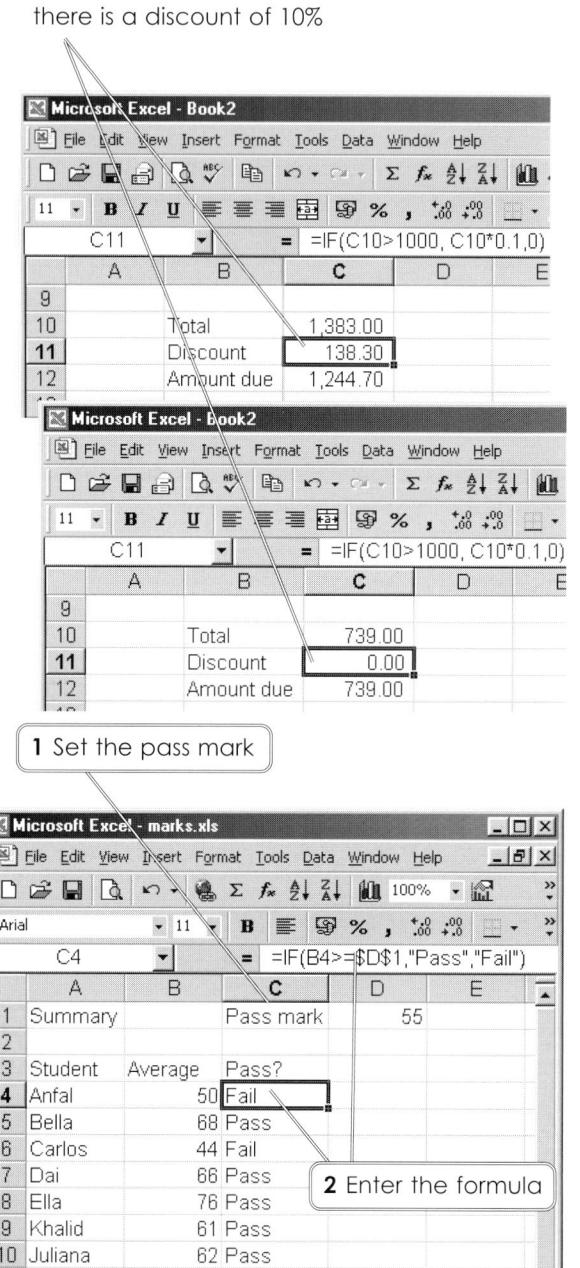

1 Set the pass mark

2 Enter the formula

3 Copy the formula

Skills builder 8:
Formulae and functions

The students in our examples don't just have to pass the tests, they must also attend a minimum number of times. If their attendance is below the minimum, they have to repeat the year. The raw attendance figures are recorded in a spreadsheet. You need to work out their average attendances and check whether or not they will have to repeat the year.

❶ Open the file *attendance.xls* in the *Cambridge/Exercise files* folder.

❷ In E4, create a formula, using the Average function, to work out the average of the values in cells B4 to D4.

❸ Copy the formula from E4 into cells E5 to E15.

❹ In F4, create a formula to display "Repeat" if the average attendance (E4) is less than the minimum (F1).

❺ Copy the formula from F4 into cells F5 to F15.

❻ How many students must repeat the year? What would happen if the minimum attendance was raised to 90%?

❼ Print to file one copy of the sheet, saving it as *attendance.prn* in your IT skills folder.

❽ Save the edited file as *newattendance.xls* in your IT Skills folder.

Your finished spreadsheet should look like this.

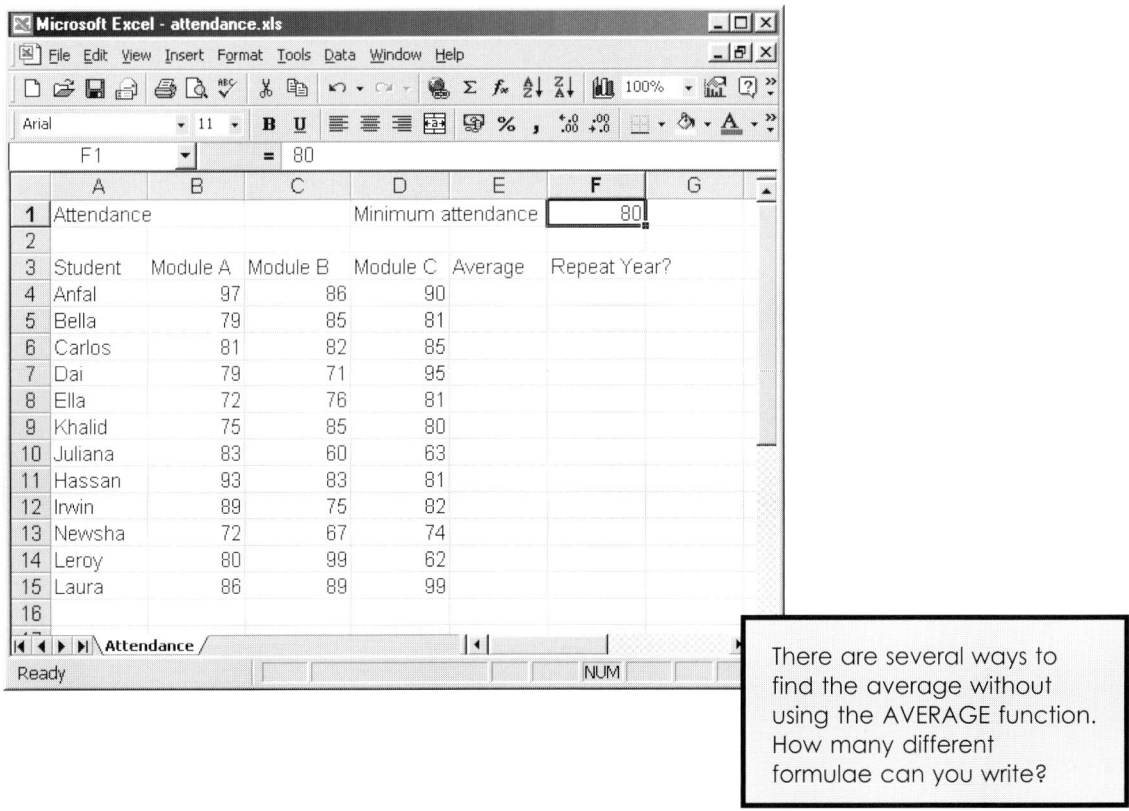

There are several ways to find the average without using the AVERAGE function. How many different formulae can you write?

AutoFormats

AutoFormats offer an instant design solution for common situations. They are all based on headed tables or lists, but with 17 alternatives to choose from you should find something there to suit most of your needs. The formatting includes number formatting, the style of text, the size of the rows and columns, and shading and borders.

If you have some formatting already in place, e.g. the number format, you can choose not to overwrite it with the AutoFormat.

Colours and shades are best avoided if you are not using a colour printer, as they will be printed in grey and could be darker than you expect – making text difficult to read.

❶ Select the table or list to be formatted, including its headers and totals.

❷ Open the **Format** menu and select **AutoFormat...**

❸ Select a format.

❹ If there are aspects you do not want to apply, click **Options…**

❺ Clear the checkboxes to turn off any unwanted formats.

❻ Click **OK**.

Tip!

Even if no format is exactly what you want, it may still be quicker to select the closest and adapt that, rather than setting all aspects of the formatting yourself.

2 Use Format > AutoFormat...

6 Click OK

4 Click Options...

3 Select a format

5 Clear the formats you do not want

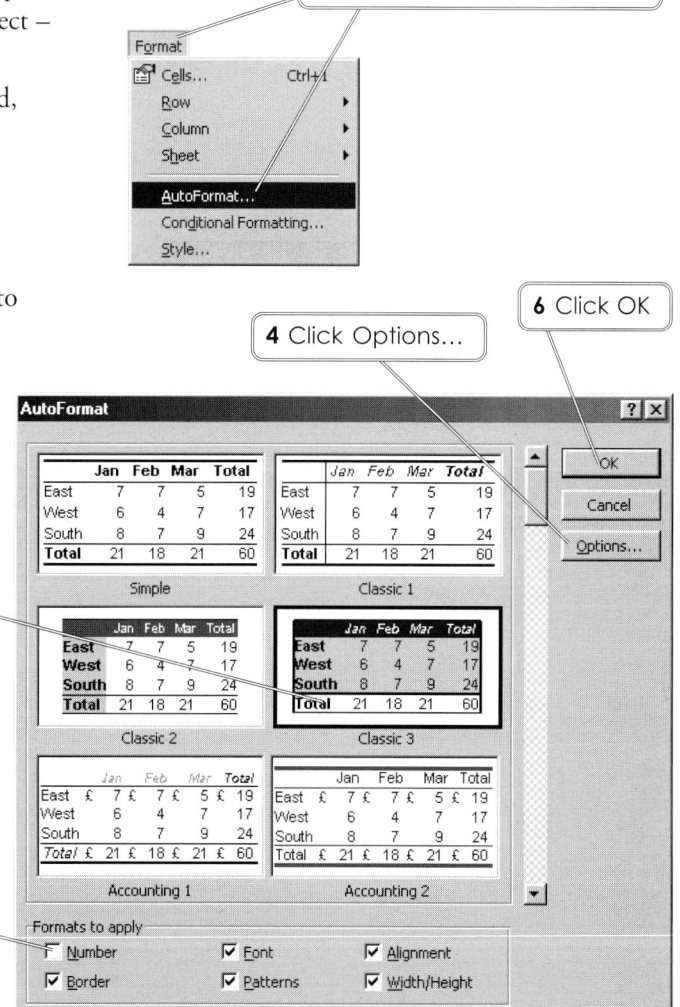

Inserting images

Clip Art and images from file can be inserted into Excel worksheets and formatted in just the same way as in Word documents.

❶ Select a cell in roughly the right place.

❷ Open the **Insert** menu and point to **Picture**.

❸ Select **Clip Art…** and insert a picture from the Clip Gallery (see pages 26 and 27).

Or

❹ Select **From File…** and locate the file on your disks (see page 25).

❺ The picture will be inserted with its top left corner on the selected cell.

❻ Click on the picture and drag to move it.

❼ Drag on a handle to change the size.

❽ Use the tools on the Picture toolbar to fine-tune its appearance (see page 28).

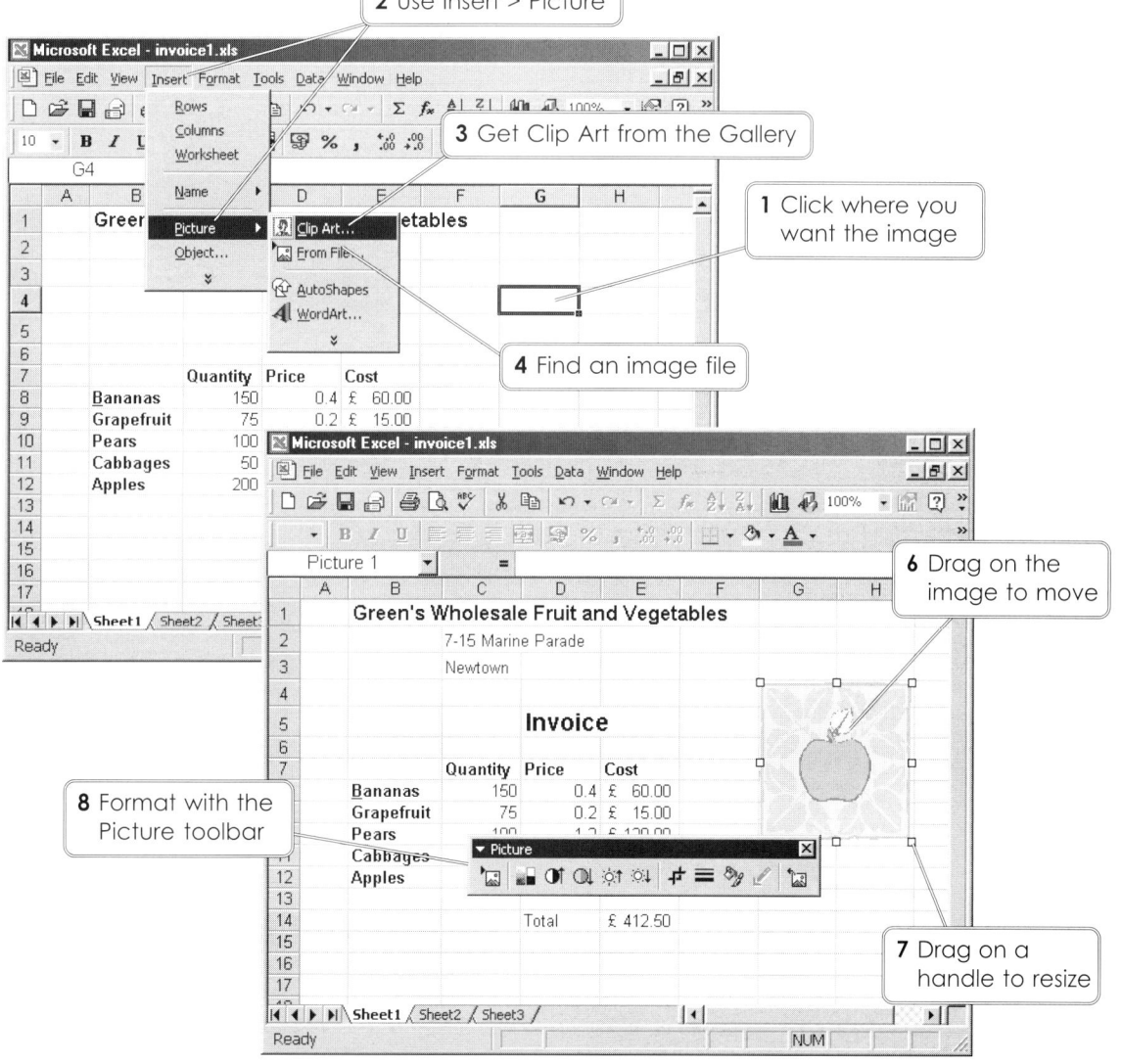

2 Use Insert > Picture

3 Get Clip Art from the Gallery

1 Click where you want the image

4 Find an image file

6 Drag on the image to move

8 Format with the Picture toolbar

7 Drag on a handle to resize

Using the computer

Word processing

Spreadsheets

Databases

Electronic communications

Presentations

Creating charts

If the data that you want to chart is organized properly in the first place, then creating a chart is very simple. If the data is not organized, the job will take a little longer, but is still not difficult.

Ideally, the data should be in a continuous block – no unwanted rows or columns in the middle – with headings above and to the side.

If the data is in rows (i.e. each row will be displayed as a line on a graph or a set of bars on a chart), the top headings will be used to label the bottom axis of the chart, and the side headings will identify the rows in the legend. Where the data is in columns, the headings will be used the other way round.

With data in this form, you can simply run the Chart Wizard, which will ask you to make a few choices, then create the graph for you.

To create a chart:

❶ Select the data, along with the headers.

❷ Click the **Chart Wizard** tool 📊.

❸ Select a **Chart type**, then a **sub-type** and click **Next**.

❹ Check the **Data range**. Click 📝 if you need to redefine the range – you will be taken back into the sheet to select the block of data.

❺ Check the **Series in Rows/Columns** setting. Click **Next**.

❻ Enter the **Chart title** and **Axis** labels, if wanted.

❼ Explore the options on the other tabs.

continued on page 56

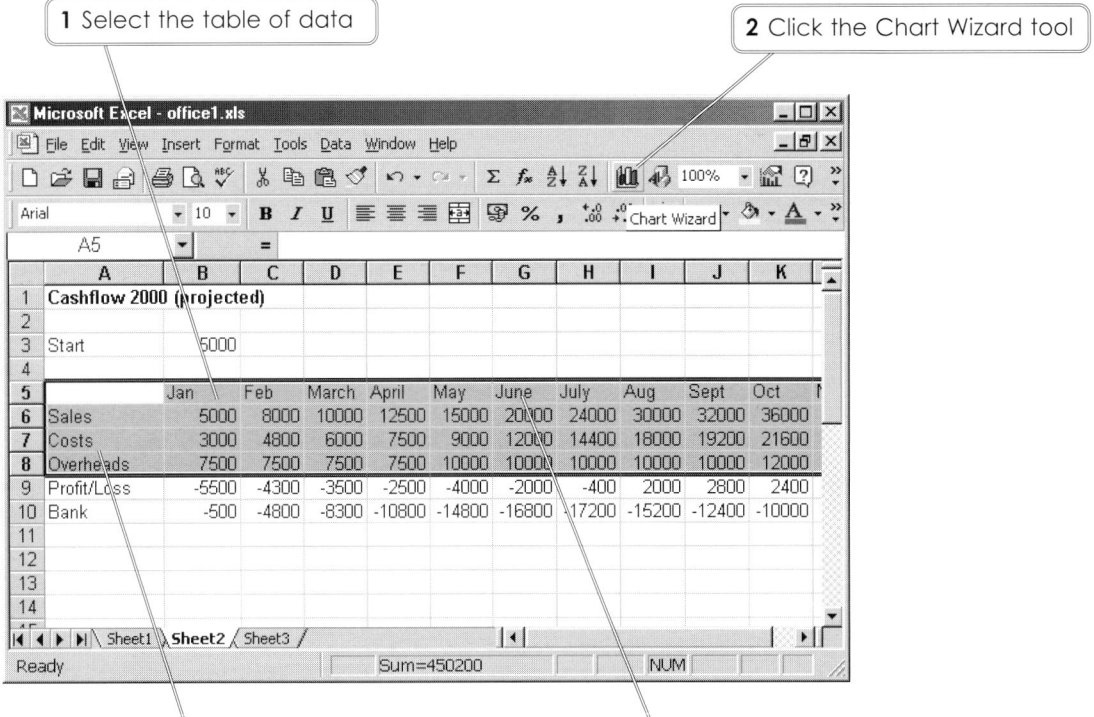

1 Select the table of data

2 Click the Chart Wizard tool

The side headings will be used as labels in the legend (see page 55)

Top headings will be used to label the X axis

54

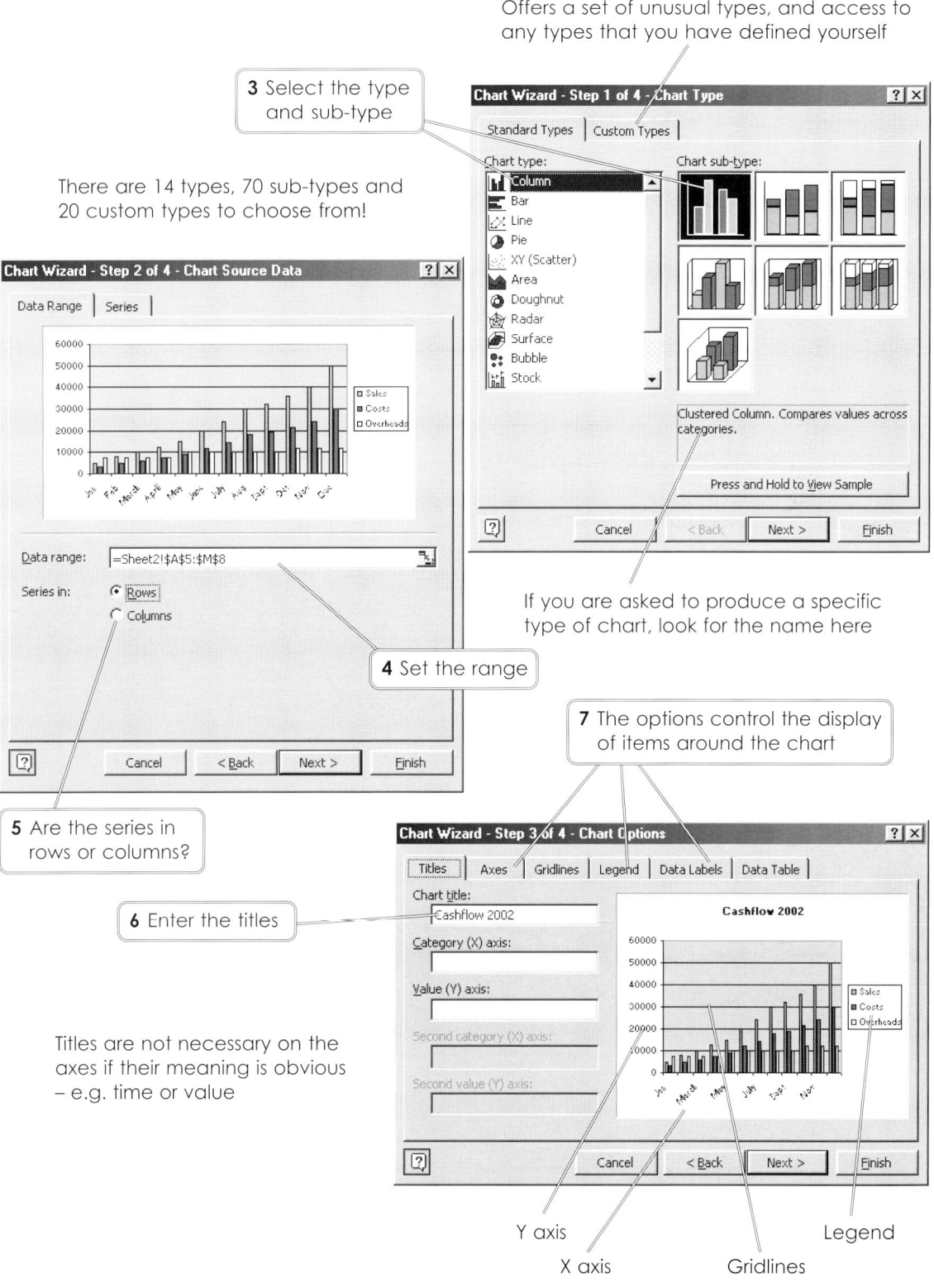

Offers a set of unusual types, and access to any types that you have defined yourself

3 Select the type and sub-type

There are 14 types, 70 sub-types and 20 custom types to choose from!

Chart Wizard - Step 1 of 4 - Chart Type

Standard Types | Custom Types

Chart type:
- Column
- Bar
- Line
- Pie
- XY (Scatter)
- Area
- Doughnut
- Radar
- Surface
- Bubble
- Stock

Chart sub-type:

Clustered Column. Compares values across categories.

Press and Hold to View Sample

Cancel | < Back | Next > | Finish

Chart Wizard - Step 2 of 4 - Chart Source Data

Data Range | Series

Data range: =Sheet2!$A$5:$M$8

Series in: ⦿ Rows ○ Columns

Cancel | < Back | Next > | Finish

4 Set the range

If you are asked to produce a specific type of chart, look for the name here

5 Are the series in rows or columns?

7 The options control the display of items around the chart

6 Enter the titles

Chart Wizard - Step 3 of 4 - Chart Options

Titles | Axes | Gridlines | Legend | Data Labels | Data Table

Chart title: Cashflow 2002

Category (X) axis:

Value (Y) axis:

Second category (X) axis:

Second value (Y) axis:

Cashflow 2002

Cancel | < Back | Next > | Finish

Titles are not necessary on the axes if their meaning is obvious – e.g. time or value

Y axis

X axis

Gridlines

Legend

Using the computer

Word processing

Spreadsheets

Databases

Electronic communications

Presentations

... continued

❽ Select where the chart is to go – as a new sheet or as an object in an existing sheet.

❾ Click **Finish**.

❿ If the chart is placed in a sheet, the Wizard will drop it into the middle – drag it into place and resize it.

Tip!

Place the chart in the same sheet as the data if you want to be able to print both on the same piece of paper.

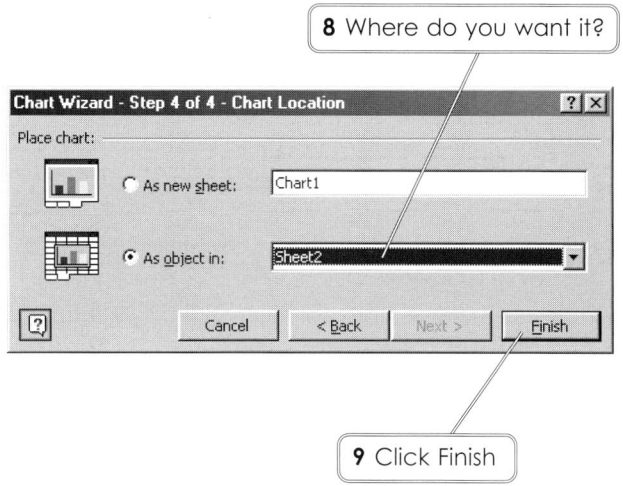

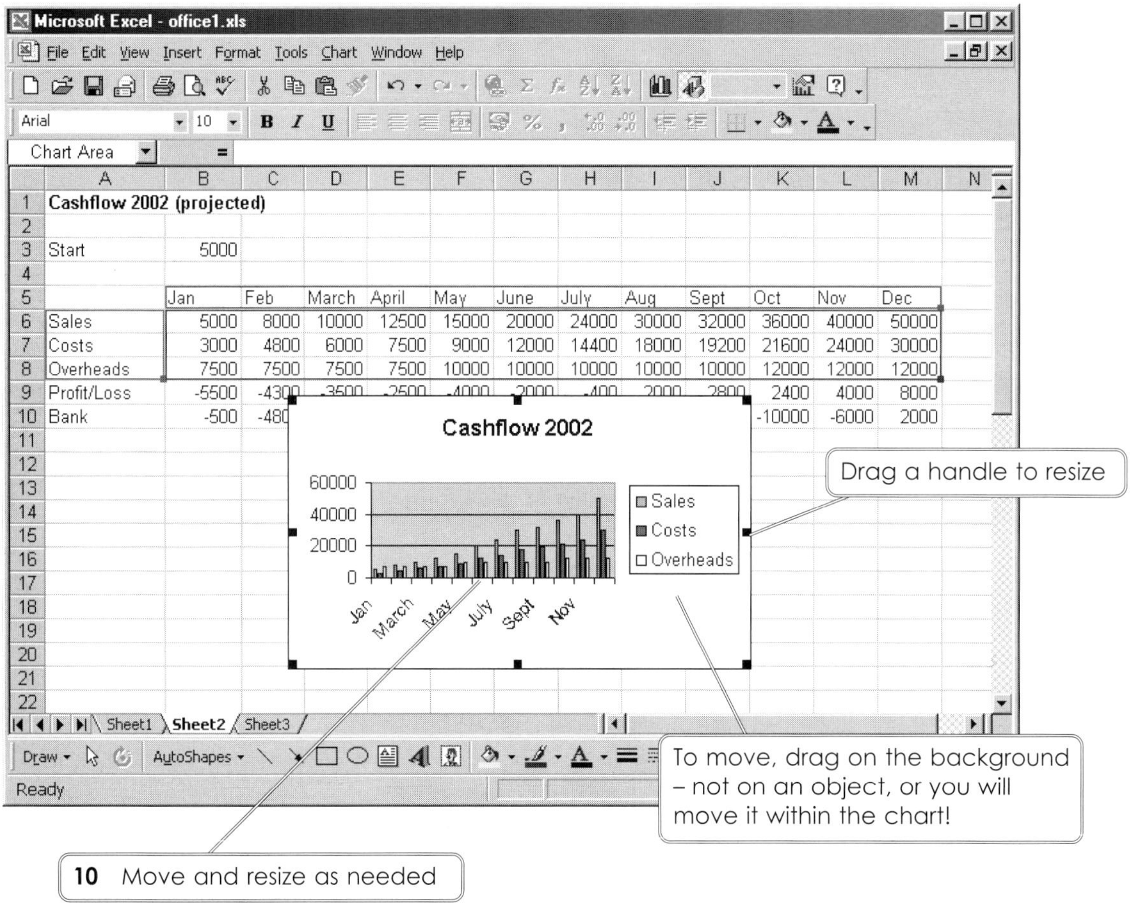

8 Where do you want it?

9 Click Finish

Drag a handle to resize

To move, drag on the background – not on an object, or you will move it within the chart!

10 Move and resize as needed

Formatting charts

Almost every aspect of a chart can be formatted individually to give you just the effect you want – right-click on any object to see the options on its context menu. Fonts, colours, line styles and other format options are set as elsewhere in Office. A few options are unique to graphs. Here, for example, is how to format a 3-D chart. Start with an existing chart – you could use the one from the last worked example.

❶ Click on the chart to select it.

❷ From the **Chart** menu select **Chart Type…**

❸ At the **Chart type** dialog box, select a 3-D option for the **sub-type** and click **OK**.

❹ Right-click on a 'wall' or on the background and select **3-D View**.

❺ In the **3-D View** dialog box:

The **Elevation** buttons raise or lower the viewpoint.

The **Perspective** buttons control the depth of field.

The **Rotation** buttons swivel it on its vertical axis.

❻ Click **Apply** to see the effect of the settings.

❼ Click **OK** when you have finished.

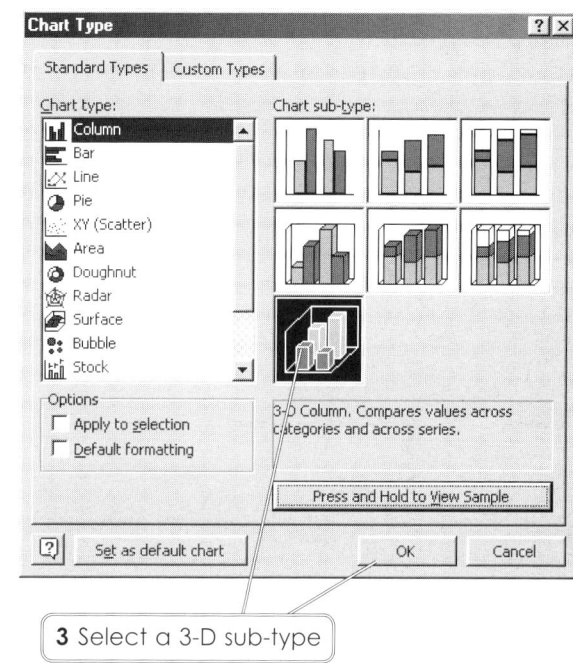

3 Select a 3-D sub-type

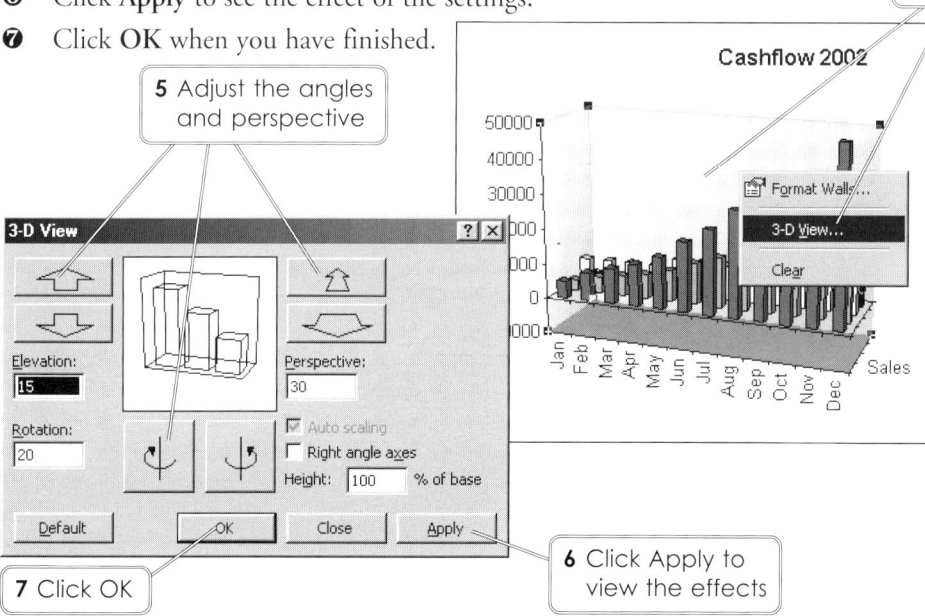

5 Adjust the angles and perspective

4 Right-click and select 3-D View

6 Click Apply to view the effects

7 Click OK

Using the computer

Word processing

Spreadsheets

Databases

Electronic communications

Presentations

57

Skills builder 9: Excel charts

This exercise draws its data from the budget worksheet from Skills builder 7.

❶ Open the file *mybudget.xls* in your IT Skills folder.

❷ In column H, create formulae, using the SUM function, to find the totals of each category of spending for January to June.

❸ Select the range A4 to A10, then hold down [**Control**] and select the range H4 to H10.

❹ Click the **Chart Wizard** button. It will now start to create a chart based on the labels in column A and the values in column H.

❺ Work through the Wizard to produce a pie chart, selecting a 3-D option.

Display the labels and percentages beside each slice.

Turn off the legend, and add the title 'Spending'.

The chart should be created on a new sheet.

❻ Open the **3-D View** dialog box, and set the Elevation to 30 and the Rotation to 90.

❼ Print the chart to file, saving it as *budgetchart.prn* in your IT Skills folder.

❽ Save the file as *budgetchart.xls*.

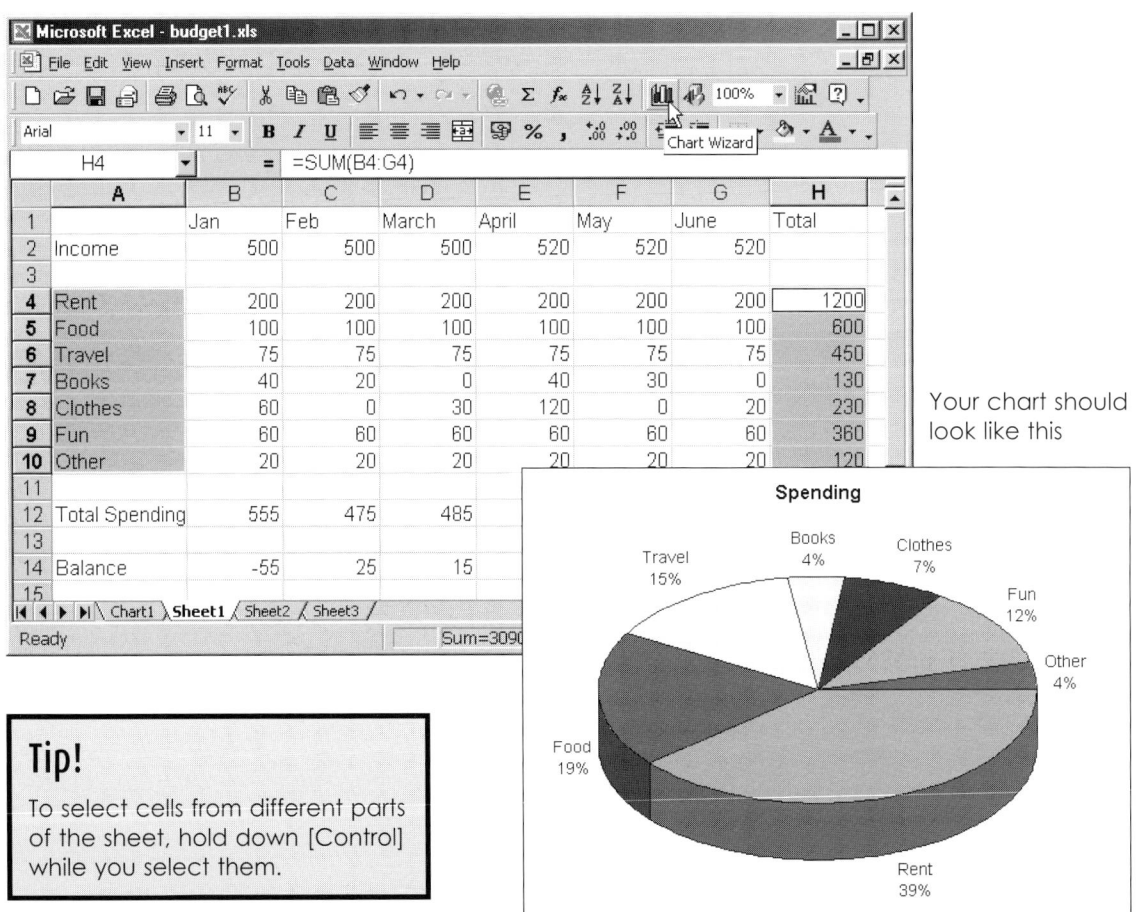

Your chart should look like this

Tip!

To select cells from different parts of the sheet, hold down [Control] while you select them.

Page Setup

As a spreadsheet can be any size, you may need to do some extra work to get it to fit neatly onto your paper when you print it. The settings are all on the Page Setup dialog box – reach it through the **Page Setup** command on the **File** menu.

Page

The **Page** tab options set the overall layout of the paper, and of the scaling.

➤ Wide sheets may well print better with the **Orientation** set to *Landscape* (sideways).

➤ If the sheet is only a little too big for the paper, then set the **Scaling** either to a % **normal size**, or make it **Fit to** a set number of pages.

➤ If the printout is for your own use, setting the **Print quality** to *Low* or *Draft* will make it print faster and use less ink or toner.

You can check the Print Preview at any time, then come back to adjust settings

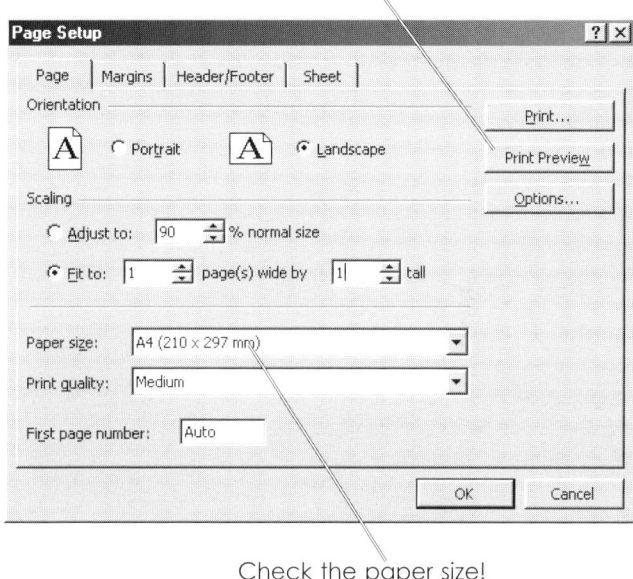

Check the paper size!

Margins

The main settings on the **Margins** tab are the widths of the margins. These can be reduced to the minimum values if it will help to produce a better fit.

Unless set otherwise, the printing will start at the top left of the page. Sometimes, especially with small sheets, the printout may look better if you turn on one or both of the **Center on page** options.

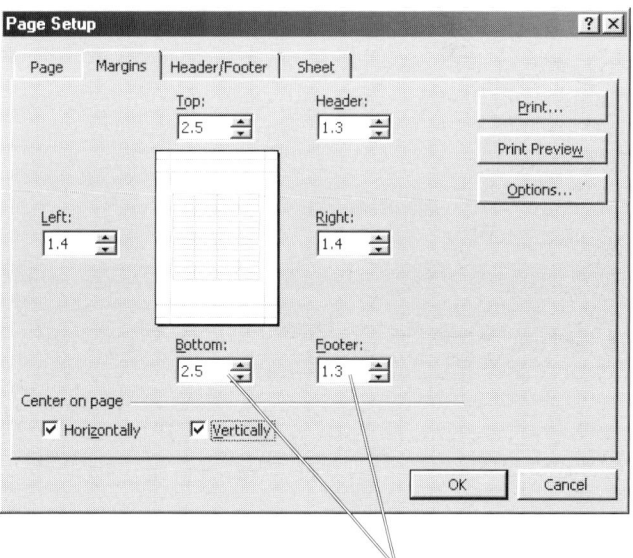

If you do not want a header or footer, the Header/Footer space can be set to 0 and the Top/Bottom margins made smaller

Using the computer

Word processing

Spreadsheets

Databases

Electronic communications

Presentations

Headers and footers

Headers and footers do not appear on the spreadsheet, but are added to the paper at printout. They can carry such information as author, filename, page number and date and time of printing, which can all help to identify the printouts. They are particularly useful with larger spreadsheets, where the main titles and headings may only be shown on the first page.

A selection of standard headers and footers are available, or you can create your own.

To add a header and/or footer:

❶ Go to the **Header/Footer** tab.

❷ Click the drop-down **Header** list and see if any of the standard headers meet your requirements. Select one if suitable, if not…

❸ Click **Custom Header…**

❹ Click into the left, center or right section, as required.

❺ Type the text (e.g. 'Page') or click an icon to insert system information.

❻ To format the text, select it and click **A** to open the **Font** dialog box. Set the font, size and style as normal.

❼ Repeat steps ❷ to ❻ for a footer.

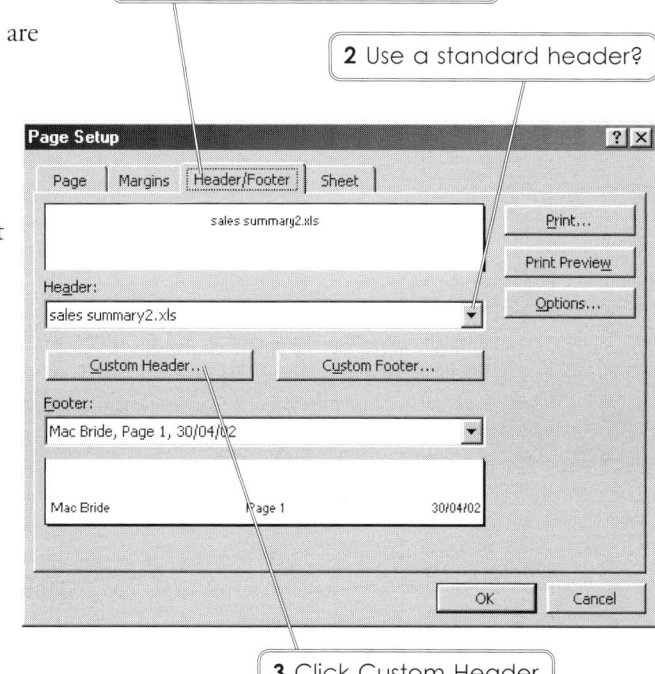

1 Go to the Header/Footer tab

2 Use a standard header?

3 Click Custom Header

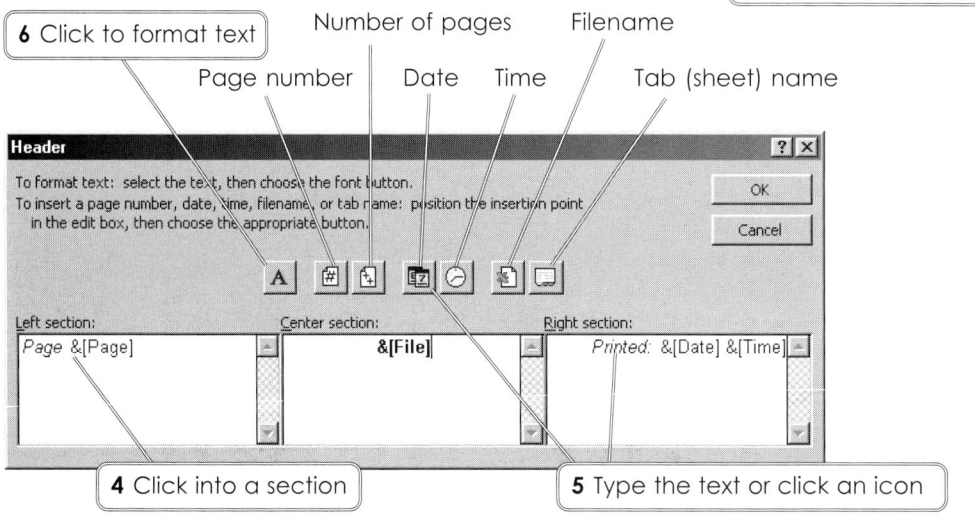

6 Click to format text

Number of pages

Filename

Page number   Date   Time   Tab (sheet) name

4 Click into a section

5 Type the text or click an icon

60

The Print area

Sometimes you will only want to print out part of a spreadsheet. For example, a sheet used for creating estimates might have areas in which prices of materials are stored or in which over-heads are calculated. You would only normally want to print out the area holding the estimate.

If the print area has not been set already, it is one of the options that can be set from the Sheet tab.

❶ Go to the **Sheet** tab.

❷ Click 🔤 at the right of the **Print area** box.

❸ The dialog box will shrink to a single line, showing the sheet clearly. Select the area to be printed.

❹ Click 🔤 to return to the dialog box.

❺ If you want to **repeat Rows** or **Columns** of headers on every page, select them, using the 🔤 icon to access the sheet.

❻ Select the **Page order** that will make for easiest reading.

Tip!

The print area can be set from the main display. Select the area, then use the command **File > Print Area > Set Print Area**.

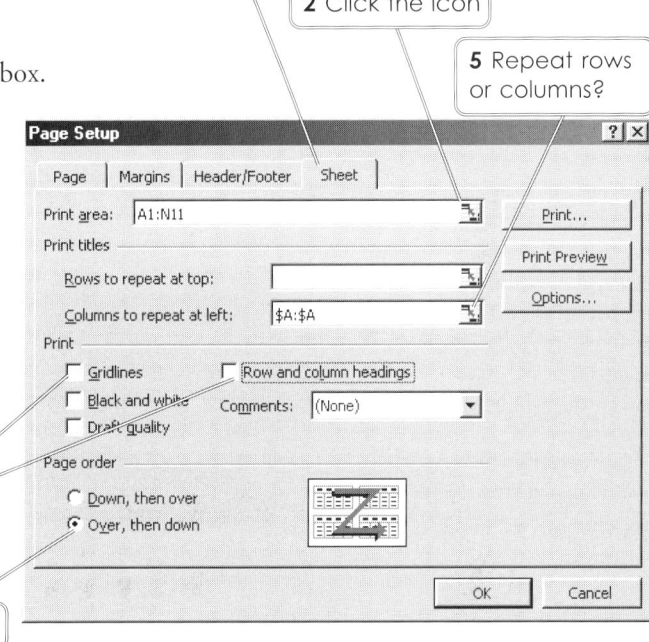

1 Go to the Sheet tab

2 Click the icon

5 Repeat rows or columns?

Gridlines and the column letters and row numbers can be printed if wanted

6 Set the page order

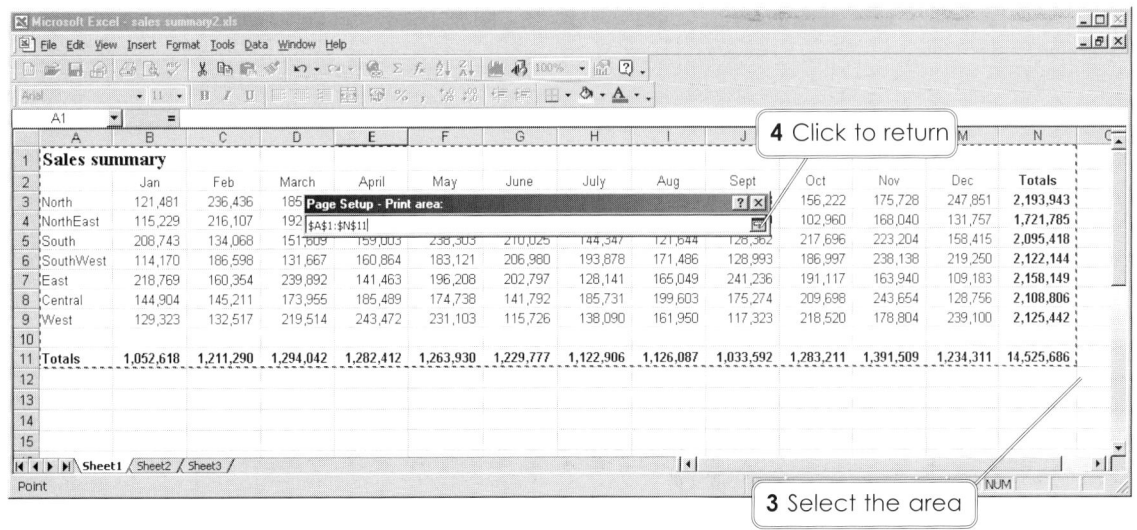

4 Click to return

3 Select the area

Using the computer

Word processing

Spreadsheets

Databases

Electronic communications

Presentations

Print Preview

The Print Preview should be used alongside the Page Setup – and the two are connected.

You can go to the Print Preview through the button on the **Page Setup** dialog box; and you can reach the Page Setup through the **Setup...** button in the Print Preview window.

The Print Preview tools

Next and **Previous**   Move back and forwards between the pages.

Zoom   Zoom in close enough to read the text and check the formatting or back to view the whole page.

Print   Send to the printer when you are happy with the preview.

Setup...   Open the **Page Setup** dialog box to adjust settings – you will be returned to the Print Preview afterwards.

Tip!

The Print Preview can also be started with the command **File > Print Preview**.

Margins   Display the margins on the preview – they can then be dragged to adjust.

Page Break Preview   Display the spreadsheet with lines to show how it will be divided when printed.

Close   Return to the spreadsheet.

Help   Open the Help system.

Print Preview, after zooming in

Note the header

Microsoft Excel - sales summary2.xls

| Next | Previous | Zoom | Print... | Setup... | Margins | Page Break Preview | Close | Help |

Page 1   sales summary2.xls   Printed: 30/04/02 10:48

Sales summary

	Jan	Feb	March	April	May	June	July
North	121,481	236,436	185,022	230,623	113,924	212,762	182,668
NorthEast	115,229	216,107	192,382	161,497	126,533	139,695	150,052
South	208,743	134,068	151,609	159,003	238,303	210,025	144,347
SouthWest	114,170	186,598	131,667	160,864	183,121	206,980	193,878
East	218,769	160,354	239,892	141,463	196,208	202,797	128,141
Central	144,904	145,211	173,955	185,489	174,738	141,792	185,731
West	129,323	132,517	219,514	243,472	231,103	115,726	138,090
Totals	**1,052,618**	**1,211,290**	**1,294,042**	**1,282,412**	**1,263,930**	**1,229,777**	**1,122,906**

Preview: Page 1 of 2   NUM

Skills builder 10: Sorting and printing

This exercise gives practice in moving data between spreadsheets, and in preparing sheets for printing.

❶ Open your *marks.xls* file created in the example on Multiple Worksheets (page 48), and the *newattendance.xls* sheet from Skills builder 8.

❷ On the Attendance sheet, select the data range A1:F15 and copy it.

❸ Go to the Summary sheet in *marks.xls* and paste in the range with its top left corner at E1.

❹ Check that the names in columns A and E are in line, then delete column E.

❺ If you used an absolute reference in the 'Repeat Year' formulae, they will now need editing as the minimum attendance figure is no longer in the same cell.

❻ Use the Page Setup to change the orientation to landscape.

❼ Add a Header – you could use a course name, e.g. 'Home Economics 2002'.

❽ In the Footer, display the page number on the left and the date on the right.

❾ Set the print area to cover the active part of the sheet – this should be A1:I16.

❿ Preview – and go back and adjust the settings if necessary – then print the sheet to file, saving it as *results.prn*. Save the worksheet as *results.xls*.

The print preview of your sheet should look like this

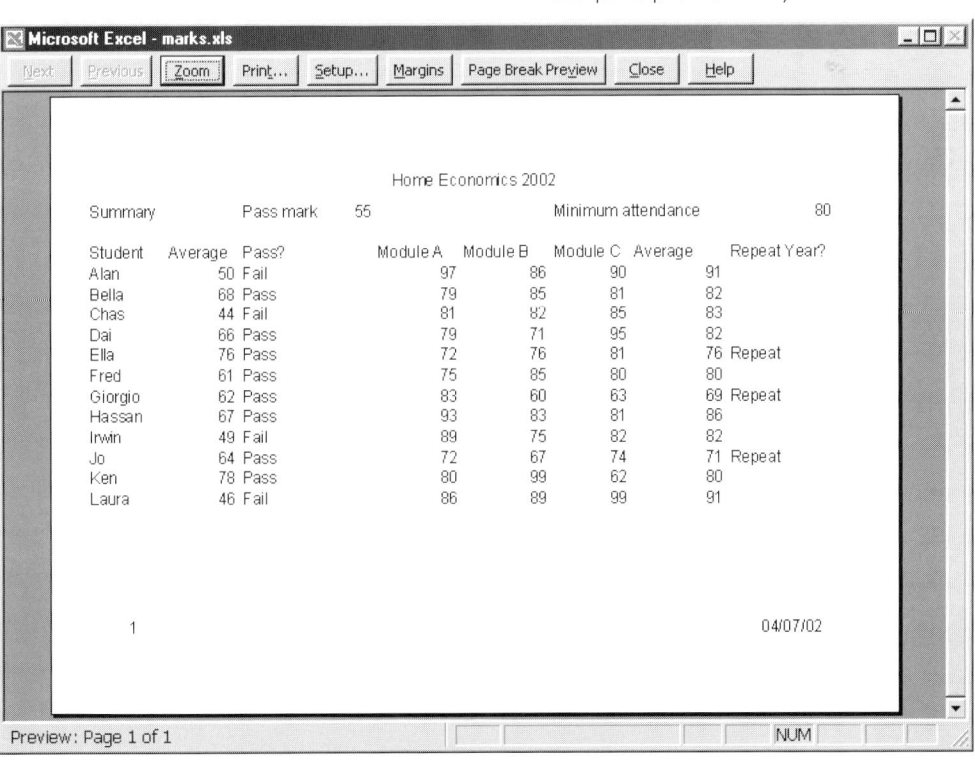

Using the computer

Word processing

Spreadsheets

Databases

Electronic communications

Presentations

Are you ready?

Get your tutor to check your work.

If you have successfully completed the skills builder exercises in this section, and are confident in using those skills, you are ready for the *Spreadsheets* test.

If you need a little more practice before taking the test, ask your tutor for the *Spreadsheets* pre-test exercise.

4 Databases

You should know how to:

- Open and close a database
- Create a simple database structure
- Enter, edit, sort and format data
- Save database files
- Print tables

You will learn how to:

- Modify a database
- Create relationships
- Write more complex queries
- Create and modify forms
- Create and modify reports

Additional resources:

- Checklist 4: Databases
- Sample files in the *Cambridge* folder

The Access screen

The layout of the screen depends upon the job that you are doing at the time (and how you choose to arrange the windows and toolbars).

The Database window

This is the control centre. Use it to create and open the tables, queries, forms and reports that make up the database.

Table window

Each table, query or other object is opened in its own window. These can be moved, minimized or resized as needed to suit the work.

The Standard toolbar

This should be open all the time. It has tools for the most commonly used tasks.

The Formatting toolbar

This opens automatically when you are designing forms and reports. It can be opened when working with tables, but note that any formatting applies to the whole table – you cannot format selected cells, fields or records.

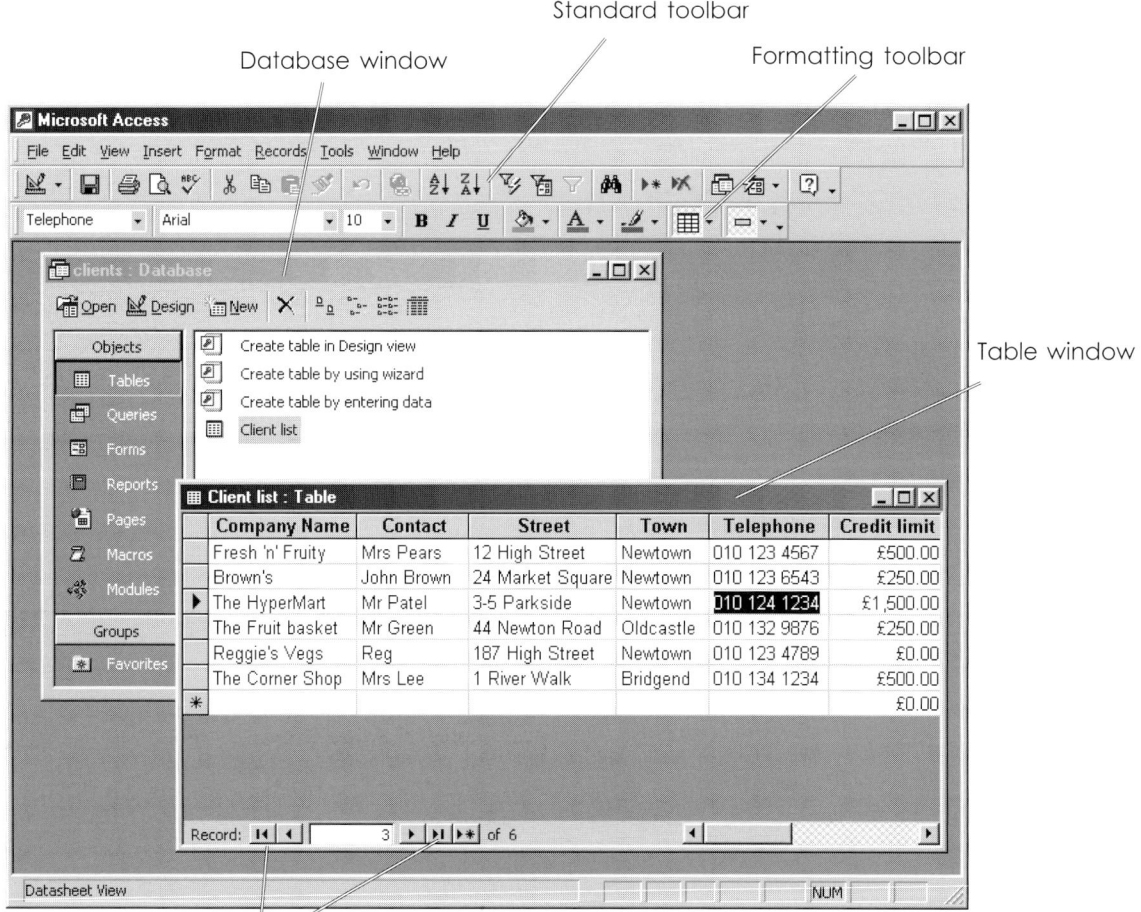

Standard toolbar

Database window

Formatting toolbar

Table window

Navigation buttons – use them when there are lots of records. With a small database it is easier to move around with the mouse or arrow keys

Modifying databases

The structure of a database can be modified at any time, even after data has been added. New tables can be added and, in existing tables, fields can be added, deleted or redefined.

Take care – you may lose data!

➤ If you delete a field, you lose all the data entered in it for any records.

➤ If you change a field's type, you will probably lose any data it contains.

➤ If you reduce the field size or change to a smaller number format, you may lose some data from some fields.

Data types and properties

Every data type has several properties which define exactly how a field handles data. Here are the most important properties at this level.

Field size

In a Text field, this sets how many characters can be stored – the default is 50, the maximum 255.

In a Number field, this sets the size and accuracy of the values that can be stored.

➤ *Integer*, whole numbers between –32,767 and +32,767 (the values that can be held in two bytes of data), used for reference codes, stock levels, etc.

➤ *Long integer*, bigger whole numbers (up to +/–2,000,000,000). Autonumbers are normally long integer.

➤ *Single* and *Double*, used for storing values with decimal fractions.

Format

This sets the appearance of data.

➤ In a *Currency* field, it determines whether or not a symbol is shown.

➤ In a *Date/Time* field you can choose whether to show the date or the time and how to display it.

> **Tip!**
>
> Backup your database file before you start to make any changes to it. Copy it to a different folder or a floppy disk.

Decimal places

This is present in Number and Currency fields, and controls the number of decimal places to display.

Indexed

This property is found with every data type, and has three settings:

➤ *No*;

➤ *Yes (Duplicates OK)*;

➤ *Yes (No Duplicates)*.

If a field is indexed, the table can be sorted on that field more quickly than if it is not indexed – though you only see the difference with very large tables.

If *Yes (No Duplicates)* is used, it ensures that the data in this field is unique – Access will prevent anyone from entering the same data that is already present in another record. It should be set for reference numbers or other identifiers.

> **Tip!**
>
> Only the core data types and the main features of Access are covered in this book. To find out about any of the more advanced features, open the Help system and browse through the contents or ask the Answer Wizard.

Using the computer

Word processing

Spreadsheets

Databases

Electronic communications

Presentations

Skills builder 11:
Modifying a table

❶ Open *clients.mdb* in the *Cambridge/Exercise files* folder.

❷ Open the table *Client list* in Design view – in the Database window, select it and click **Design**.

❸ Select the *Company name* field.

❹ Click into **Field Size** and change it to 30.

In the same way, set *Contact* to 20, *Town* to 30 and *Telephone* to 15.

❺ Select the *Credit limit* field and click into the **Format** property.

❻ Click the arrow that appears on the right and select *Standard* from the drop-down list.

❼ Select the *Last order* field, drop down its **Format** list and select *Medium Date*.

❽ Add a new field, called *Reference*, with the Number data type, setting *Integer* as its Field Size.

❾ Click 🖫 to save your changes. You will be warned that data may be lost as you have made some fields smaller. Click **OK**.

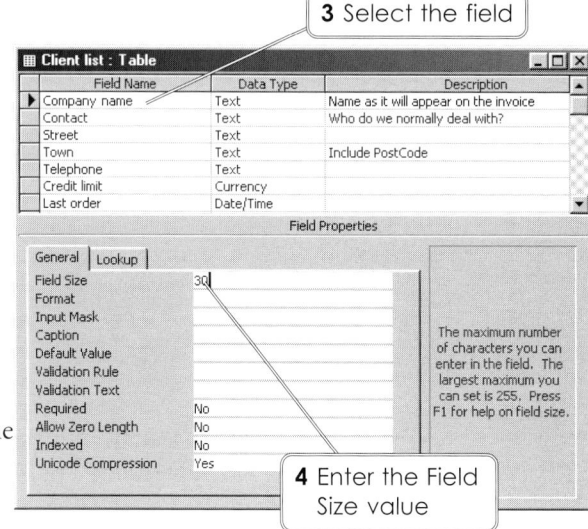

3 Select the field

4 Enter the Field Size value

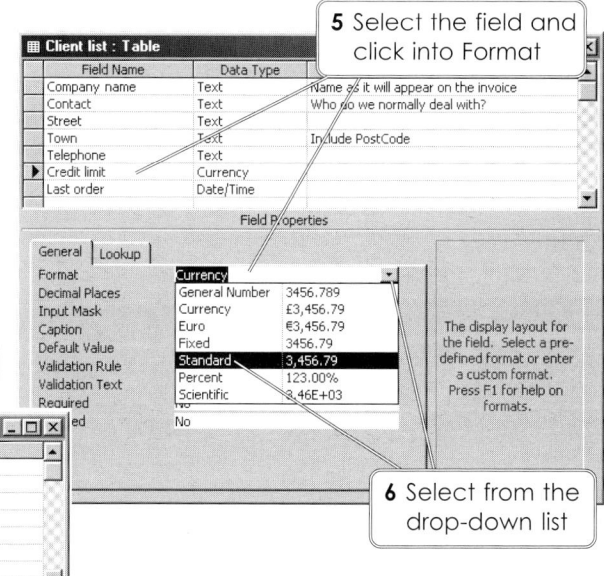

5 Select the field and click into Format

6 Select from the drop-down list

7 Set the Date/Time Format

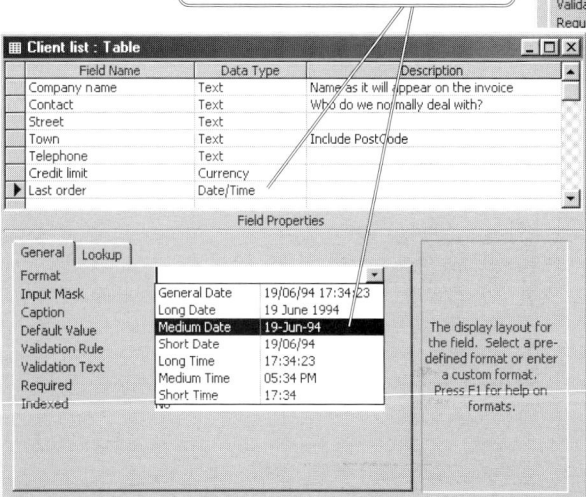

> **Tip!**
>
> If you want to help with any of the properties of data types, click into the box for the property and press [F1]. The Help system will open at the relevant page.

Relational databases

A relational database is one which has two or more tables, which are linked by shared data in specific fields. The link is normally a one-to-many relationship, where one record in the first table is linked to many in the second.

For example, a firm might have a stock database, consisting of a *Products* table and a *Suppliers* table, each having a field called *SupplierID*. When the firm starts to use a new supplier, its name, address and other details are entered into the *Suppliers* table. When a new item is taken on, its details are entered into the *Products* table. For the product's supplier, all that is needed is the *SupplierID*. When it is time to order new stock, the *SupplierID* link will pull the name and address from the *Suppliers* table.

Linking tables in this way saves time and reduces errors in data entry. It also saves data storage space. Think of the alternative. If you had to enter the details of the supplier for every item in the *Products* table, how much bigger would that table be? How much longer would it take to enter each new product record?

ID	Name	Description	Price	Stock Level	SupplierID
1	Typist chair	Gas lift, armless	£29.99	8	1
2	Executive chair	High back, tilting	£89.99	2	1
3	Budget desk	Ash finish, 5 drawer	£119.99	5	2
4	Budget cabinet	Ash finish, 1.4m	£109.99	3	2

The linked fields do not have to have the same name
– but it makes the link more obvious

SupplierID	Name	Street	Town	Telephone
1	Chairs, etc.	14 Railway Arches	Hightown	555 12345
2	OffEquip	Unit 3, Western Industrial Estate	Redbridge	555 45624

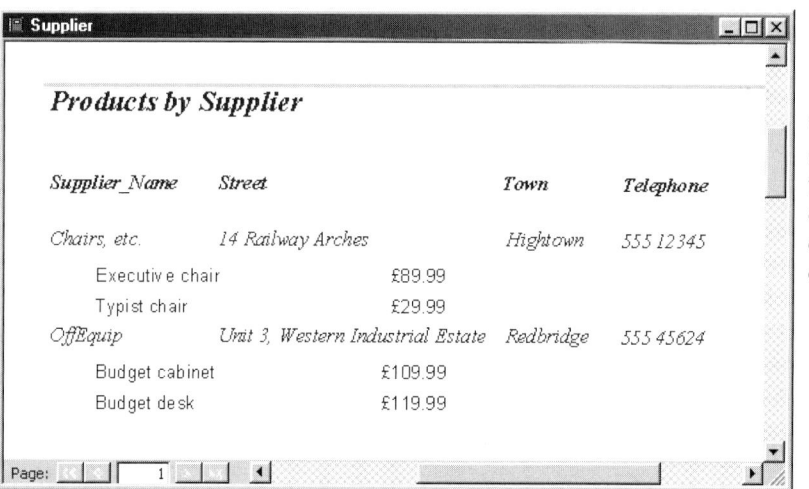

When tables are linked, data can be drawn from them to produce combined reports, as in this example where products are grouped by supplier

Using the computer

Word processing

Spreadsheets

Databases

Electronic communications

Presentations

Making relationships

The first step in creating a relational database is to set up the tables. These may be added to an existing database, or started in a new database. Here we do it by creating a new database.

First set up the tables:

❶ Run Access and start to create a new database. Save it as '*stock*' in your IT Skills folder.

❷ Create the tables. Define the *Products* table as shown on the right. Make *ID* the primary key – select it and click 🔑.

❸ Define the *Supplier* table, as shown, setting *SupplierID* as the primary key.

❹ Save both tables.

❺ Take the tables into Datasheet view and add the sample data shown on page 69.

Then join them together:

❶ From the **Tools** menu select **Relationships…**

❷ When the **Relationships** window appears, open the **Relationships** menu and select **Show Table…**

continued…

> **Tip!**
>
> Before you start to set up a database, work out what will be stored in each table, and which fields will be used to link them.

Products

Name	Type	Field size
ID	Autonumber	Long Integer
Name	Text	50
Description	Text	100
Price	Currency	
Stock level	Number	Integer
SupplierID	Number	Integer

Supplier

Name	Type	Field size
SupplierID	Autonumber	Long Integer
Name	Text	20
Street	Text	50
Town	Text	30
Telephone	Text	12

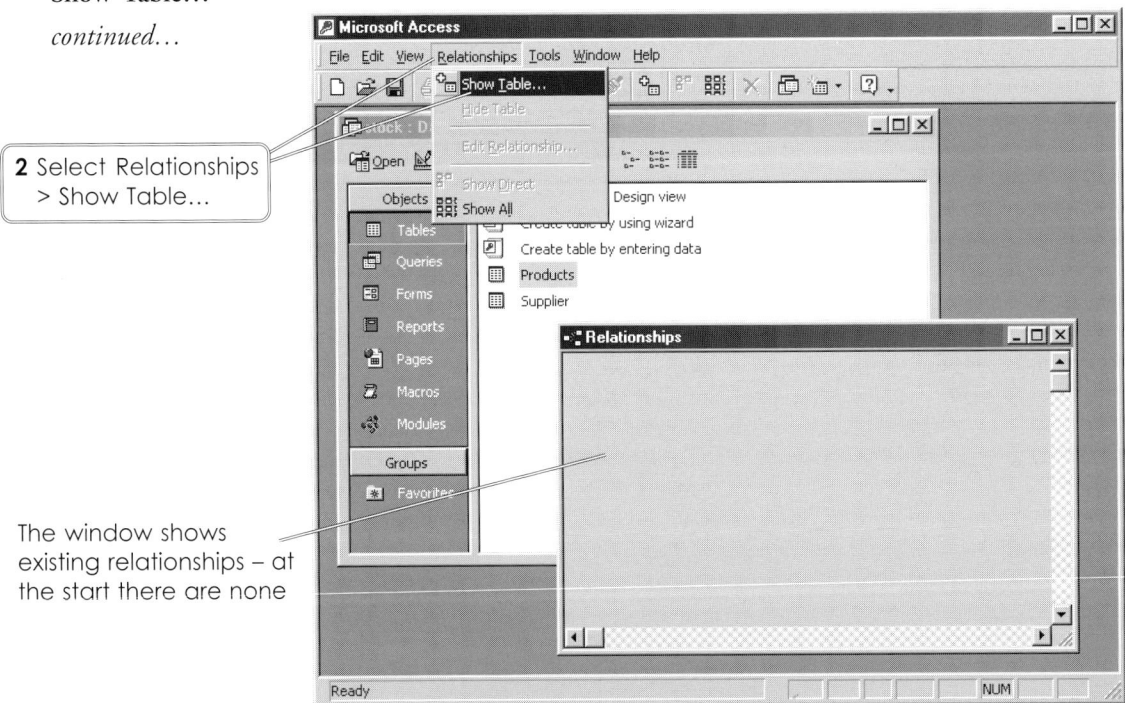

2 Select Relationships > Show Table…

The window shows existing relationships – at the start there are none

❸ At the **Show Table** dialog box, select each table and click **Add** to add the table to the Relationships display.

❹ Click **Close**.

❺ Select the field to be linked from one table and drag it onto the field in the other table.

❻ At the **Edit Relationships** dialog box, check that it lists the correct fields and click **Create**.

❼ Click 🖫 to save the new relationship.

❽ Click ⊠ to close the window.

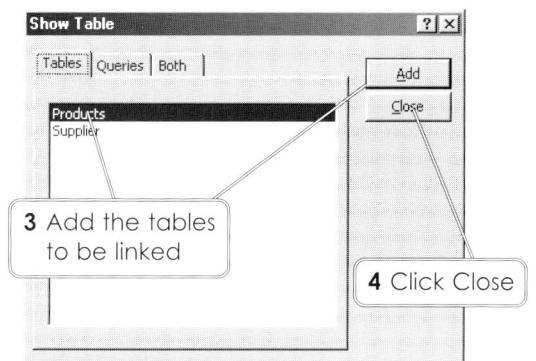

3 Add the tables to be linked

4 Click Close

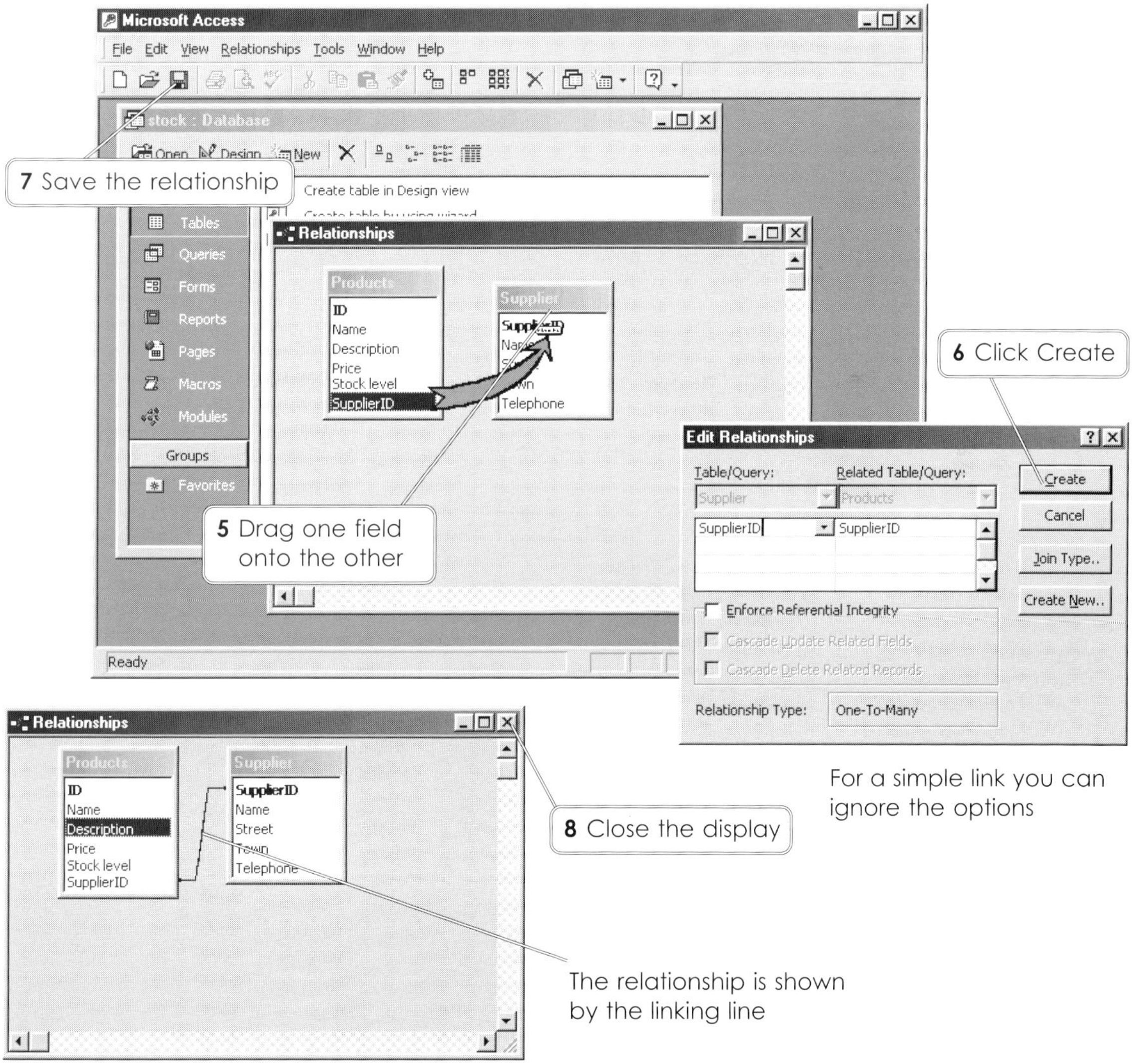

7 Save the relationship

5 Drag one field onto the other

6 Click Create

8 Close the display

For a simple link you can ignore the options

The relationship is shown by the linking line

Using the computer

Word processing

Spreadsheets

Databases

Electronic communications

Presentations

Skills builder 12:
Relationships

In this exercise you will extend the *Stock* database that we have just created, adding a new table, *Category*. This will be linked to the *Products* table through a new field.

❶ Create a table in Design view, containing the fields *ID* and *Description* – see right.

❷ Save the table design, then enter the four records shown here (or something similar).

❸ Open the *Products* table in Design view, and add the field *CategoryID*, a Number data type, set to Long Integer. Save the changes.

❹ From the **Tools** menu, select **Relationships** to open the **Relationships** dialog box.

❺ Open the **Relationships** menu and select **Show Table…**

❻ Add the Categories table to the display and click **Close**.

❼ Drag the *CategoryID* field from *Products* onto the *ID* field in *Categories*, then click **Create** at the **Edit Relationships** dialog box.

❽ Click 🖫 to save the new relationship and close the window.

Categories (design)

Name	Type	Field size
ID	Autonumber	Long Integer
Description	Text	20

Categories (data)

ID	Description
1	Chairs
2	Tables
3	Cabinets
4	Shelves

The Relationships window should look like this after step ❼

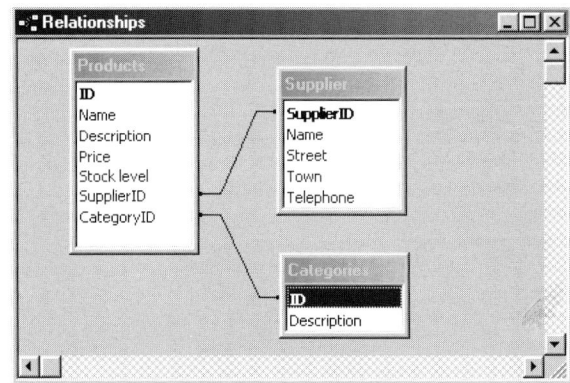

72

Queries using operators

Simply entering a value for the Criteria cell will only find exact matches. Very often you want those that fall into a range, e.g. customers owing more than a certain amount. To find these we can use the *relational operators*.

Operator	Meaning
>	Greater than
<	Less than
<>	Not equal to
>=	Greater than or equal to
<=	Less than or equal to

These can be used on any type of value, not just numeric, e.g. '<=M' in a *Surname* field would match those people whose surname began with anything from 'A' to 'M'. '>31/12/01' will find any dates after the end of 2001.

To add a field to the query, double-click on it in the field list

To remove a field, click on the thin bar at the top of the column, then press [Delete]

AND and OR queries

A query may have several criteria.

If two or more criteria must be met, then you have a logical AND. For example, in a student database, to find students who were over 16 AND played football, you would set '>16' as the criteria in the *Age* field and 'Football' in the *Sports* field. Both criteria must be true for the record to be retrieved.

AND can be used to set several criteria in a single field, e.g. clients whose last order was after 1/1/02 AND before 31/1/02. You could select these by writing '>1/1/02 AND <31/1/02' in the Criteria cell of the *Last order* field.

If either two or more alternative values may be matched, you have a logical OR. For example, you could create a query to select clients in Oldcastle or Bridgend. Notice the **or:** row in the query design grid. To set up OR queries, write the first value in the Criteria cell, then the alternative value in the **or:** cell of the same field.

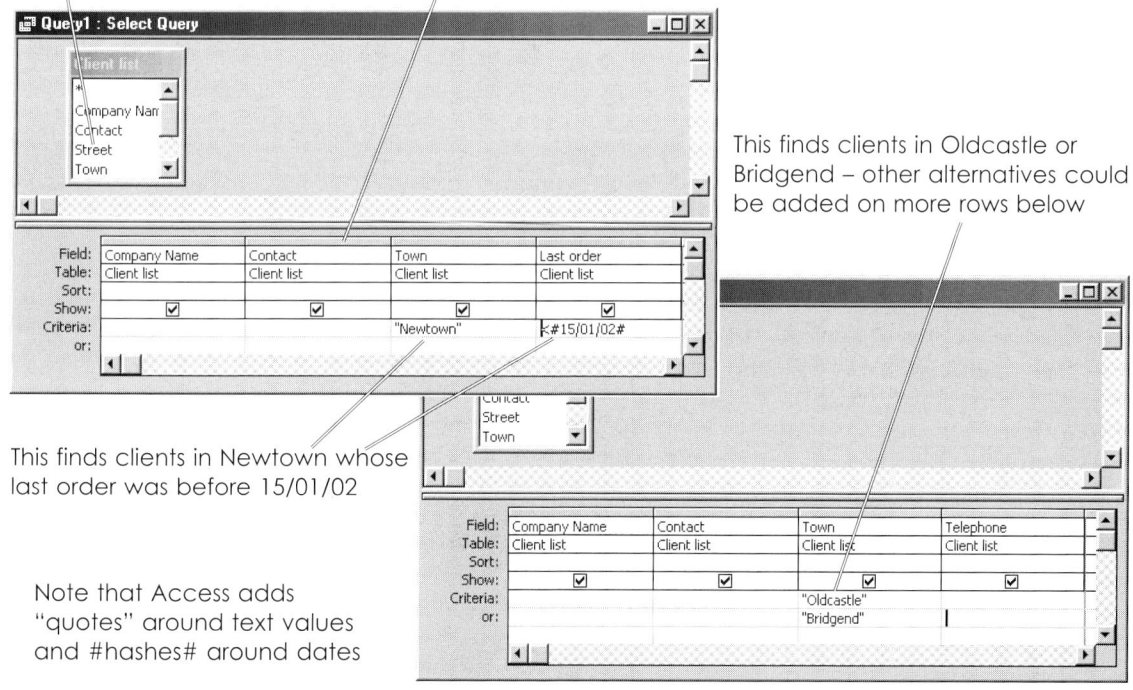

This finds clients in Oldcastle or Bridgend – other alternatives could be added on more rows below

This finds clients in Newtown whose last order was before 15/01/02

Note that Access adds "quotes" around text values and #hashes# around dates

Using the computer

Word processing

Spreadsheets

Databases

Electronic communications

Presentations

Multi-table queries

In a relational database, a query can be used to bring together data from more than one table. For example, in a stock database, you might use a query to find those items that needed restocking. If the query included details of the supplier as well as of the products, then the *dynaset* would have all that was needed to reorder stock.

To create a multi-table query:

❶ Select **Queries** in the **Object** list in the database window, then click on **Create query by using Wizard**.

❷ Select a table from the **Tables/Queries** list.

❸ Add fields from the **Available Fields** display to the **Selected Fields**.

❹ Repeat steps ❷ and ❸ to add fields from one or more other tables.

❺ Click **Next**, then complete the query as usual.

❻ Choose **Modify the query design** at the end if you want to set criteria.

You do not have to include the link field in the query – this query would still relate the right supplier details to each product without it

Tip!

In Access, the table that is produced when a query is run is called a *dynaset*.

2 Select a table

3 Add fields

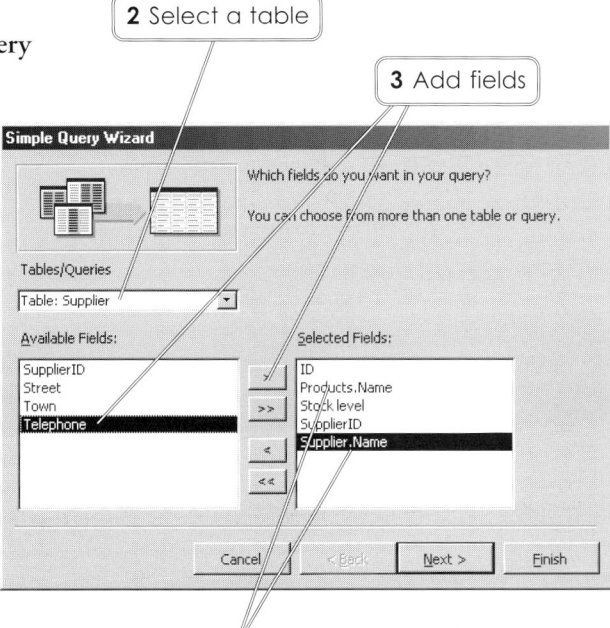

If fields have the same name, then the table names are prefixed to the field names to identify them

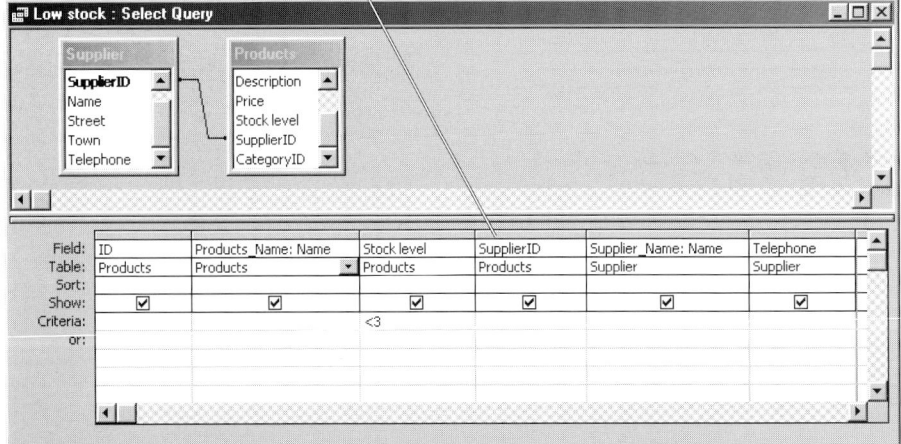

Sorting the dynaset

The records in a dynaset are normally shown in their natural order, but they can be sorted if required. Sorting can be useful. For example, in an accounts database, sorting clients by amount owing makes it easy to see the bad payers; sorting a student database by classes groups the classes' members.

To produce a sorted database:

❶ Start the query as usual.

❷ Click the **Sort** cell for the field you wish to sort on.

❸ A drop-down list arrow button appears at the end of the cell. Click the button to reveal the sorting choices:

Ascending;

Descending;

(not sorted).

❹ Select the order.

❺ Complete the query and run it as usual.

> ## Tip!
>
> A sort can be based on more than one field. The priority of sorting is determined by the order of the fields in the query – those on the left having higher priority. If you know that you will want to sort on more than one field, add fields to the Selected Fields list in the desired order of priority when you are setting up the query with the wizard.

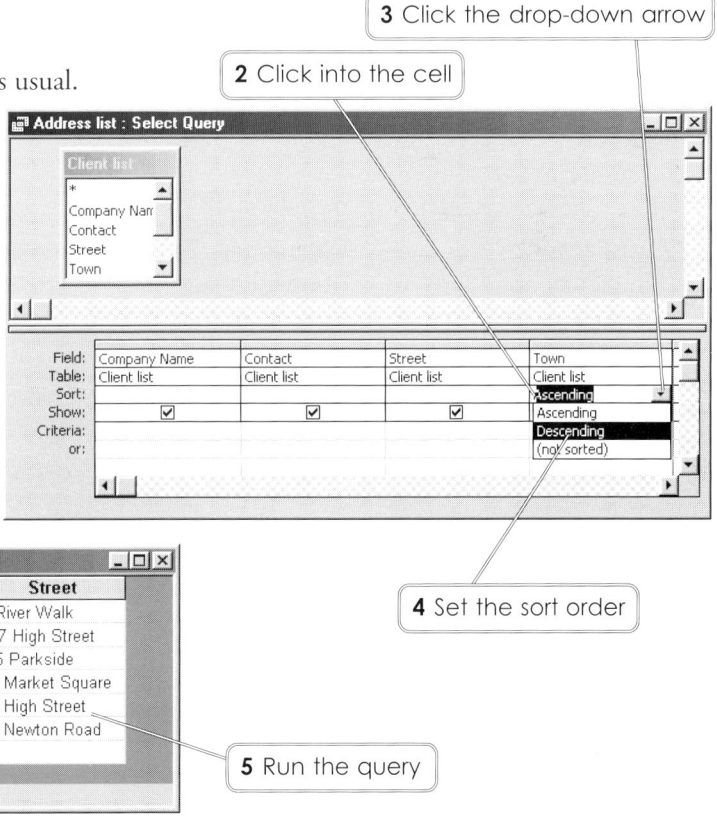

3 Click the drop-down arrow

2 Click into the cell

4 Set the sort order

5 Run the query

Using the computer

Word processing

Spreadsheets

Databases

Electronic communications

Presentations

Skills builder 13:
Further queries

This exercise gives practice in more complex queries, and sorting and printing a dynaset. It uses an estate agent's database of houses. The aim is to find houses under £100,000 in Redbridge.

❶ Open the file *property.mdb* in the *Cambridge/ Exercise files* folder.

❷ Using the Simple Query Wizard, set up a query that will include the fields *Address 1, Town, Bedrooms* and *Price*. Save it as *Redbridge under 100k*.

❸ Modify the query so that it selects those records with Redbridge in the Town field and where the price is under 100,000.

❹ Run the query.

❺ Sort the dynaset into ascending order of price.

❻ Print the dynaset.

Address 1	Town	Bedrooms	Price
34, Adelaide Rd	Redbridge	1	£35,000.00
Flat 4, 367 Woodside Lane	Redbridge	1	£39,000.00
56, Bodmin Drive	Redbridge	3	£50,000.00
158, Moss Lane	Redbridge	2	£60,000.00
34, The Grove	Redbridge	3	£65,000.00
4, St Paul's Avenue	Redbridge	3	£67,000.00
15, Pownall Lane	Redbridge	3	£80,000.00
67, Steal Rd	Redbridge	5	£87,000.00

Your printout should look like this

Forms

Tables provide a compact way to display data, but they are not user-friendly. They can show 40 or more records on one screen, but if there are more than 10 or so fields, or if some fields contain a lot of text, you cannot easily see all the data for one record, or locate a field for editing.

Forms offer a alternative way to view data. A form displays the data from one record at a time, and takes all the space it needs to present it clearly. It is normally easier to enter, edit and read data on a form than in a table.

To create a simple form:

❶ In the Database window, select *Forms* in the **Objects** bar.

❷ Select **Create form by using wizard**.

❸ Select a table from the **Tables/Queries** list.

❹ Add the fields to display on the form – if you want them all, click >> . Click **Next**.

❺ Choose a layout and click **Next**.

   continued…

> **Tip!**
>
> Forms are linked to tables (or dynasets), and are simply another way of accessing their data. When data is entered into a form, it is stored in the linked table.

1 Select Forms

2 Use the wizard

3 Select a table

You can use a form to display the dynaset from a query or the data from more than one table in a relational database

5 Pick a layout

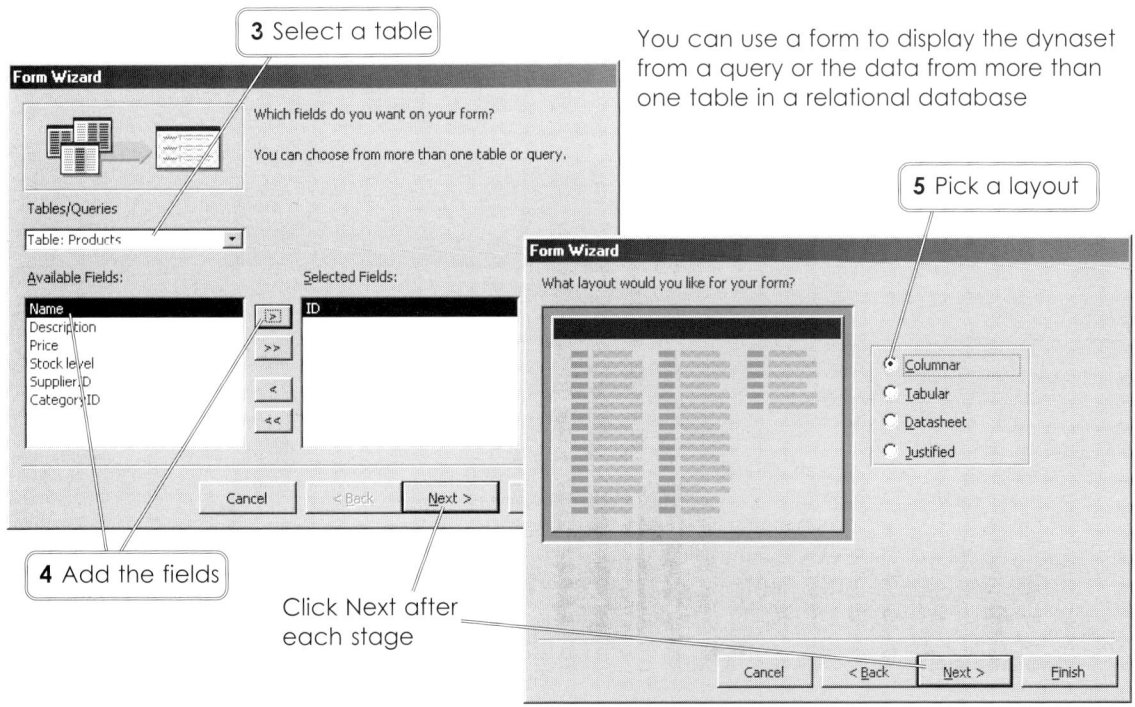

4 Add the fields

Click Next after each stage

Using the computer

Word processing

Spreadsheets

Databases

Electronic communications

Presentations

⑥ Choose a style and click **Next**.

⑦ Give the form a title.

⑧ Choose whether to open the form to view the data or to modify the design, and click **Finish**.

Tip!

If the style or layout are not exactly how you want them, they can be modified later.

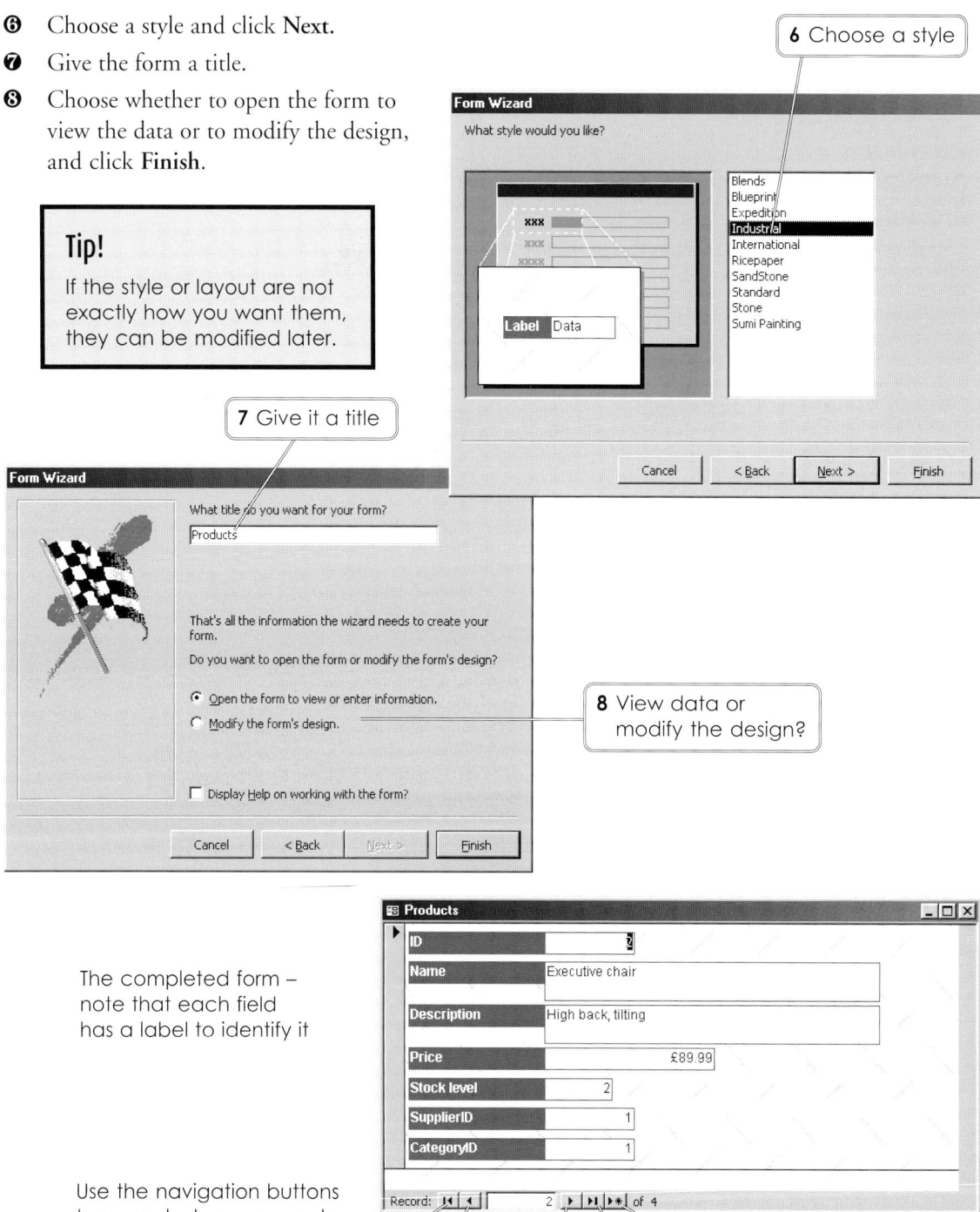

6 Choose a style

7 Give it a title

8 View data or modify the design?

The completed form – note that each field has a label to identify it

Use the navigation buttons to move between records

First
Previous
Next
Last
New record

Modifying a form

The layout, size, font and colours of fields and labels can be changed easily. The techniques are the same as in the other Office applications.

❶ Click 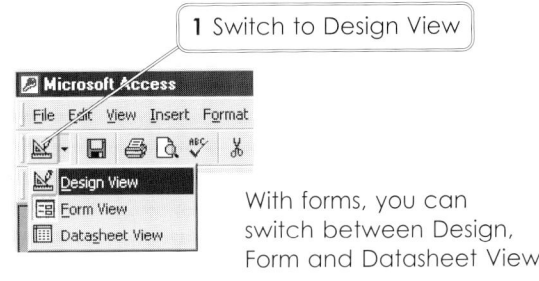 to switch to Design View.

❷ Fields must be selected before they can be moved, resized or formatted.

To select a field or label, click on it once.

To select several fields or labels at once, hold down [**Shift**] and click on each in turn.

❸ *To set the font, style, size, colours and borders*, use the Formatting toolbar buttons.

❹ *To move a field*, drag on any of its edges – the cursor will turn into a hand when it is in a suitable place for moving.

❺ *To resize a field*, drag on a handle.

1 Switch to Design View

With forms, you can switch between Design, Form and Datasheet View

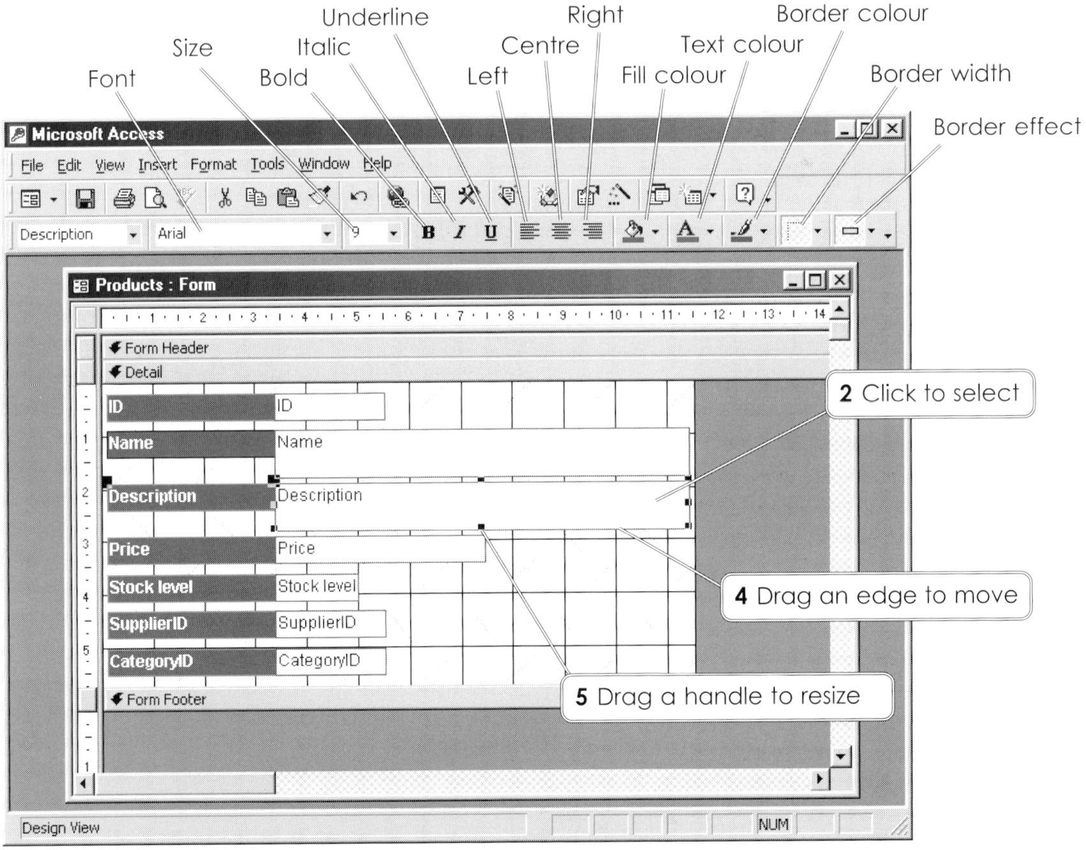

3 Use the Formatting toolbar

Font
Size
Bold
Italic
Underline
Left
Centre
Right
Fill colour
Text colour
Border colour
Border width
Border effect

2 Click to select

4 Drag an edge to move

5 Drag a handle to resize

Using the computer

Word processing

Spreadsheets

Databases

Electronic communications

Presentations

Reports

Tables, dynasets and forms can all be printed, but database printouts are normally through reports.

A simple report is little more than a table print-out, but it can be much more than this. Records can be grouped and sorted by one or more fields. Grouping brings together all the records with the same value in the grouping field, and heads each group with that value, e.g. a report could list clients grouped first by region, then by town within each region, and in alphabetical order of name in each town grouping.

To create a simple report:

❶ In the Database window, select *Reports* in the **Objects** bar.

❷ Select **Create report by using wizard**.

❸ Select a table or query from the **Tables/ Queries** list.

❹ Add the fields to display on the form – if you want them all, click >> – and click **Next**.

❺ If the records are to be grouped by the data in a field, select the field and click > , then click **Next**.

> **Tip!**
>
> Reports can also show summaries, totals, averages or other calculations from the data within groups of records. This feature is beyond the level of this course.

1 Select Reports

2 Use the wizard

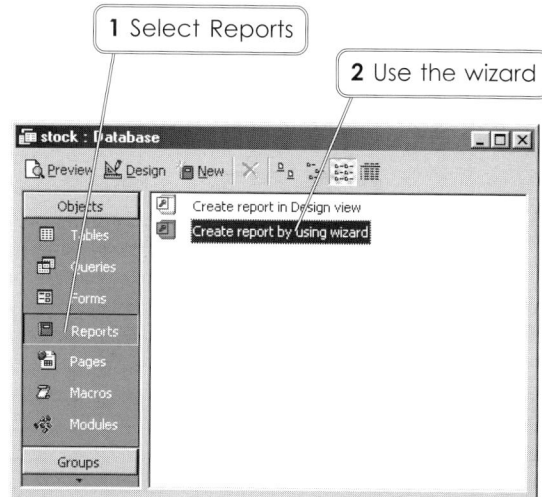

3 Select the table or query

Here, Town has been added as a grouping level

5 Group on a field?

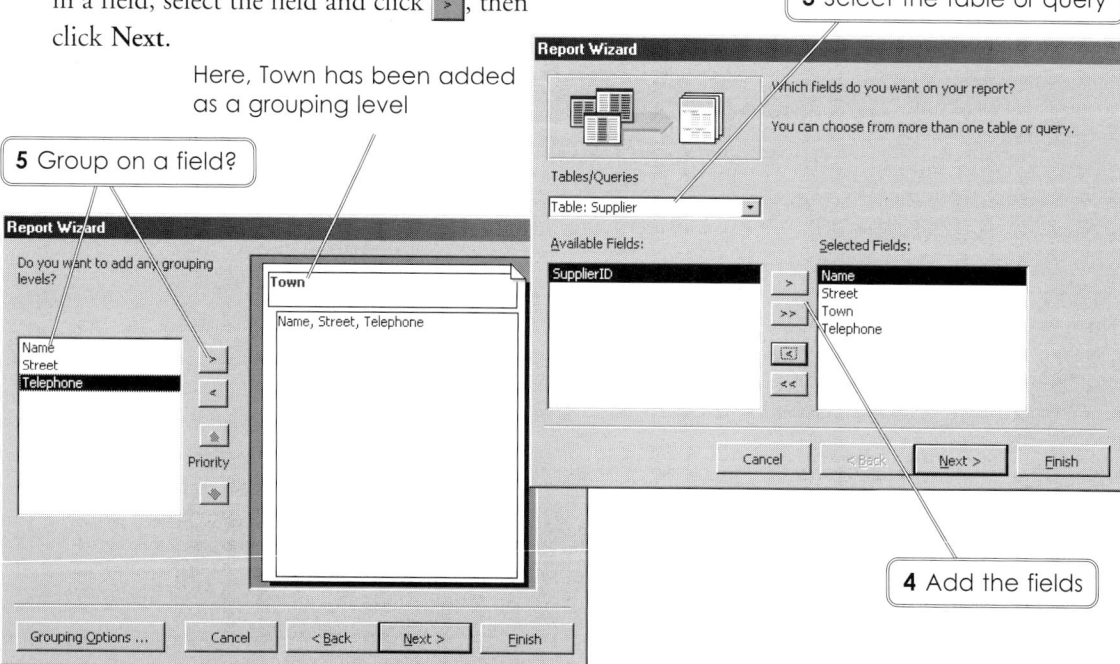

4 Add the fields

80

⑥ If the records are to be sorted by the data in a field, select the field from the drop-down list, then click **Next**.

❼ Choose a layout, then click **Next**.

❽ Choose a style, then click **Next**.

❾ Give the report a title, then click **Next**.

❿ Choose whether to preview the report or to modify the design, and click **Finish**.

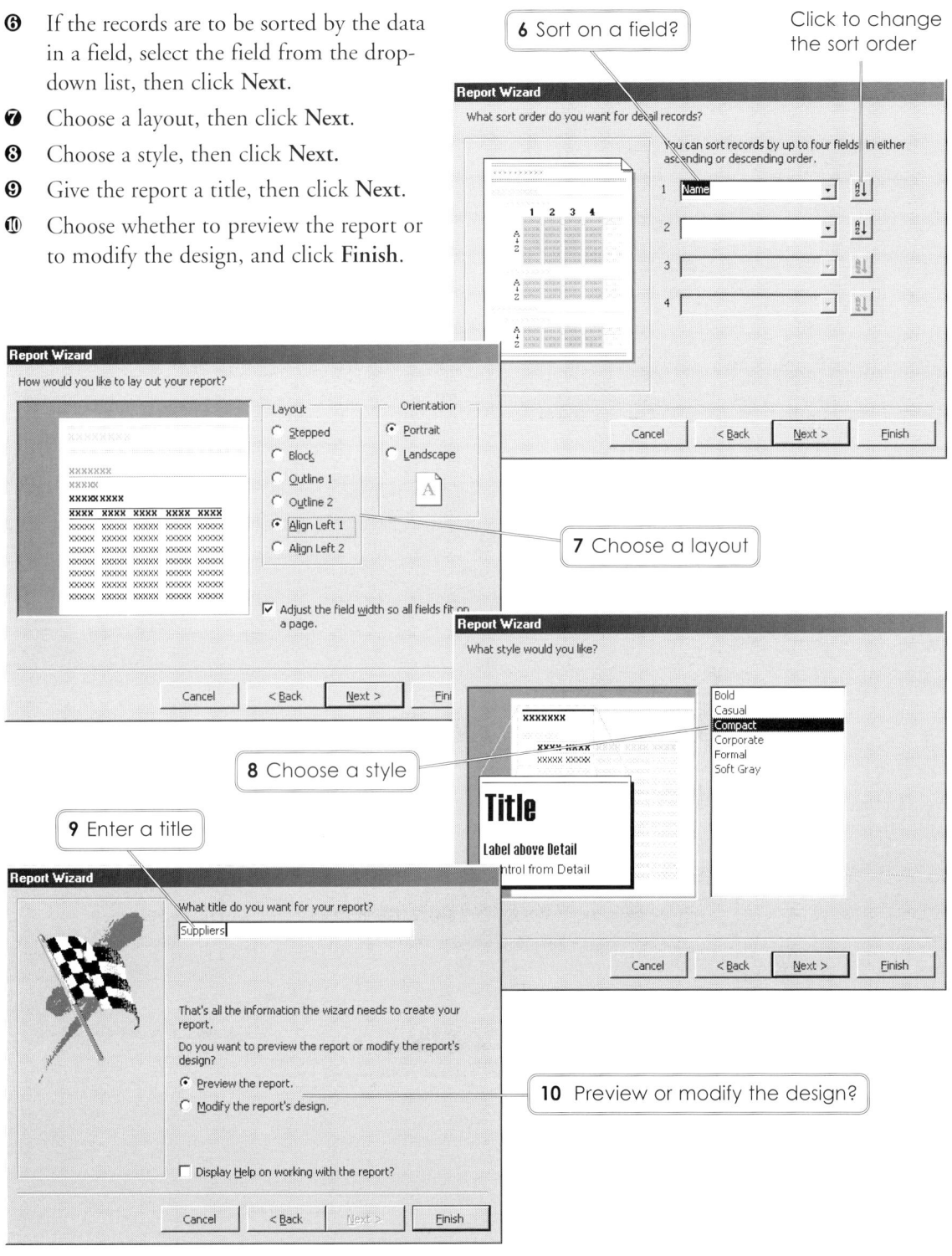

6 Sort on a field?

Click to change the sort order

7 Choose a layout

8 Choose a style

9 Enter a title

10 Preview or modify the design?

Using the computer

Word processing

Spreadsheets

Databases

Electronic communications

Presentations

Report structure

Reports have a more complex structure than forms. Every report has five areas, plus one for each level of grouping. The areas may be left blank, or closed away, but their heading bars remain visible in Design view.

Report header

Anything written in this area appears once at the very start of the report. The title is placed here by the wizard. The header is also often used to show the report's author and the company name.

Page header

Anything here will be printed at the top of every page of the report. The page number, report title and date of printing are often inserted into the header.

Group header

There will be a group header for every level of grouping. It is printed above each new group, and normally contains the label and data of the grouping field.

Detail

The selected fields from each record are shown here. The labels for these fields will normally be written into the group header (if present) or page header, to avoid pointless duplication.

Page footer

This appears at the bottom of every page, and can carry the same kinds of information as the header.

Report footer

This appears once, at the end of the report.

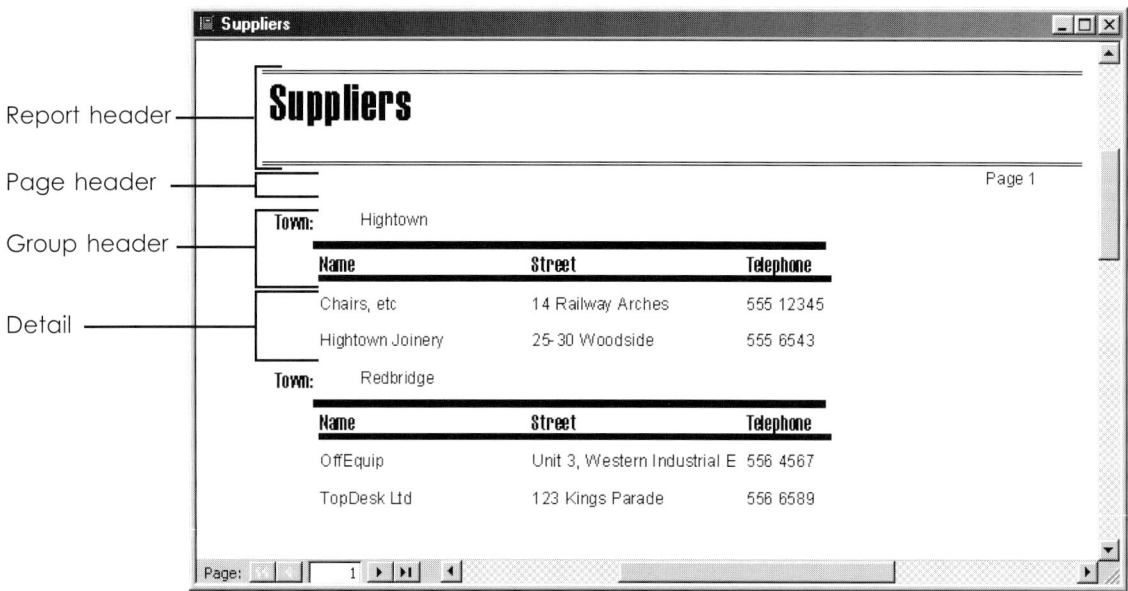

Report header

Page header

Group header

Detail

Modifying a report

To select, move and format fields and labels:

➤ Use the same techniques as in a form.

To change the depth of an area:

❶ Point to the top of the bar below the area (or the bottom of the report footer bar, if its area is closed) – the pointer will become ⬍ and a thin guideline will appear – drag this up or down as required.

To add text:

❷ Open the **View** menu and select **Toolbox**.

❸ Select the Label tool and draw an outline on the report where you want the text to go.

❹ Click into the outline and type your text.

To add the page number:

❺ Open the **Insert** menu and select **Page Numbers…**

❻ Select the **Format** and **Position** then click **OK**.

To add the date and time:

❼ Open the **Insert** menu and select **Date and Time…**

❽ You can include either the date or time or both. Set your options and click **OK**.

❾ The date/time will be inserted into the report header. Drag it into place as required.

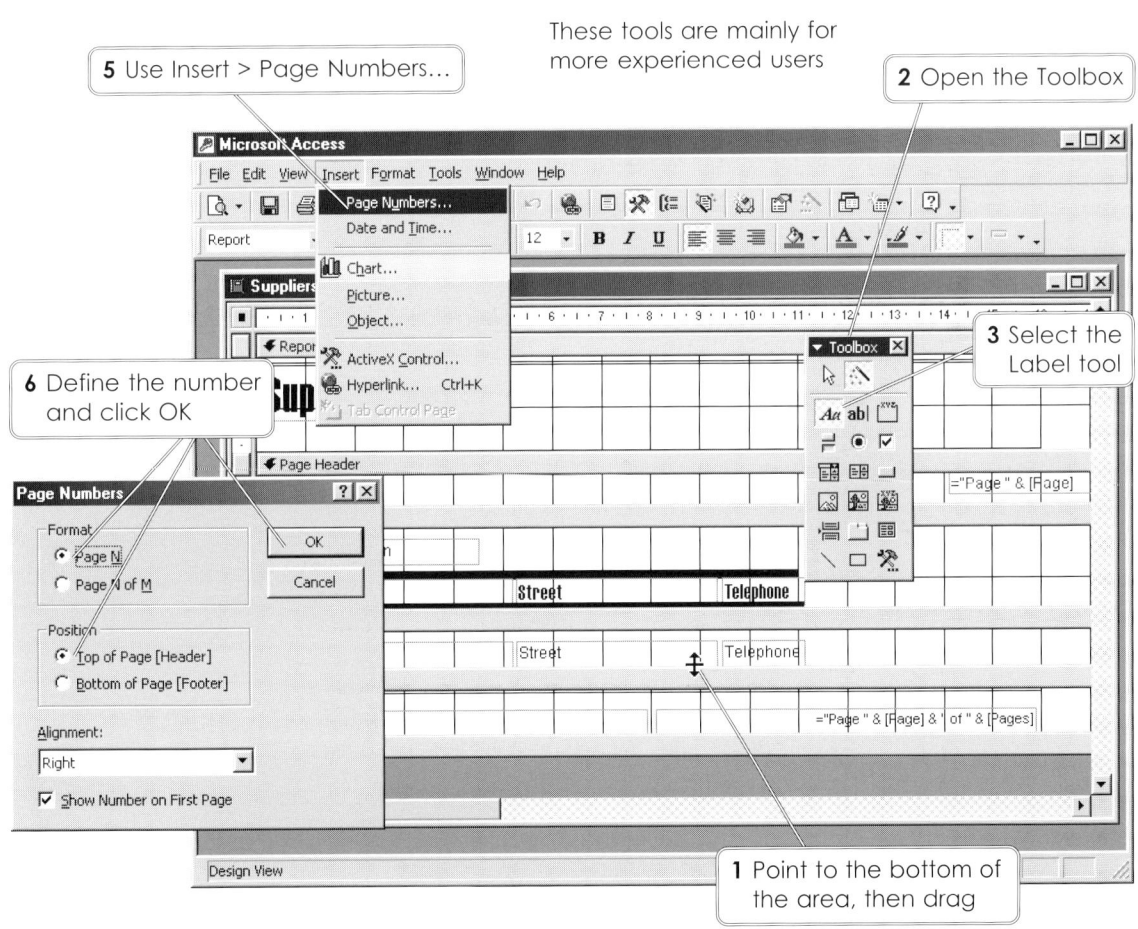

These tools are mainly for more experienced users

5 Use Insert > Page Numbers…

2 Open the Toolbox

3 Select the Label tool

6 Define the number and click OK

1 Point to the bottom of the area, then drag

Using the computer

Word processing

Spreadsheets

Databases

Electronic communications

Presentations

Skills builder 14:

Forms and reports

❶ Open *clients.mdb* in the *Cambridge/Exercise files* folder.

❷ Create a form suitable for data entry. It must contain all the fields in the client table. Use any suitable layout and style. Call the form 'Client Data Entry'.

❸ Modify the new form in Design view.

Increase the font size of all the fields to 10.

Make the labels bold, then enlarge any that are not wide enough to display their text.

Select all the fields (and their labels) and use the options on the **Format** menu to increase their horizontal and vertical spacing.

❹ Save the changes by clicking 💾.

❺ Use the wizard to create a report based on the client table. It should have the fields: *Company name, Contact, Street, Town* and *Telephone*.

Set *Town* as a group, and have the report sorted on *Company name*.

❻ Take the report into Design View, and set the fonts so that the details are all in Times New Roman and the headings and labels in Arial. Adjust the label and field sizes if necessary, so that the text is fully visible.

❼ Print the report to file, saving it as *clients.prn*.

Are you ready?

Get your tutor to check your work.

If you have successfully completed the skills builder exercises in this section, and are confident in using those skills, you are ready for the *Databases* test.

If you need a little more practice before taking the test, ask your tutor for the *Databases* pre-test exercise.

Your new form should look like this...

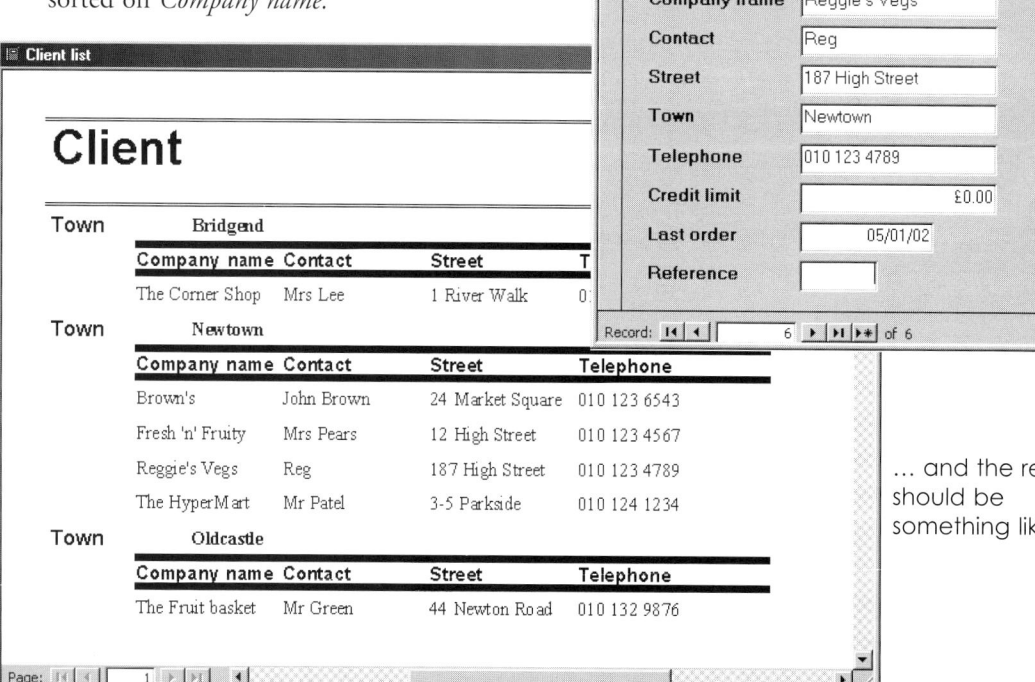

... and the report should be something like this.

5 Electronic communications

You should know how to:

- Start and use Internet Explorer
- Use search engines
- Start Outlook Express
- Read incoming messages
- Search for messages and organize their storage

You will learn how to:

- Set browser options
- Use URLs to go to sites and pages
- Search from within Internet Explorer
- Save data from Web pages and print pages
- Use Favorites
- Send, reply to and forward messages
- Copy text from messages
- Send and receive files by e-mail
- Use the Address Book

Additional resources:

- Checklist 5: Electronic Communications

Internet Explorer

Internet Explorer (IE) is a browser – software to display Web pages and handle the hyperlinks between them. The main features of the screen, and the key tools are summarised here.

The **Address bar** shows you where you are. You can type a URL here to go to a page.

The **Toolbars** can be turned on or off as needed, using the options on the **View** menu.

The **Explorer bar** can be opened on the left of the screen to give simpler navigation when searching the Internet, or when using the Favorites or History.

The **Status bar** at the bottom shows how much of an incoming file has been loaded, or the URL when you point to a link. It can be turned off if not needed, using the **View** menu option.

The Toolbar

Back   Go back to the page visited previously.

Forward Go forward, after you have been back.

Stop   Stop downloading the current page.

Refresh Reload the page. Click this if a page fails to load properly.

Home   Go to your 'home page' (see page 87).

Search   Run an online search in the Explorer bar (see page 90).

Favorites Open the Favorites in the Explorer bar.

History Open the History in the Explorer bar.

Mail   Runs the linked e-mail software (normally Outlook Express)

Print   Print the current page.

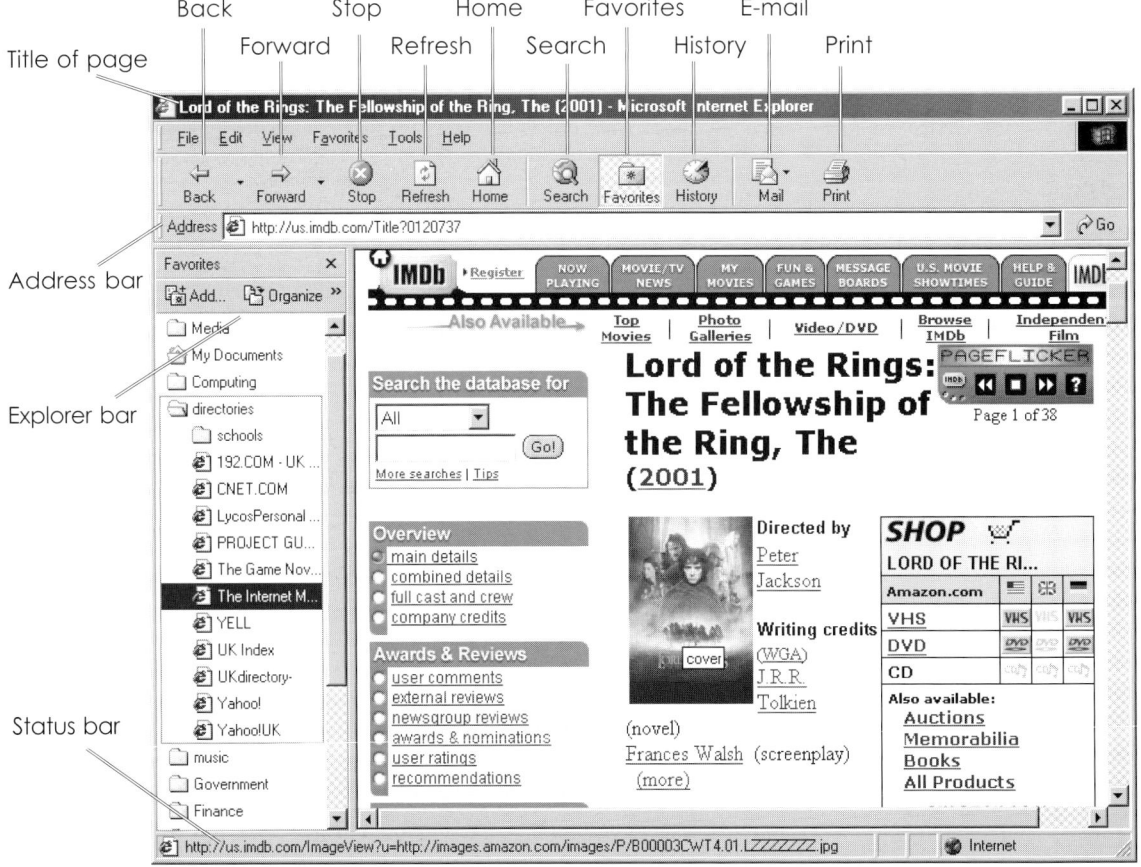

Internet options

IE has many options that you can set to suit the way you browse. Two of the key ones are covered here. Take time to see what else is there, but if you are not sure what effect a change will have – leave the setting alone!

To set the options:

❶ Open the **Tools** menu and select **Internet Options...**

Your home page

When you first start IE, it will connect to your designated home page. This can be any page on the Web, e.g. a search engine, or it can be left blank, so that IE does not go to a specific page when it starts.

To set the home page:

❷ Go to the **General** tab.

❸ Type the address to use as the home page.

Or

❹ Click **Use Blank** to start with a blank display.

Languages

If you visit sites that have alternative text in several languages, you can choose which to display, and which should have priority.

To add a language:

❺ On the **General** tab, click **Languages...**

❻ Click **Add...**

❼ Choose the language and click **OK**.

❽ Select a language and use **Move Up** or **Move Down** to change its priority.

❾ Click **OK**.

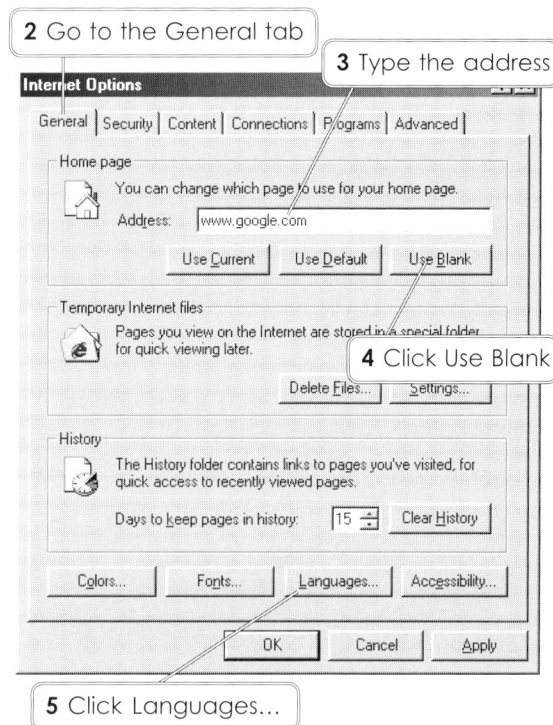

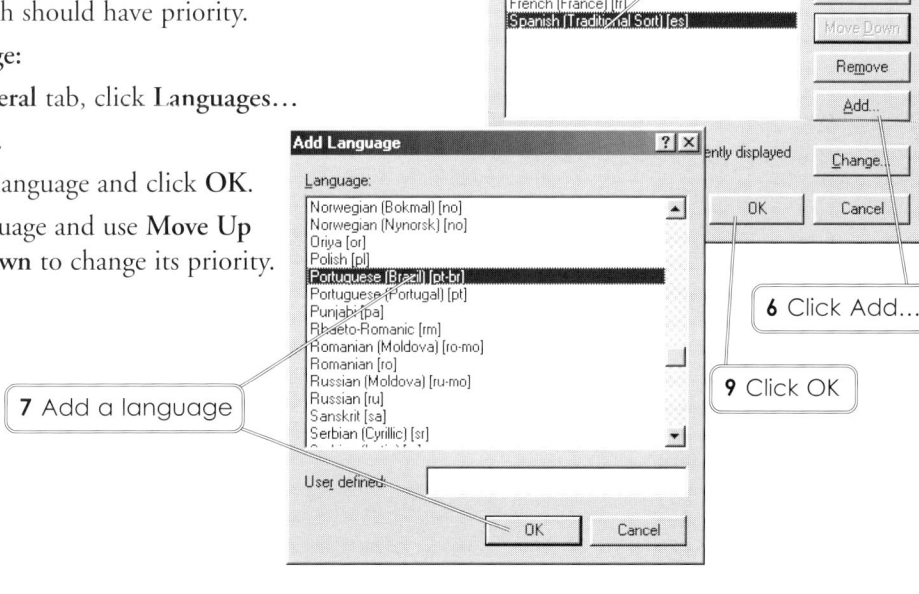

Using the computer

Word processing

Spreadsheets

Databases

Electronic communications

Presentations

Show pictures

The pictures on a Web page may be an essential part of the display or used for navigating, or they may be merely decorative or even advertisements. All pictures take longer than text to download.

If you are in a hurry, you can turn off the display of pictures. You will then see 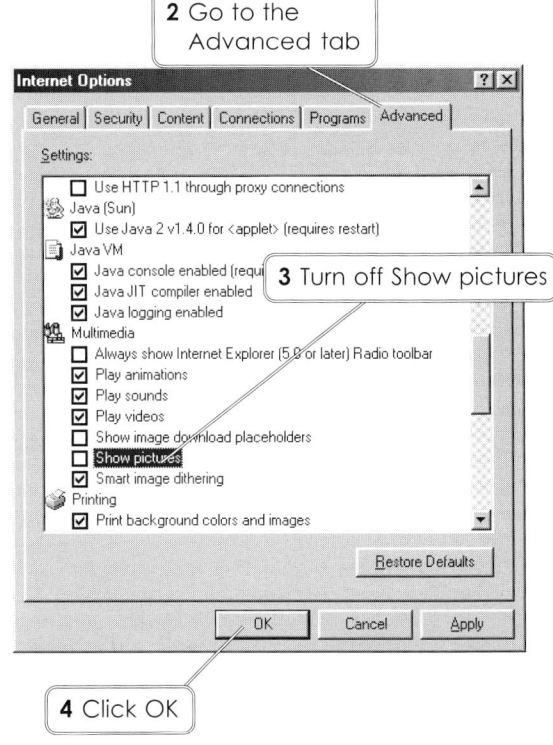 in place of each image, usually accompanied by its name or a description. If you want to see an image, it can be individually downloaded and viewed.

To turn images off:

❶ Open the **Tools** menu and select **Internet Options…**

❷ Go to the **Advanced** tab.

❸ Scroll down to the **Multimedia** section, and clear the tick by **Show pictures**.

❹ Click **OK**.

To show a picture:

❺ Right-click on the 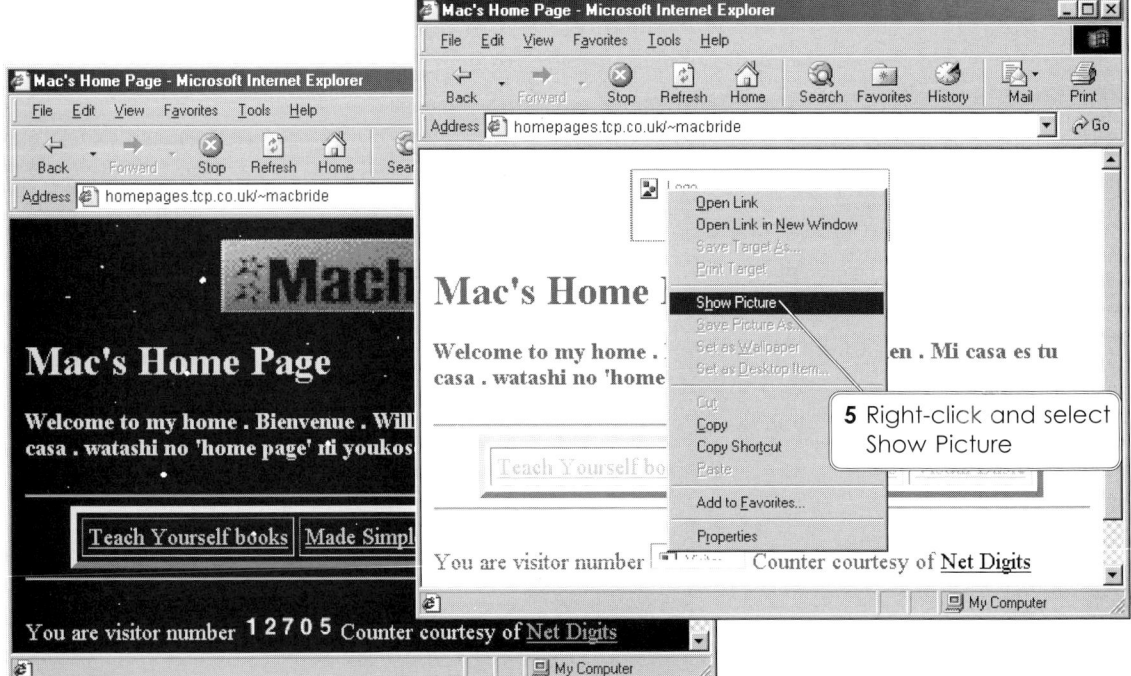 icon to get the context menu and select **Show Picture**. The picture will then be downloaded and displayed.

URLs, sites and pages

Every Web site and every Web page – in fact, every file of any kind on the Internet – has its own identifier, or URL (Uniform Resource Locator). The URLs of Web sites and pages are highly variable, but there are certain patterns which are worth knowing.

Web site URLs

The URL of a Web site typically takes this shape:

www.organisation_name.type.country

www reminds you that this is on the World Wide Web.

organisation_name may be the actual name of the organisation, or an abrieviation of the name.

type tells you the nature of the organisation. The most commonly used types are:

com	commercial (USA or international)
co	commercial (in other countries)
edu	educational/academic (USA)
ac	educational/academic (non-USA)
gov	government
net	network service provider
org	non-profit-making organization

country is omitted if the organization is in the USA, or operates internationally.

Examples:

www.microsoft.com
Microsoft, a US/international company

www.bbc.co.uk
BBC, a UK-based company

www.metoffice.gov.uk
The UK government's Meteorological Office

www.cam.ac.uk
Cambridge University, an academic establishment in the UK

www.yamaha-motor.co.jp
Yamaha Motor Company, in Japan

> **Tip!**
> A **Web site** is a collection of **Web pages**, normally stored on a computer run by the organization that maintains the site.

Web page URLs

Within a Web site, each page has its own URL. This will typically consist of the site name, one or more folder names and the page name, all separated by / (forward slashes). The page name will normally end in .htm or .html, showing that it was written in HTML. For example, this is the Thailand area page at Yahoo's weather site:

http://weather.yahoo.com/regional/THXX.html

On some sites, pages are not held as files, but are constructed on demand by drawing data from a database. For example, the page illustrated in *Skills builder 15* (page 96) has this URL:

http://visibleearth.nasa.gov/cgi-bin/
viewrecord?11465

Using URLs

If you give an URL to the browser, it will connect directly to the site or page, but the URL must be typed exactly right to work – even one wrong character is enough to produce the 'Error 404: File not Found' message.

If you want to go to a specific page in a site, use the URL if it is straightforward. If the page URL is long and complex, go to the top level of the site and use the site's navigation or search tools to find the page. For example, to find out about Japanese art in the Edo period, you could go to:

www.ibiblio.org/wm/paint/tl/japan/edo.html

Or start at the entrance of the Web Museum …

www.ibiblio.org

… and work through from there.

Using the computer

Word processing

Spreadsheets

Databases

Electronic communications

Presentations

Searching from IE

There are two ways to search the Web from IE.

Search engines

These are sites which hold databases of Web pages, and offer tools for searching through those databases so that you can find Web pages matching your requirements.

Popular search engines include:

Google	www.google.com
AltaVista	www.altavista.com
Excite	www.excite.com
MSN Search	search.msn.com

To run a search at any of these, simply type a few words to describe what you are looking for into the labelled box and click the **Search** button.

Explorer bar searches

The search is actually performed at MSN or your service provider's search engine, but it has one big advantage over a search run directly at a search engine. The search, and its results, stay within the Explorer bar, which makes it much easier to browse through the results.

To search in IE:

❶ If you are not already online, connect to the Internet.

❷ Click [Search] to start a search in the Explorer bar.

It doesn't matter where you are when you start a search in the Explorer bar – I happened to have been searching at MSN

2 Click the Search button

3 Type your keywords

4 Start the search

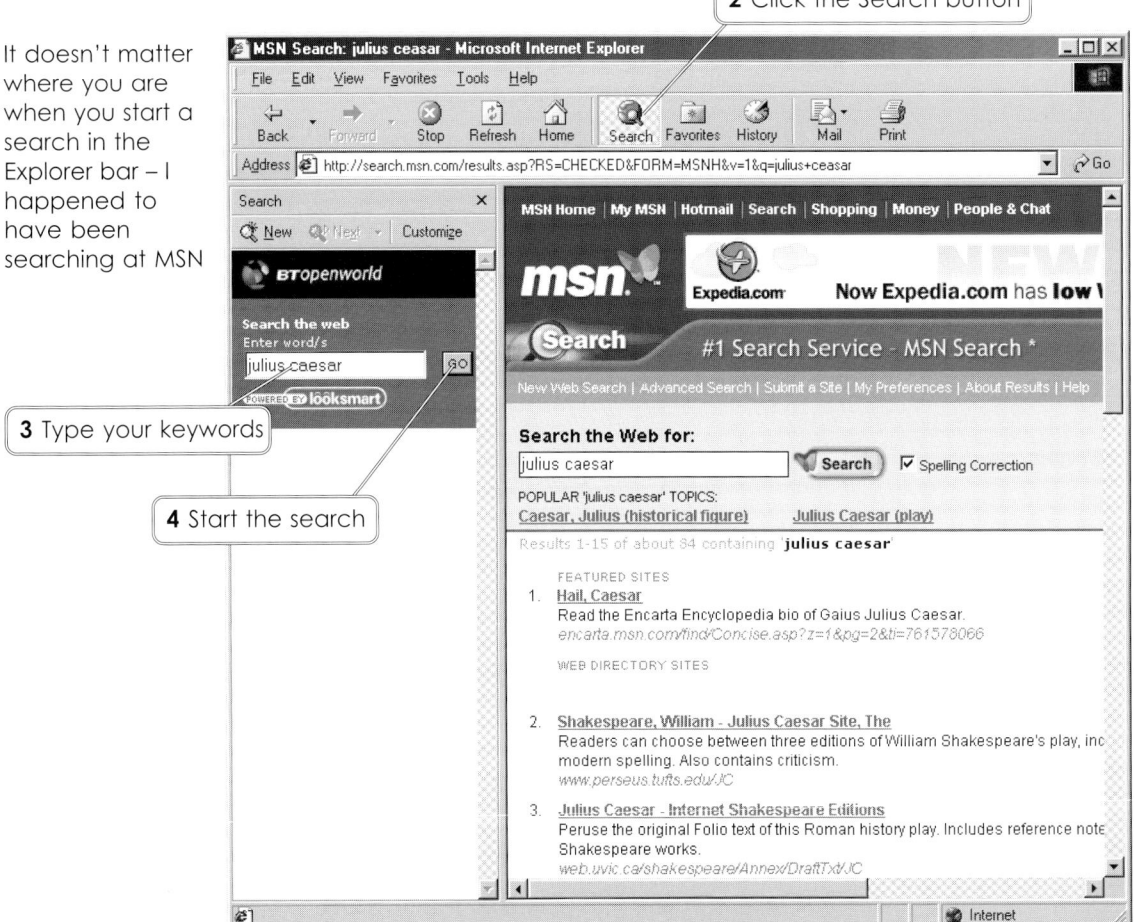

❸ Type one or more keywords to describe what you are looking for.

❹ Click the **Go** button (**Search** in IE4).

❺ When the results appear, click on a link to open its page in the main display area.

The results list will stay open in the Explorer bar, so you can pick up other links from here at any point.

❻ If you want to try some more results, scroll down to the bottom of the page and click the **Next>>** link that you will find there. There will be a delay as IE has to return to the search site to collect the links.

Tip!

A 'keyword' is simply one that describes what you are looking for. You can give any number of keywords, but normally two or three will be enough.

Using the computer

Word processing

Spreadsheets

Databases

Electronic communications

Presentations

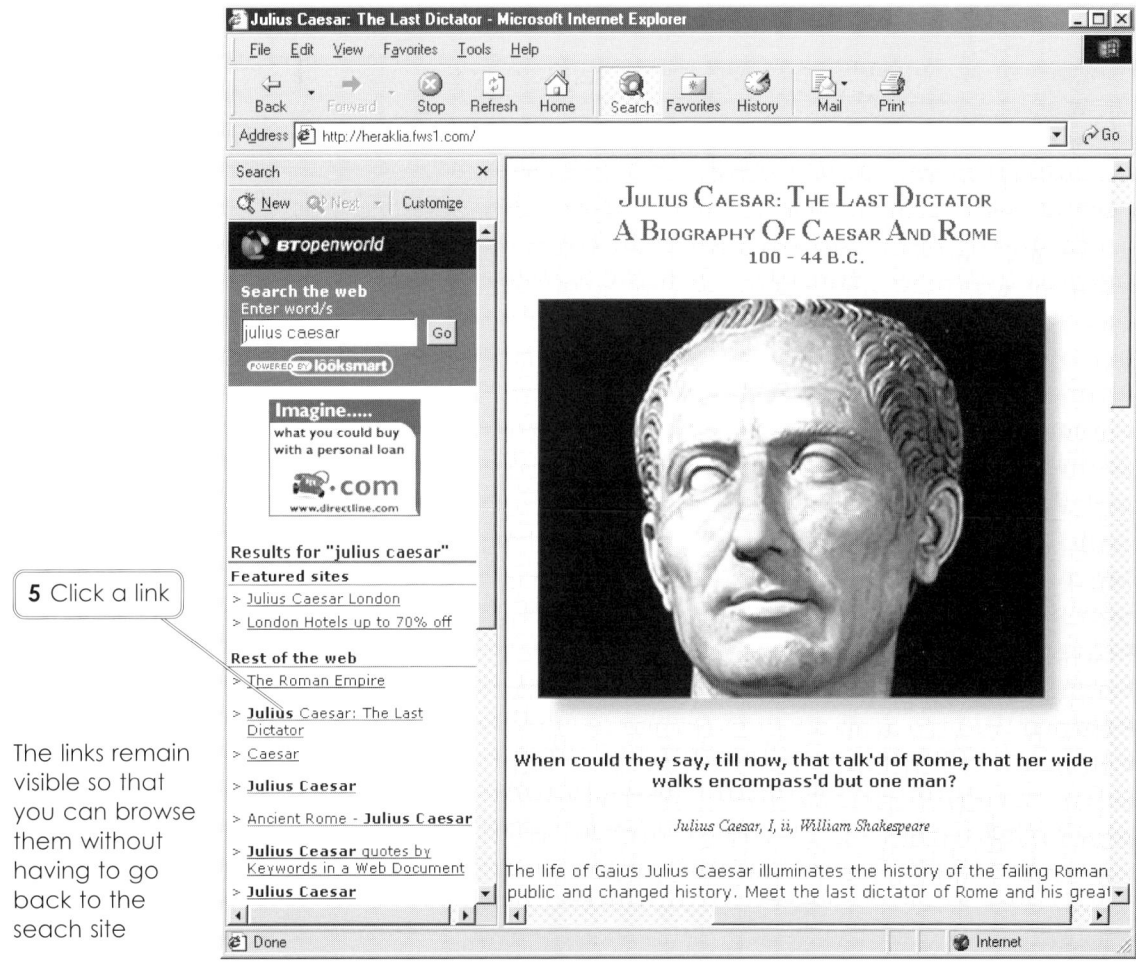

5 Click a link

The links remain visible so that you can browse them without having to go back to the seach site

Data from Web pages

There are three main ways to save information from Web pages.

To save an image:

❶ Right-click on the image and select **Save Picture As…**

❷ Go to the required folder.

❸ Enter or edit the **File name**.

❹ Click **Save**.

To save selected text:

❺ Highlight the text, then right-click on it and select **Copy.** Paste it into Notepad or Word and save it from there.

To save a page:

❻ Open the **File** menu and select **Save As…**

❼ Go to the required folder, and edit the **File name** to identify the page clearly.

❽ If you just want the text of the page, set the **Save as type** to *Text File*.

❾ If you want to save the page complete with its images and other files set the **Save as type** to *Web Page complete*. The files will be saved in a subfolder with a related name – e.g. if the page is 'Mount Etna.htm', the files will be stored in 'Mount Etna_files'.

❿ Click **Save**.

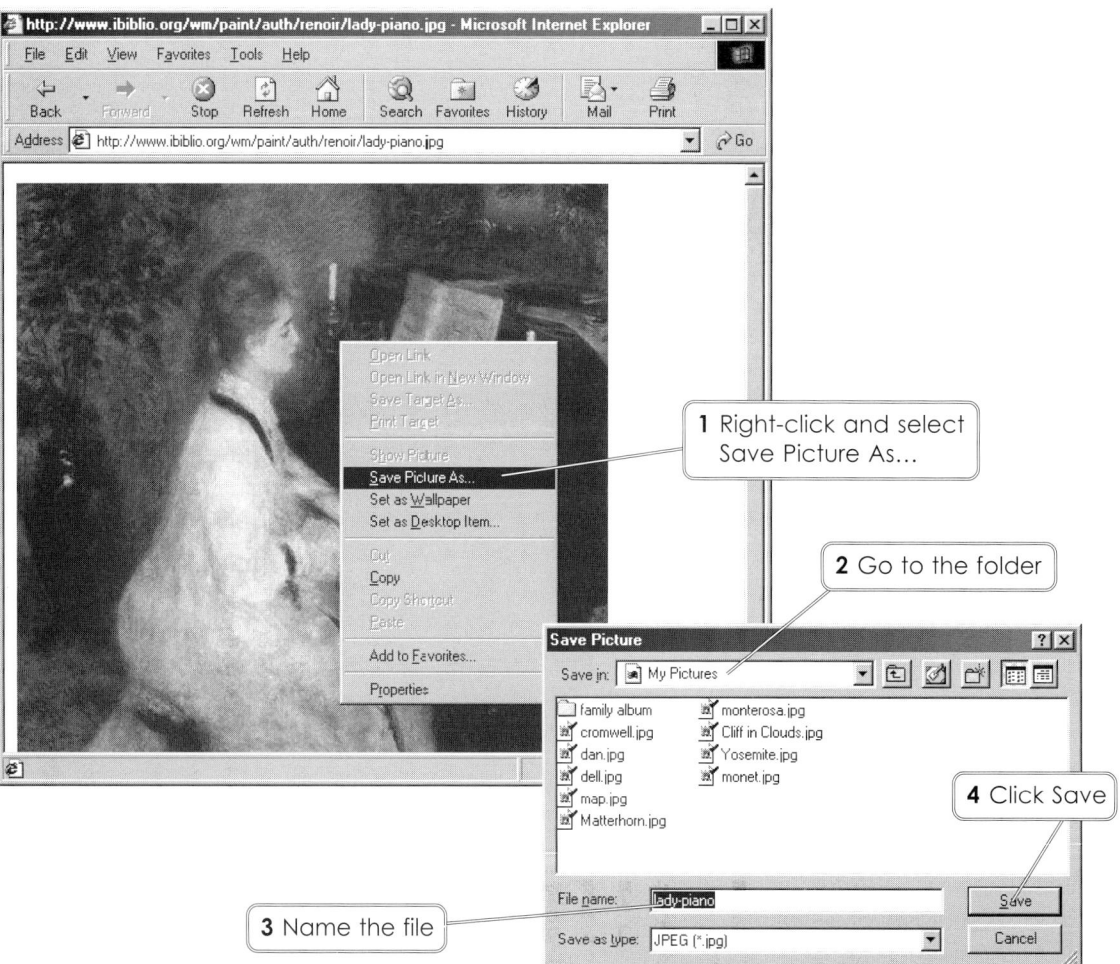

1 Right-click and select Save Picture As…

2 Go to the folder

3 Name the file

4 Click Save

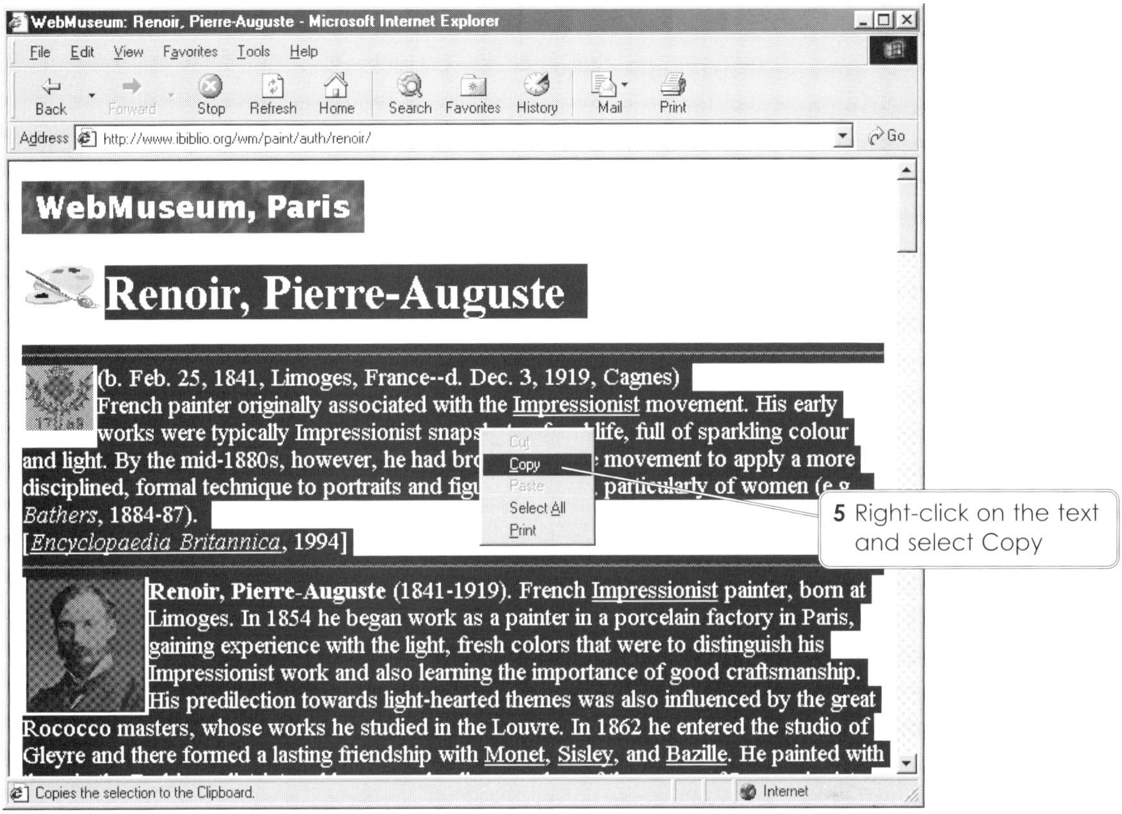

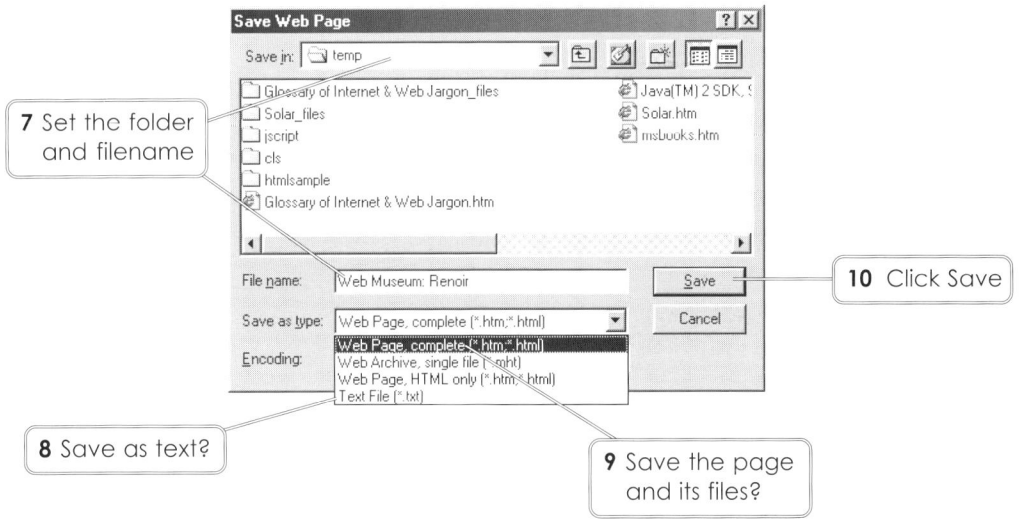

5 Right-click on the text and select Copy

7 Set the folder and filename

8 Save as text?

9 Save the page and its files?

10 Click Save

Printing Web pages

The current Web page can be printed, once it has fully loaded.

To print the entire page:

❶ Click the **Print** button .

To print part of the page:

❷ Select the text and images.

❸ Open the **File** menu and select **Print…**

❹ In the **Print** range, click **Selection**.

❺ Click **OK**.

> ### Tip!
> Screens and sheets of paper are very different shapes. If you want to know how the printout will look before you print, use File > Print Preview.

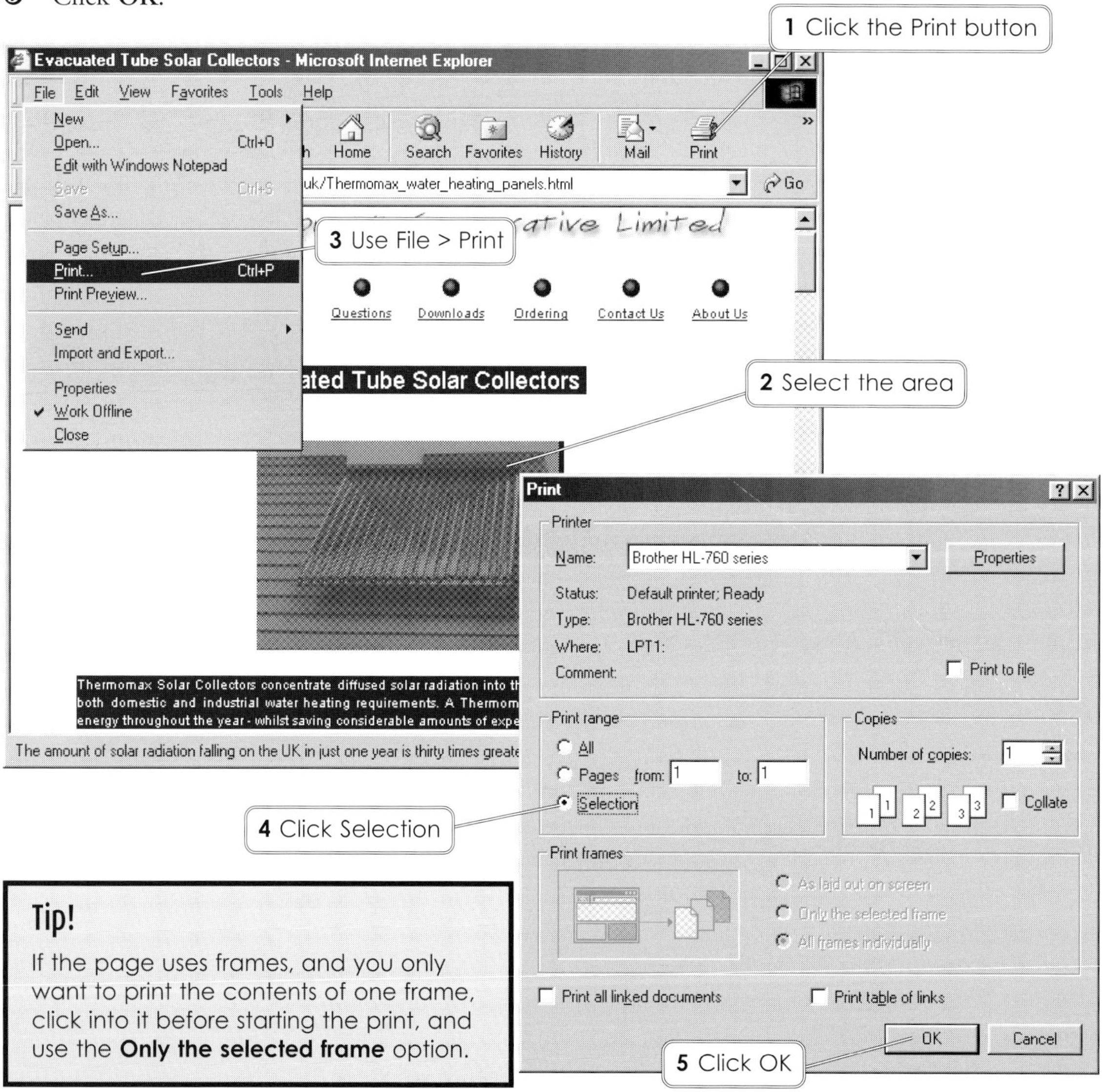

1 Click the Print button

3 Use File > Print

2 Select the area

4 Click Selection

5 Click OK

> ### Tip!
> If the page uses frames, and you only want to print the contents of one frame, click into it before starting the print, and use the **Only the selected frame** option.

Favorites

The History list only keeps the links for a limited time. If you want a permanent link to a page, add it to your *Favorites*.

To add a page:

❶ When you are at a site that you know you want to revisit, open the **Favorites** menu and select **Add to Favorites…**

❷ At the **Add Favorite** dialog box, edit the name, if necessary.

❸ To add to the main list, click **OK**.

❹ To store the Favorite in a folder, click **Create in>>** to fully open the dialog box, select the folder and click **OK**.

To return to a Favorite:

❺ Click ⬛ to display your Favorites in the Explorer bar.

Or

❻ Open the **Favorites** menu.

❼ Click on a link, opening folders as needed.

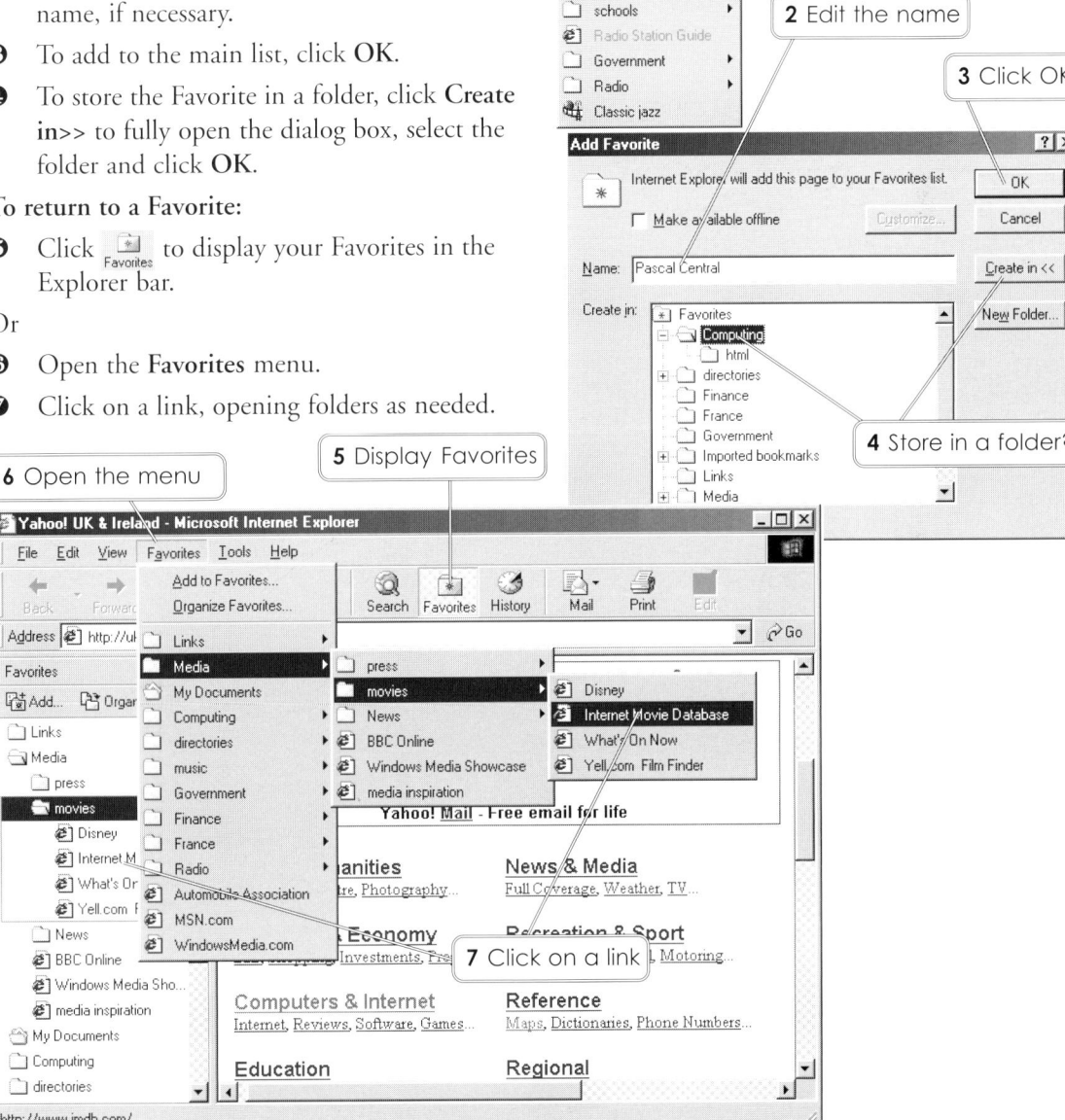

Using the computer

Word processing

Spreadsheets

Databases

Electronic communications

Presentations

Skills builder 15:
Data from the Web

❶ Run Internet Explorer.

❷ NASA, the American Space Agency, has a superb collection of Earth-from-space photographs. Go to the URL:

http://visibleearth.nasa.gov/Regions/

❸ Add a link to the page to your Favorites list.

❹ Select a region. You will be offered a choice of images. Select one.

❺ You will see a thumbnail of the image, along with a description and details of its origin. You will be offered several files in JPEG format. Select one – bigger files give sharper images but take longer to load.

❻ Save the image in your IT Skills folder.

❼ Go to AltaVista (www.altavista.com) or Google (www.google.com).

❽ Run a search for 'Ludovic Zamenhof'. What is his claim to fame? Find a site that gives a brief outline of his life and/or work.

❾ Print the page.

❿ Copy the main text to Word and save it as a document file in your IT Skills folder.

The introductory page for a photograph at Visible Earth. NASA has other collections of Earth and space pictures. Its main page is at www.nasa.gov

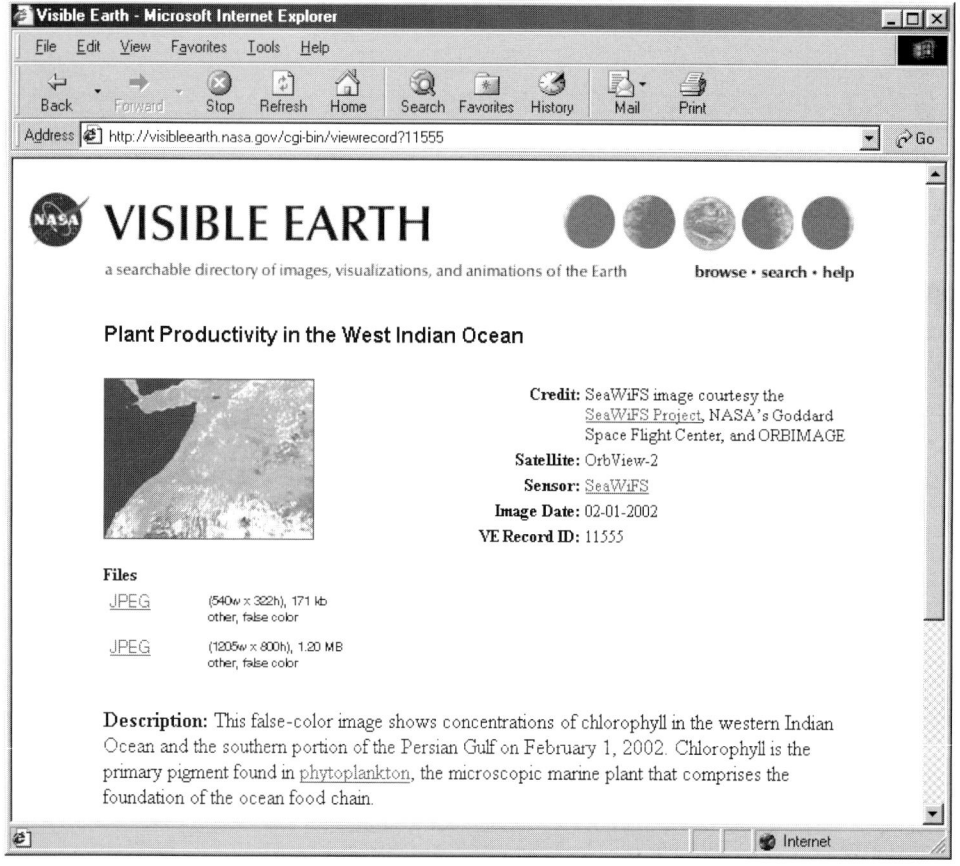

Outlook Express

Outlook Express is the e-mail software that accompanies IE and is normally supplied with Windows. It is efficient and easy to use, though there are plenty of features for advanced users.

Most parts of the screen display are optional – the most useful are the Folder list, Toolbar and Preview pane.

To turn screen elements on or off:

❶ Open the **View** menu and select **Layout…** to open the **Window Layout Properties** dialog box.

❷ Tick the checkboxes to show or clear them to hide the elements.

❸ Click **OK**.

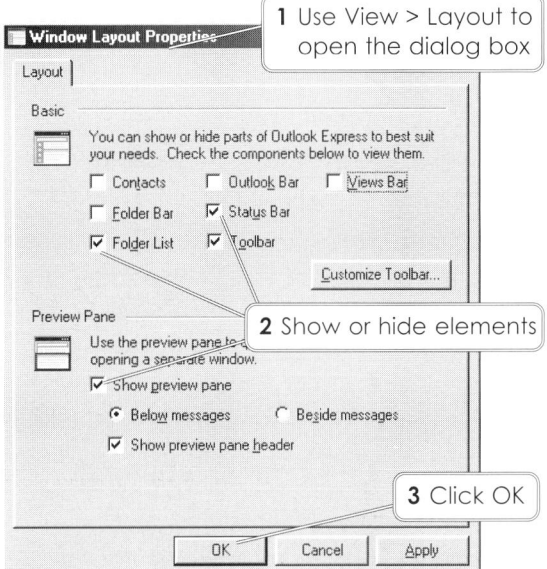

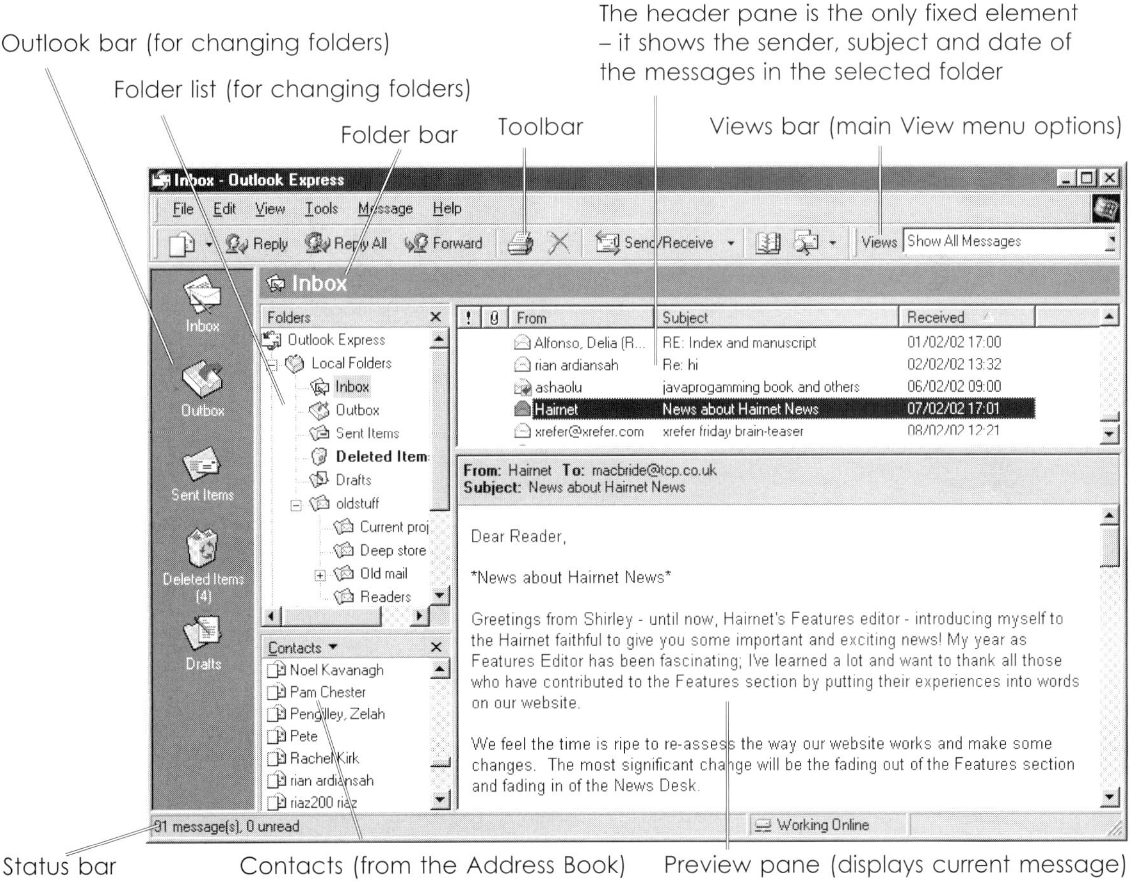

1 Use View > Layout to open the dialog box

2 Show or hide elements

3 Click OK

The header pane is the only fixed element – it shows the sender, subject and date of the messages in the selected folder

Outlook bar (for changing folders)

Folder list (for changing folders)

Folder bar

Toolbar

Views bar (main View menu options)

Status bar

Contacts (from the Address Book)

Preview pane (displays current message)

Outlook Express options

Outlook Express has a lot of options! Most are best left at their default settings, but there are a few that you might like to look at.

➤ Use **Tools > Options** to open the dialog box.

On the **General** tab, you can set when to send and receive messages, defining how often to go online to check for new messages. Turn the options off if you prefer to control the process directly, by clicking the **Send/Receive** button on the Toolbar.

The key options on the **Send** tab, are **Automatically put people I reply to in my Address Book** (see page 104) and **Include message in reply** (see page 100). Both may be best turned on – you can easily delete unwanted Address Book entries or shorten and edit the original message when replying.

When you 'delete' a message, it is actually sent to the *Deleted Items* folder, and will stay there – and can be read, copied or moved – until it is deleted from that folder. If you like, you can turn on the option on the **Maintenance** tab so that Outlook empties the folder automatically on exit.

A signature is a small file that can be added to the end of your outgoing messages. It might carry your contact details, or advertise your business, or just be interesting or decorative.

To add a signature, go to the **Signatures** tab, and define one there.

Turn on these to send and receive automatically

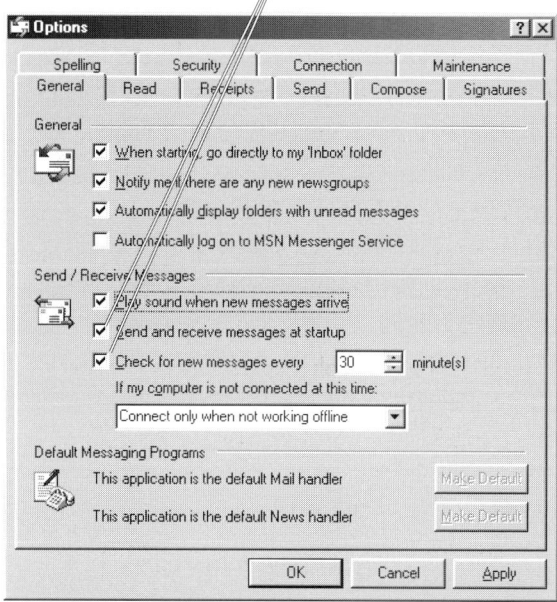

Turn on if your PC is always online or can be connected easily. Turn off if you prefer to store messages in the Outbox then send them all at once when you click the Send/Receive button.

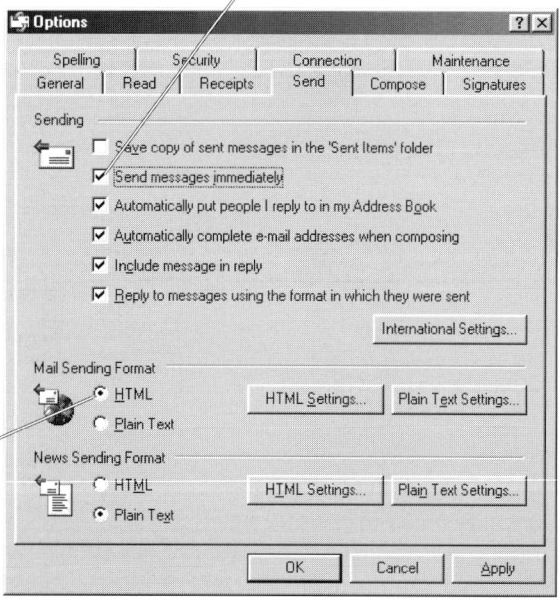

HTML allows you to format your messages, adding colour and emphasis. Most people now have Outlook Express or similar software that can handle HTML

Sending e-mail

Messages are written in the New Message window. The main part of this is an editor, but at the top are these four fields:

➤ **To:** is the address of the recipient.

➤ **Cc:** is for Carbon copies – the addresses, if any, to whom you want to send copies.

➤ **Bcc:** is for Blind carbon copies – the people in this set are not visible to other recipients.

➤ **Subject:** will appear in the header. It should outline the purpose of the message so that your recipients know what is coming.

The editor in Outlook Express offers the sort of capabilities that you would find in a word-processor. You will find the usual font, size, style, colour and alignment options. You can also insert images, or text from other documents.

When you have finished, you can send the message immediately if you are online, or store it in the Outbox for sending when you go online.

To create a new message:

❶ Use **File > New > Mail Message** or click ⬚ ▾.

❷ Click 🔟 **To:** to open the Address Book.

❸ Select the recipient and click **To: ->** or **Cc: ->** to add the address to the To or Cc sets.

❹ Click **OK**.

❺ Type a **Subject** – keep it brief but clear.

❻ Type your message.

❼ Click **Send**. The message will either be sent immediately or placed in your Outbox for mailing when you next click **Send/Receive**.

Using the computer

Word processing

Spreadsheets

Databases

Electronic communications

Presentations

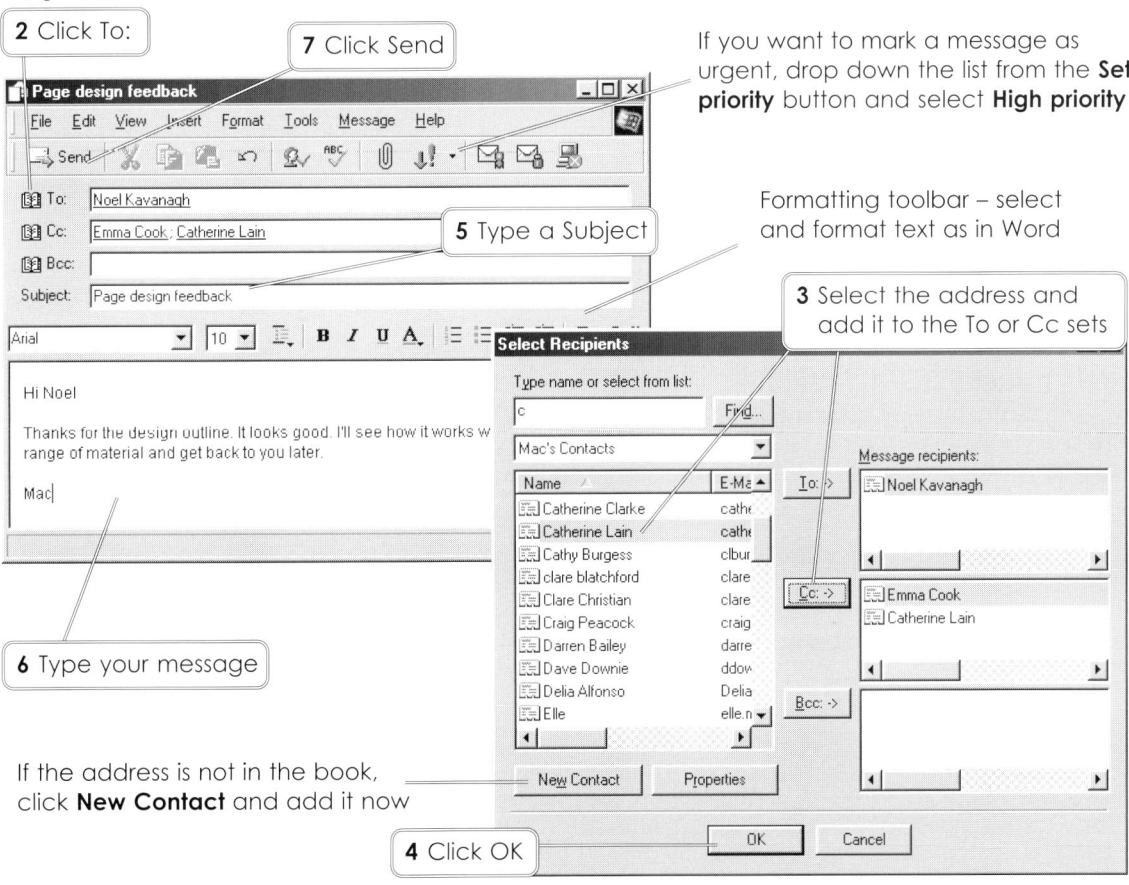

2 Click To:

7 Click Send

If you want to mark a message as urgent, drop down the list from the **Set priority** button and select **High priority**

5 Type a Subject

Formatting toolbar – select and format text as in Word

3 Select the address and add it to the To or Cc sets

6 Type your message

If the address is not in the book, click **New Contact** and add it now

4 Click OK

Reply and forward

You can reply to an incoming message, or forward it on to another person. Click these buttons on the toolbar to:

Reply reply to the sender;

Reply All reply to the sender, and to all who received a copy of the message;

Forward forward the message to another person.

When you forward a message, its text is copied into the New Message window.

When you reply, the text will be copied if the **Include message in reply** option is turned on (see page 98). It can be useful to include the original text, so that it is clear to the recipient which message you are replying to. You can even work through long messages, adding text after each point.

In all of these, the Subject line is copied, with either Re: (reply) or Fwd: (Forward) at the start.

To reply to or forward a message:

❶ Select the message.

❷ Click a reply or forward toolbar button.

❸ When *replying*, the address will be copied into the **To:** field. When *forwarding*, you will need to enter the recipient's address.

❹ Delete any of the original text that you don't want.

❺ Add your own text.

❻ Send the message as normal.

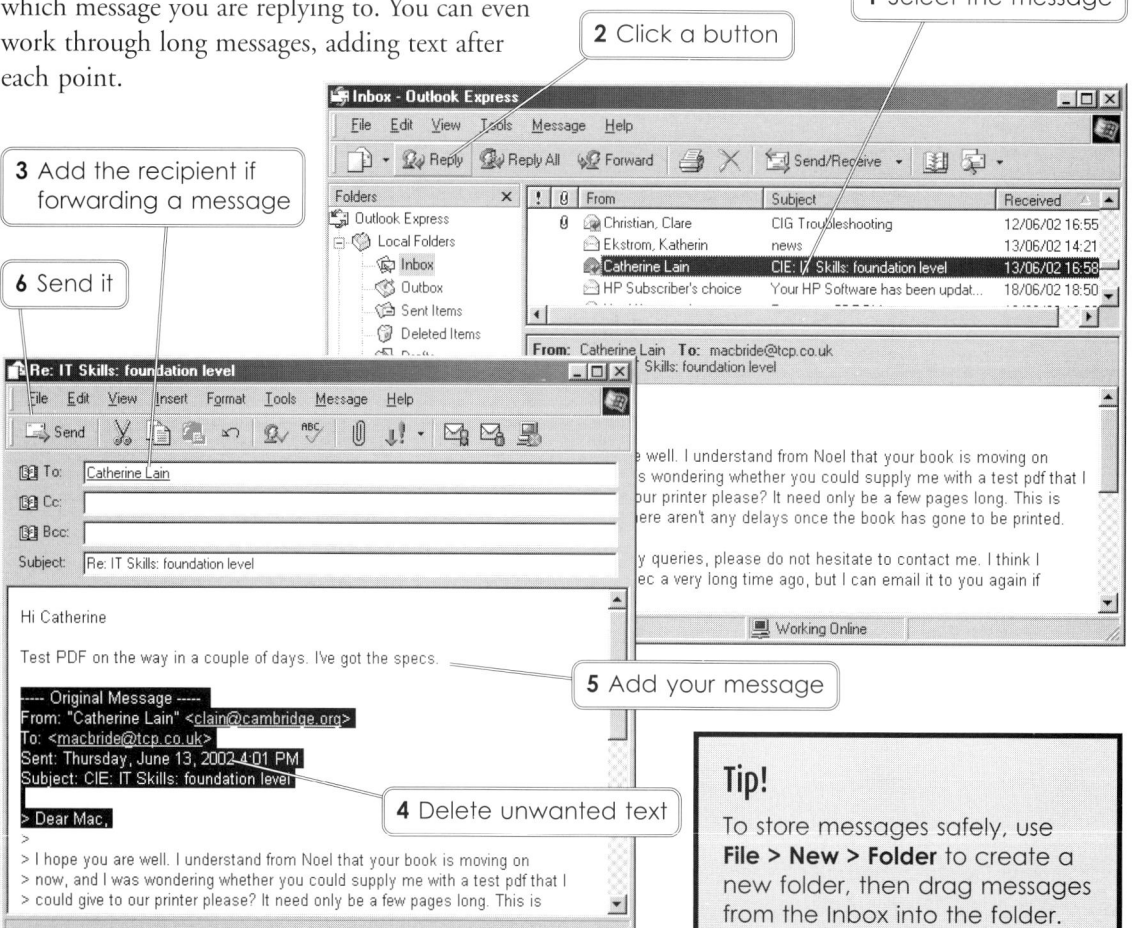

1 Select the message

2 Click a button

3 Add the recipient if forwarding a message

6 Send it

5 Add your message

4 Delete unwanted text

Tip!

To store messages safely, use **File > New > Folder** to create a new folder, then drag messages from the Inbox into the folder.

Copying between messages

Reply and forward copy the whole message into the new one. You can then edit out any text that you don't need, but if you only want to re-use a small part of a message, it may be quicker to copy it and paste it into a new message.

To copy between messages:

❶ Open the source message.

❷ Select the text.

❸ Open the **Edit** menu and select **Copy**.

❹ Start a new message as normal.

❺ Paste in the copied text with **Edit > Paste**.

Copying from messages

If you want to use the whole of a message in another application, you can save it as text then reopen the text file.

❶ Select the source message.

❷ Use **File > Save As**, and set the **Save as type** to text.

This saves the entire message, including the From, To and Subject headers.

If you only want part of the text, it is simpler to use Copy and Paste.

Using the computer

Word processing

Spreadsheets

Databases

Electronic communications

Presentations

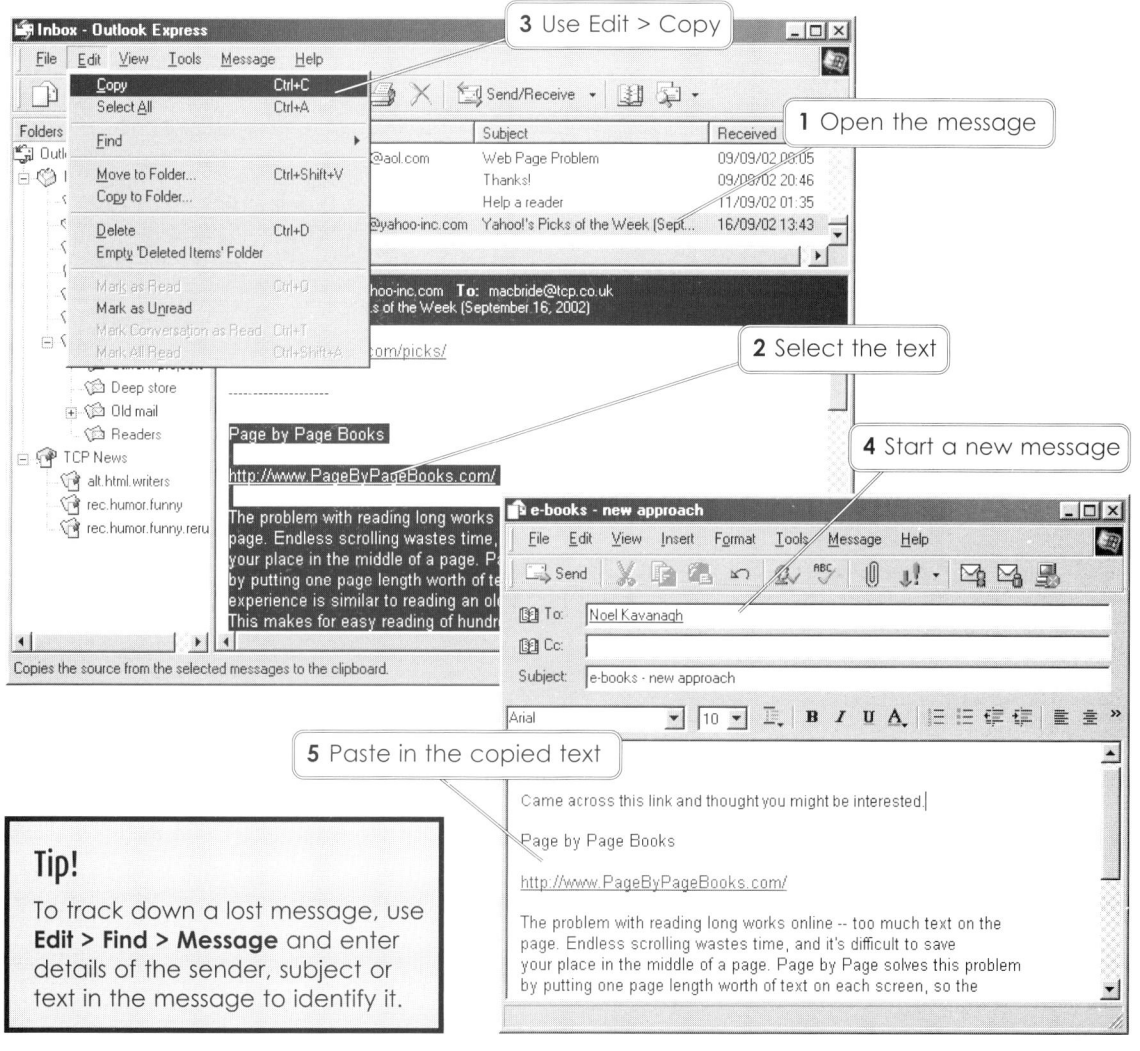

3 Use Edit > Copy

1 Open the message

2 Select the text

4 Start a new message

5 Paste in the copied text

Tip!

To track down a lost message, use **Edit > Find > Message** and enter details of the sender, subject or text in the message to identify it.

Attaching files

Images, documents and other files can be sent by e-mail, attached to messages. As the mail system was designed for transmitting plain text, these data files must be converted to text for transfer, and back again on receipt. Fortunately Outlook Express will do the conversions for you – all you have to do is identify the file to attach, or select a folder to store an incoming attachment.

You can use attachments to send documents, samples, images – even whole books – to people, and it is reliable and efficient, but there are a few problems you should be aware of.

When a file is converted for transmission, it gets about 50% bigger, and it can take some time to send – or receive – messages with attachments. For example, the screenshot below is around 650kb, and as an attached file would be just under 1Mb. E-mail is transmitted at around 3kb per second, so it would take around 5 minutes to send this picture. In contrast, the text of the message will go through in 5 or 10 seconds.

When you collect your messages, they are downloaded from your service provider in the order in which they were received, and if there is a huge attachment on an early message, you have to download that before you can receive later ones. This can be very annoying, especially if you know that there is an urgent message after it in the queue. Do not send people big files unless they really want them!

Finally, note that some old e-mail software cannot handle attachments, and some organizations restrict the type of attachments that can be received. Check that your recipients can receive attachments before sending anything important.

To attach a file:

❶ Start to create a new message as usual.

❷ Open the **Insert** menu and select **File Attachment…** or click 📎 .

❸ Locate and select the file and click **Attach**.

❹ Repeat for other files, if wanted.

❺ Complete and send the message.

1 Start the message

2 Click Attach File

> **Tip!**
> With a long file there will be a delay after you click **Send** while the file is converted.

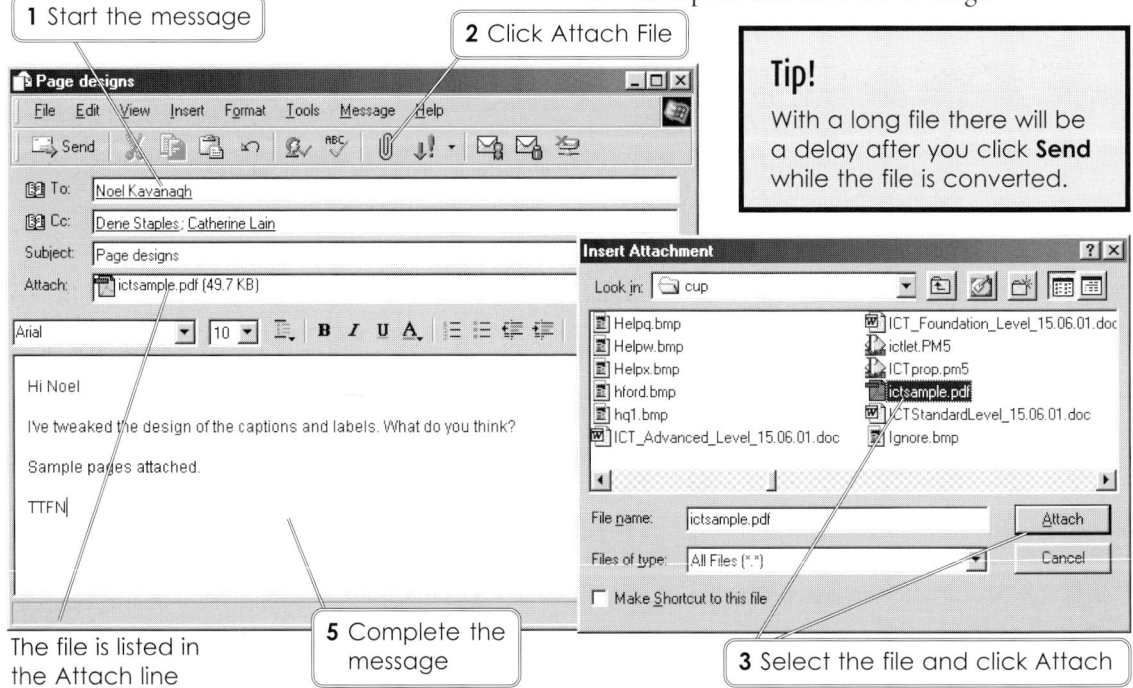

The file is listed in the Attach line

5 Complete the message

3 Select the file and click Attach

Detaching files

Detaching files is simple. Files can be opened directly from the message, or saved to disk for viewing later. *Caution is essential as computer viruses can be spread through attached files.*

❶ Select the message.

❷ Click 📎 in the preview pane header.

❸ If you want to save the file(s), click **Save Attachments...**

❹ Select the folder and click **Save**.

❺ To open a file, select it from the list.

❻ At the **Open Attachment Warning** dialog box, select **Open it** if you are sure it is safe, and click **OK**. The file will be opened (as long as there is a program on your computer that can handle it).

Using the computer

Word processing

Spreadsheets

Databases

Electronic communications

Presentations

Avoiding viruses

Follow these rules to reduce the chances of being infected by viruses:

❖ *Never open a file from an unknown source*, and only open them from known sources if you are expecting them.

❖ *Never open an executable file* – one with an .exe, .com, .bat, .vb extension.

❖ Word documents may have viruses hidden in macros. Make sure that the Security level is set to high – use **Tools > Macro > Security** to set the level.

❖ Install anti-virus software *and use it.*

A paperclip indicates an attached file

You can save the file from this box

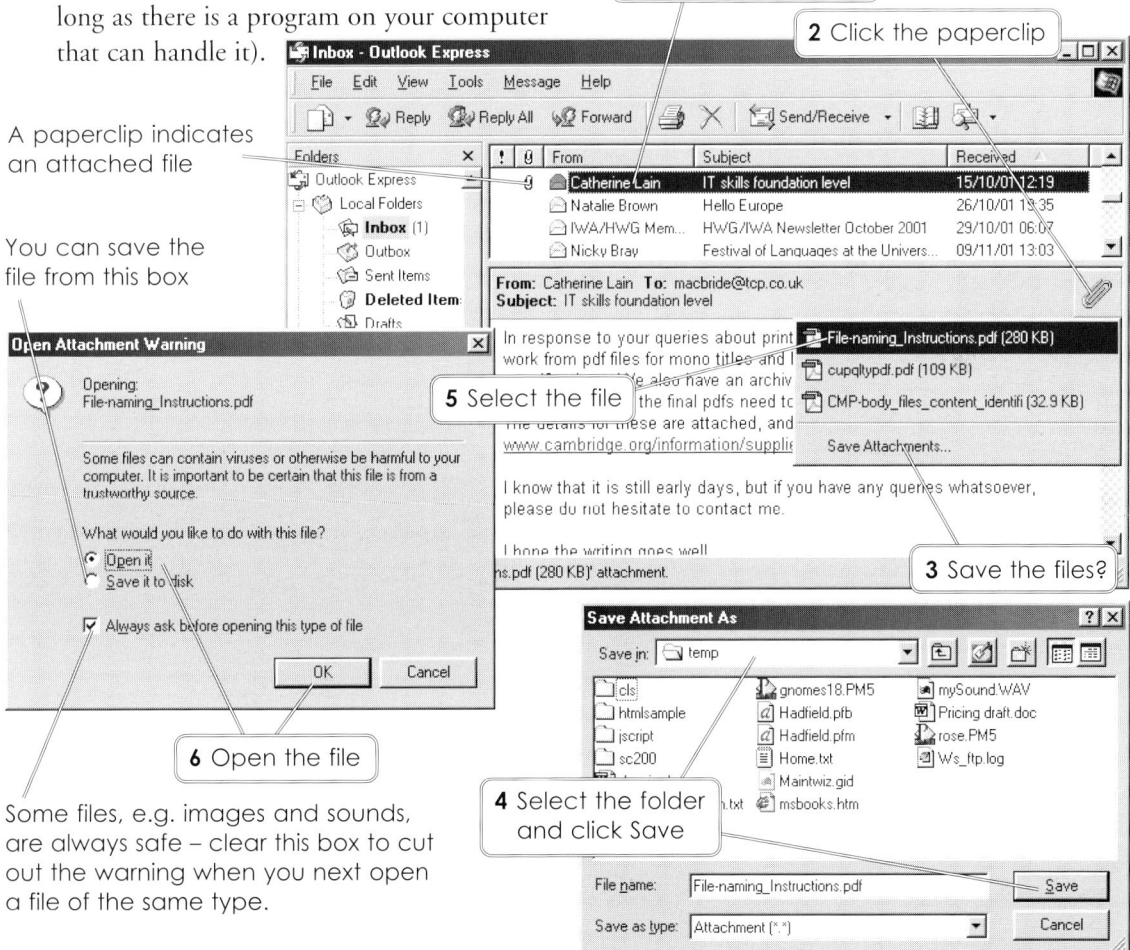

1 Select the message

2 Click the paperclip

5 Select the file

3 Save the files?

6 Open the file

4 Select the folder and click Save

Some files, e.g. images and sounds, are always safe – clear this box to cut out the warning when you next open a file of the same type.

The Address Book

If you are going to write to someone, you must have their e-mail address – and if you are going to write to them often, you should keep the address in your Address Book. This can hold not only e-mail addresses, but also postal addresses, phone numbers and other details.

You can add an address to your book at any time, whether you are online or offline.

❶ Open the **Tools** menu and select **Address Book...** or click 📖.

❷ At the **Address Book** window, open the **File** menu or click the **New** button and select **New Contact...**

❸ On the **Personal** tab type the person's **First**, and **Last** (and **Middle**?) names and e-mail address.

❹ If they have several addresses, click **Add** and enter the others, **Add**ing each one.

❺ Go to the other tabs to add further details.

❻ Click **OK**.

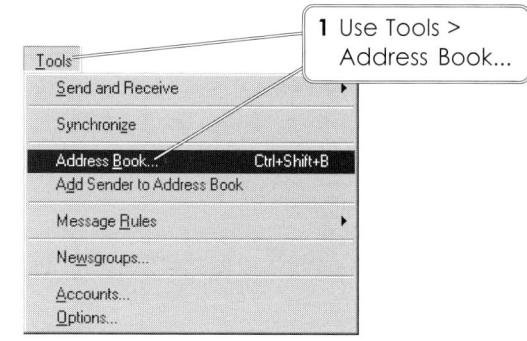

1 Use Tools > Address Book...

2 Set up a New Contact

To edit an existing entry, select it then click Properties

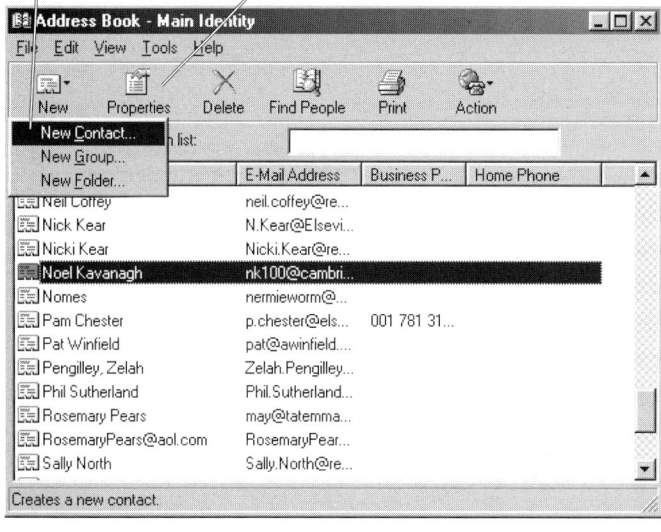

> ## Tip!
>
> You can add people's addresses to your book as you reply to them. Either turn on the option to add them automatically (see page 98), or start to reply, then right-click on the address in the To: line and select Add to Address Book.

3 Type the name and address

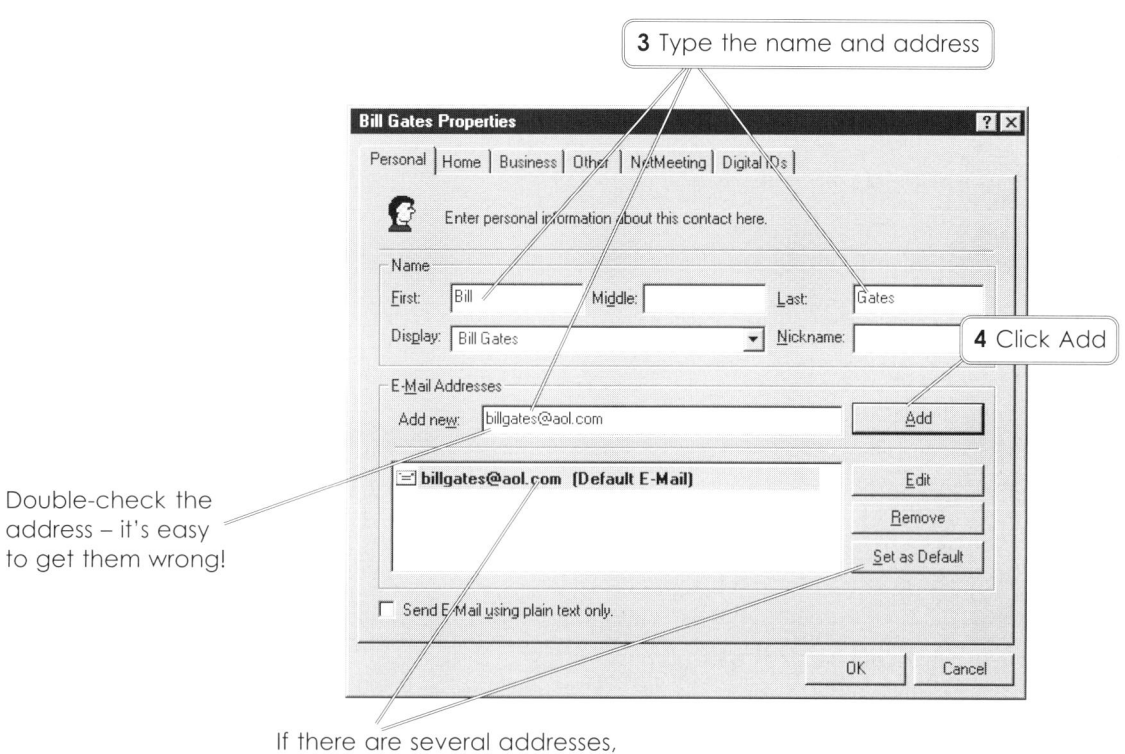

4 Click Add

Double-check the address – it's easy to get them wrong!

If there are several addresses, set one as the Default.

5 Add other details if required

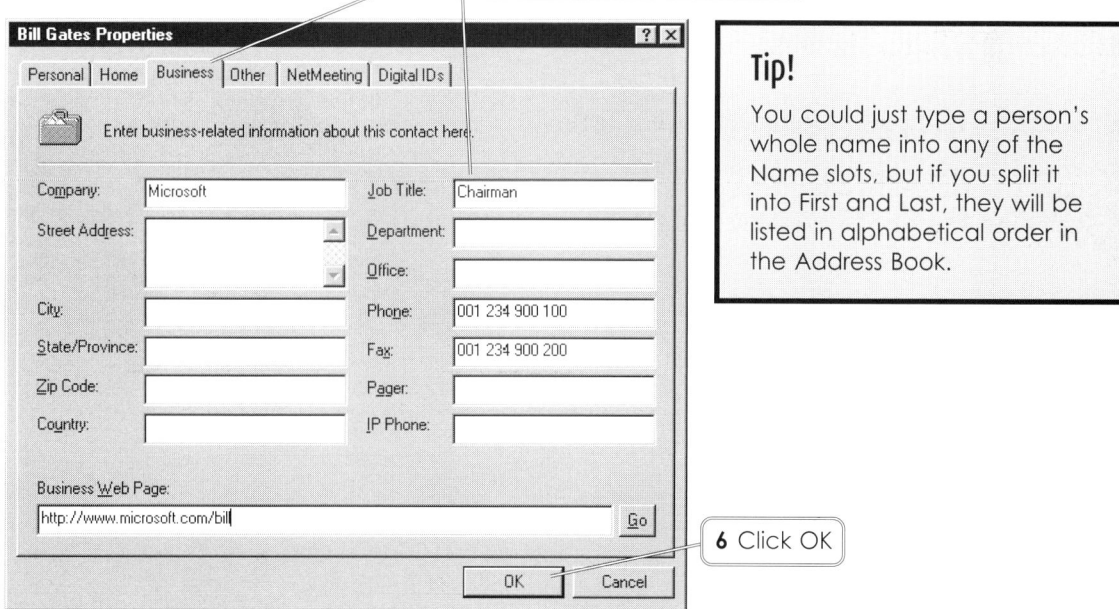

Tip!

You could just type a person's whole name into any of the Name slots, but if you split it into First and Last, they will be listed in alphabetical order in the Address Book.

6 Click OK

Skills builder 16:
Using e-mail

This exercise asks you to send an e-mail with an attached file to someone, and to detach a file from an incoming message.

Before you start, swap e-mail addresses with another member of your group, or with a friend, and arrange to exchange files with them.

❶ Run Outlook Express and start to send a new message.

❷ At the **New Message** window, click 🖳 To: to open the Address Book.

❸ Click **New Contact**, and add your contact's name and e-mail address, then click **To: ->**.

❹ Enter a suitable subject line and type a brief message.

❺ Attach a Word document or other file.

❻ Click **Send**. If necessary, go online and click **Send/Receive** to actually send the mail.

When your e-mail partner has sent you a message with an attached file…

❼ Open the message and read it.

❽ Click 📎 and save the file in your IT Skills folder.

❾ Create a new e-mail folder, calling it 'Stored mail' and move the message into it.

6 Presentations

You should know how to:

- Start a new presentation
- Create slides
- Enter and format text
- Manage slides
- Set up and run a slide show

You will learn how to:

- Modify slides
- Use the drawing tools
- Insert objects and images
- Create graphs and organization charts
- Add animation and transition effects
- Create and print notes pages
- Run custom shows

Additional resources:

- Checklist 6: Presentations
- Sample files in the *Cambridge* folder

The PowerPoint screen

The screen has three panes:

➤ The **Slide pane** is where you build up and display the slides – normally one at a time.

➤ The **Outline pane** shows only the text.

➤ The **Notes pane** holds the notes that can be printed out to accompany the slides.

The PowerPoint display has six views.

➤ In **Normal view** the Slide, Outline and Notes panes are all open and accessible.

➤ In **Outline view** the Outline pane takes most space. Use this view when you want to concentrate on the text.

➤ In **Slide view** the Outline pane is reduced to a slim strip. Use this for work on the layout.

➤ **Slide Sorter view** shows thumbnails (small pictures) of the slides. Use this view for rearranging the order.

➤ **Slide Show view** runs the presentation.

➤ **Notes Page view** shows the slide and its notes, as it will appear when printed.

You can switch between the first five views using the buttons at the bottom left of the status bar.

To get to Notes Page view, open the **View** menu and select it from there.

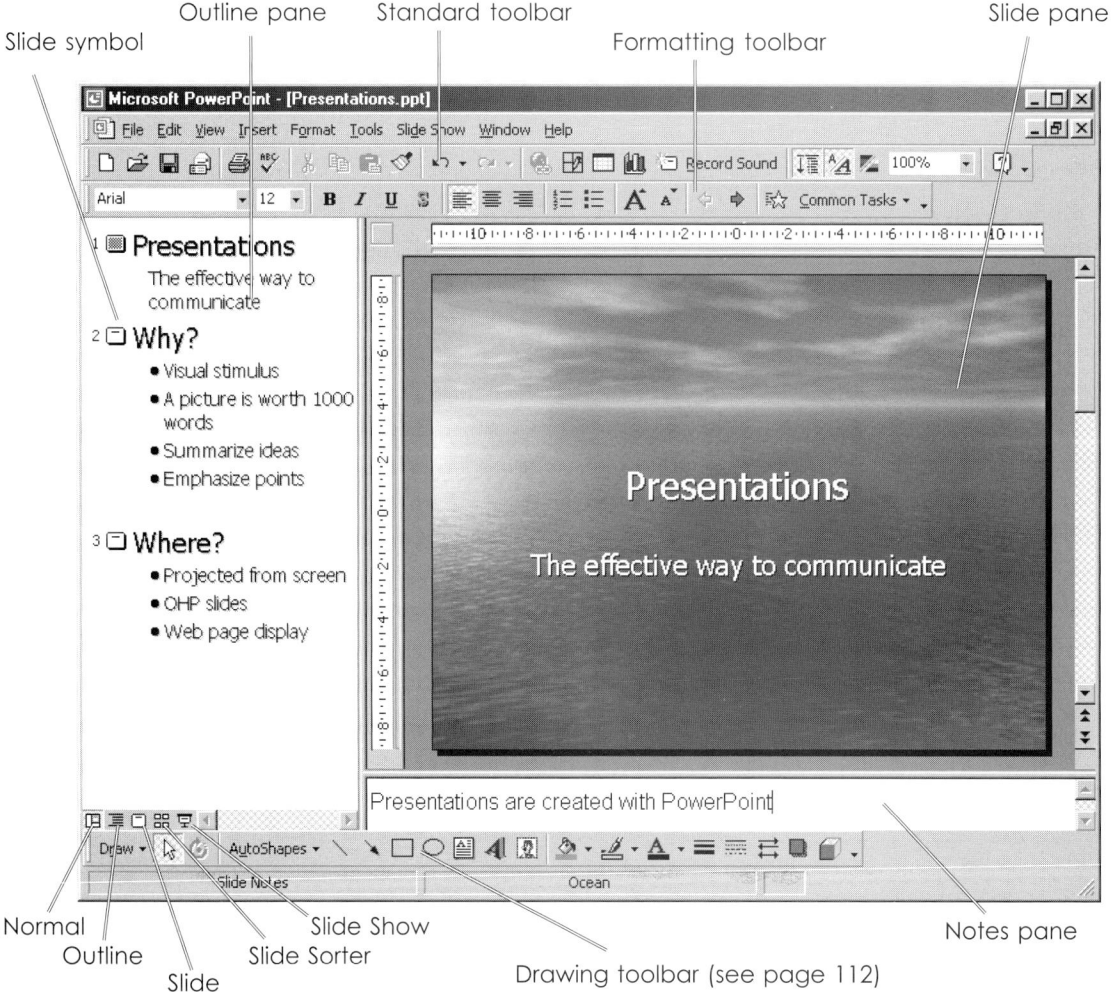

108

Master Slides

The Master Slide sets the default design for the slides in your presentation. Unless you change them individually, the slides will use the colours and text formats set here. They will also display any images or footers that you insert into the Master Slide.

To edit the Master Slide:

❶ Open the **View** menu, point to **Master** and select **Slide Master**.

❷ Select the title text or a bullet level.

❸ Set the font, style and size of the text.

❹ If you want to add a footer, click into the Footer area and type the text.

❺ Click **Close** to return to Normal view.

Tip!

The Title slide is not affected by changes to the Master Slide. Its design and formats are set on the Title Master Slide.

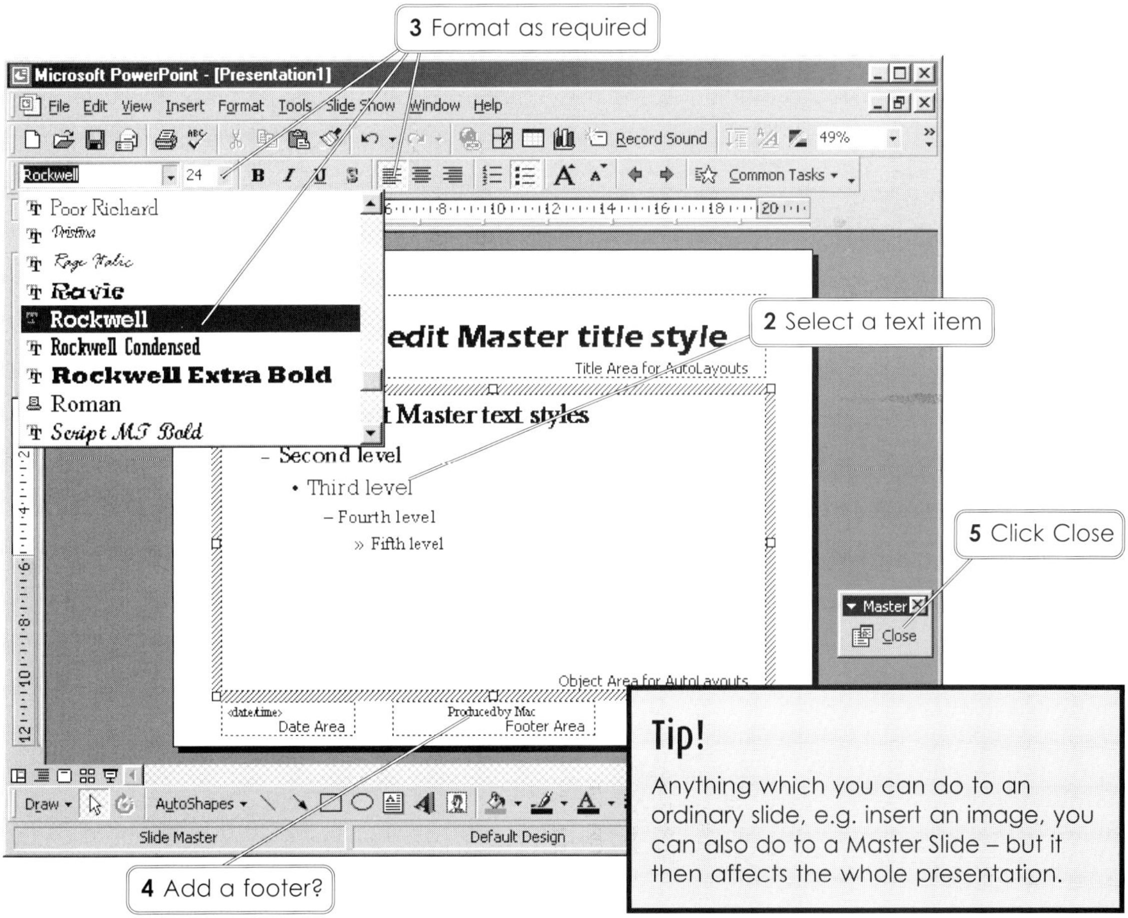

1 Use View > Master > Slide Master

3 Format as required

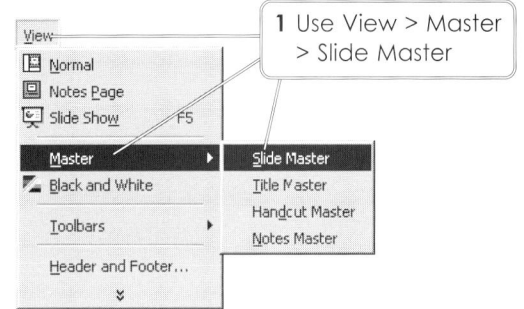

2 Select a text item

5 Click Close

4 Add a footer?

Tip!

Anything which you can do to an ordinary slide, e.g. insert an image, you can also do to a Master Slide – but it then affects the whole presentation.

Modifying slides

AutoLayouts are the simplest way to start new slides, but the placeholders – the blank text boxes or areas for other objects – are not always in the right place. This is not a problem as they can easily be moved, resized or deleted, or new ones inserted.

Working with text boxes

The title, subtitle and bullet list placeholders are all text boxes, but with different formatting.

The main thing to remember when working with text boxes is that you must click on the outline if you want to do something with the whole box – click inside it when you want to edit its text.

❶ Click once on the box to select it.

To resize:

❷ Drag on a handle to pull a corner or side in or out as needed.

To move:

❸ Click anywhere on the thick grey outline and drag the box to its new position.

To delete:

❹ Click on the thick grey outline then press [Delete].

To add a new box:

❺ Click on the Text Box tool 🔲 on the Drawing toolbar (see page 112).

❻ Drag an outline where you want the box.

❼ Click into the new box and type the text.

❽ Format the text as required.

> **Tip!**
>
> The placeholders for objects are moved and resized in a similar way to text boxes.

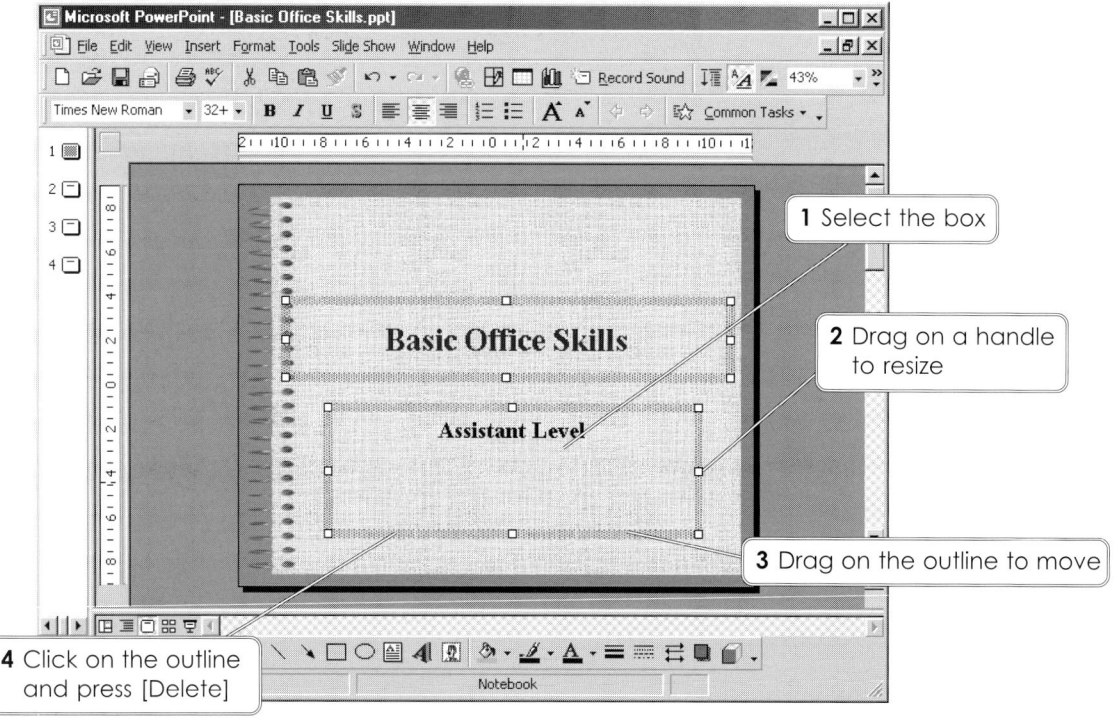

110

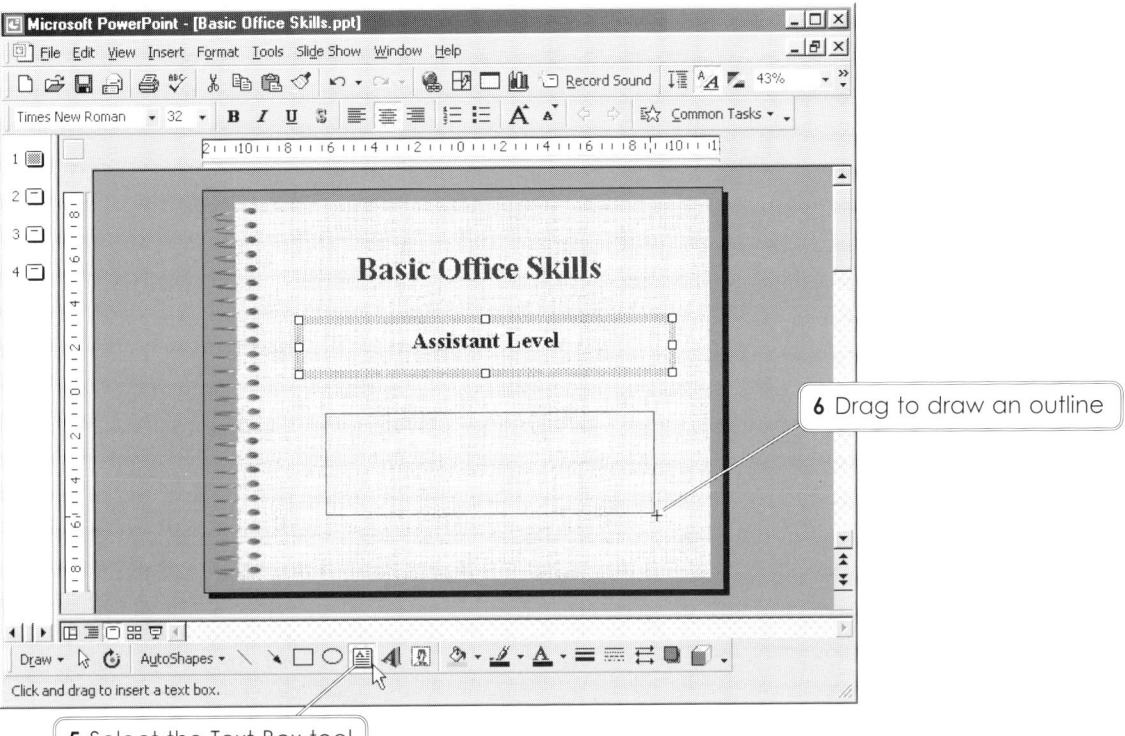

6 Drag to draw an outline

5 Select the Text Box tool

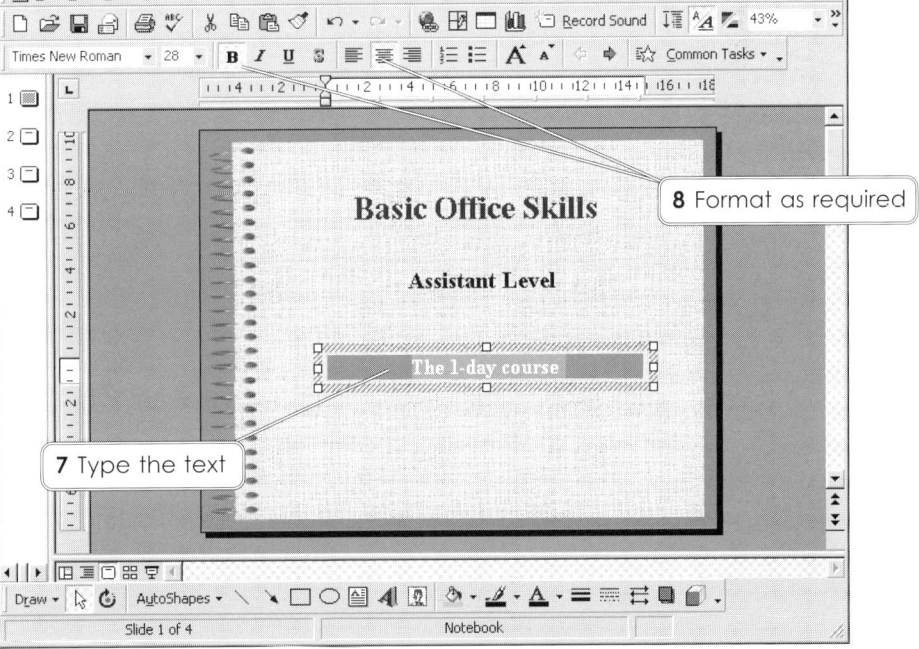

8 Format as required

7 Type the text

Drawing lines or arrows

PowerPoint has a good set of tools for drawing lines, arrows, rectangles, ovals and other shapes. At the simplest level, you might just draw dividing lines between blocks of text, or arrows to point to important items. If you have the time and the ability, you can create complex images with these tools – many of the Clip Art pictures have been drawn with them.

Lines and arrows are drawn and formatted in the same way – in fact, you can turn a line into an arrow, or an arrow into a line.

To draw a line/arrow:

❶ Click the **Line** or **Arrow** tool.

❷ Click where you want the line/arrow to start and drag across the slide to draw it.

To adjust its length or angle:

❸ Click on the line/arrow to select it, then drag on a handle.

To change the thickness:

❹ Click the **Line Style** button and select from the pop-up list.

To make it dashed or dotted:

❺ Click the **Dash Style** button and select from the pop-up list.

To change the line/arrow style:

❻ Click the **Line Style** or **Arrow Style** button and select from the list.

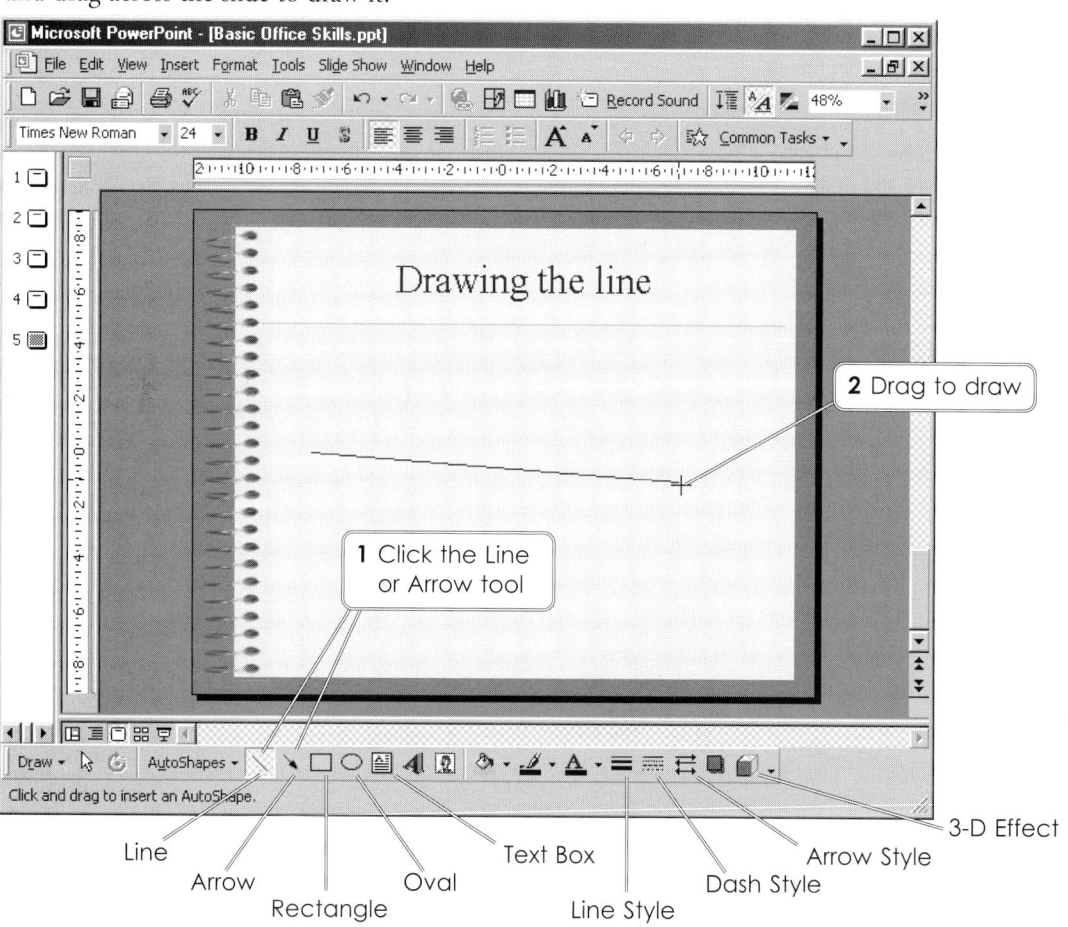

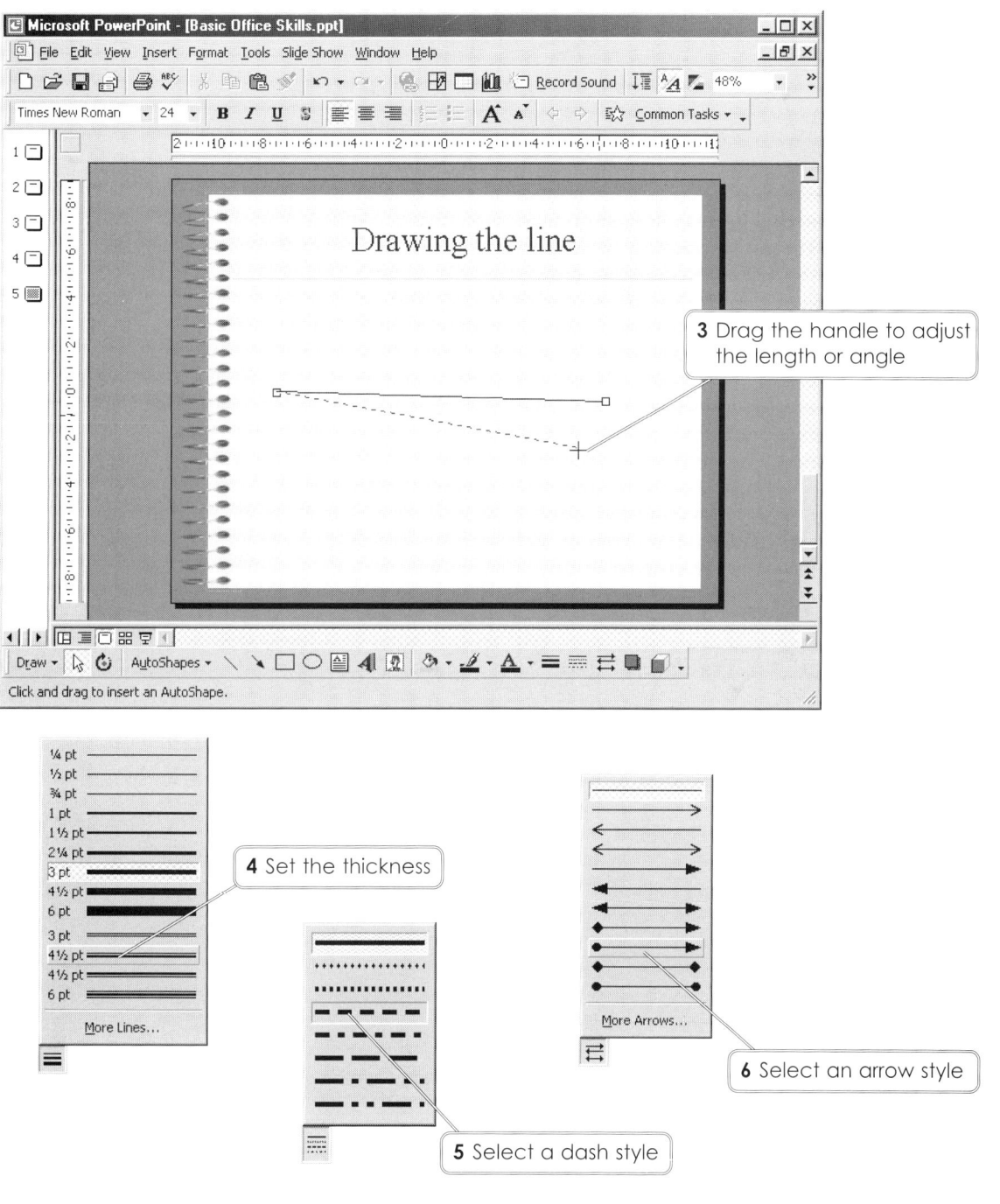

Using the computer

Word processing

Spreadsheets

Databases

Electronic communications

Presentations

Rectangles and ovals

These are both drawn in the same way, with one minor difference. You create a rectangle by clicking where you want one corner to go and dragging across to its opposite. With an oval, you have to imagine the rectangle into which the oval will fit, then drag across from corner to corner. It's easier than it sounds – an outline shows how the oval will look, and if it is not in the right place or the right size, you can change it later.

To draw a rectangle/oval:

❶ Click the **Rectangle** or **Oval** tool.

❷ Click where one corner of the (enclosing) rectangle will go.

❸ Drag across to the opposite corner, using the outline as a guide.

To resize a rectangle/oval:

❹ Click on the shape to select it.

❺ Drag on a handle to adjust the shape.

To move a rectangle/oval:

❻ Click anywhere within the shape and drag it into its new position.

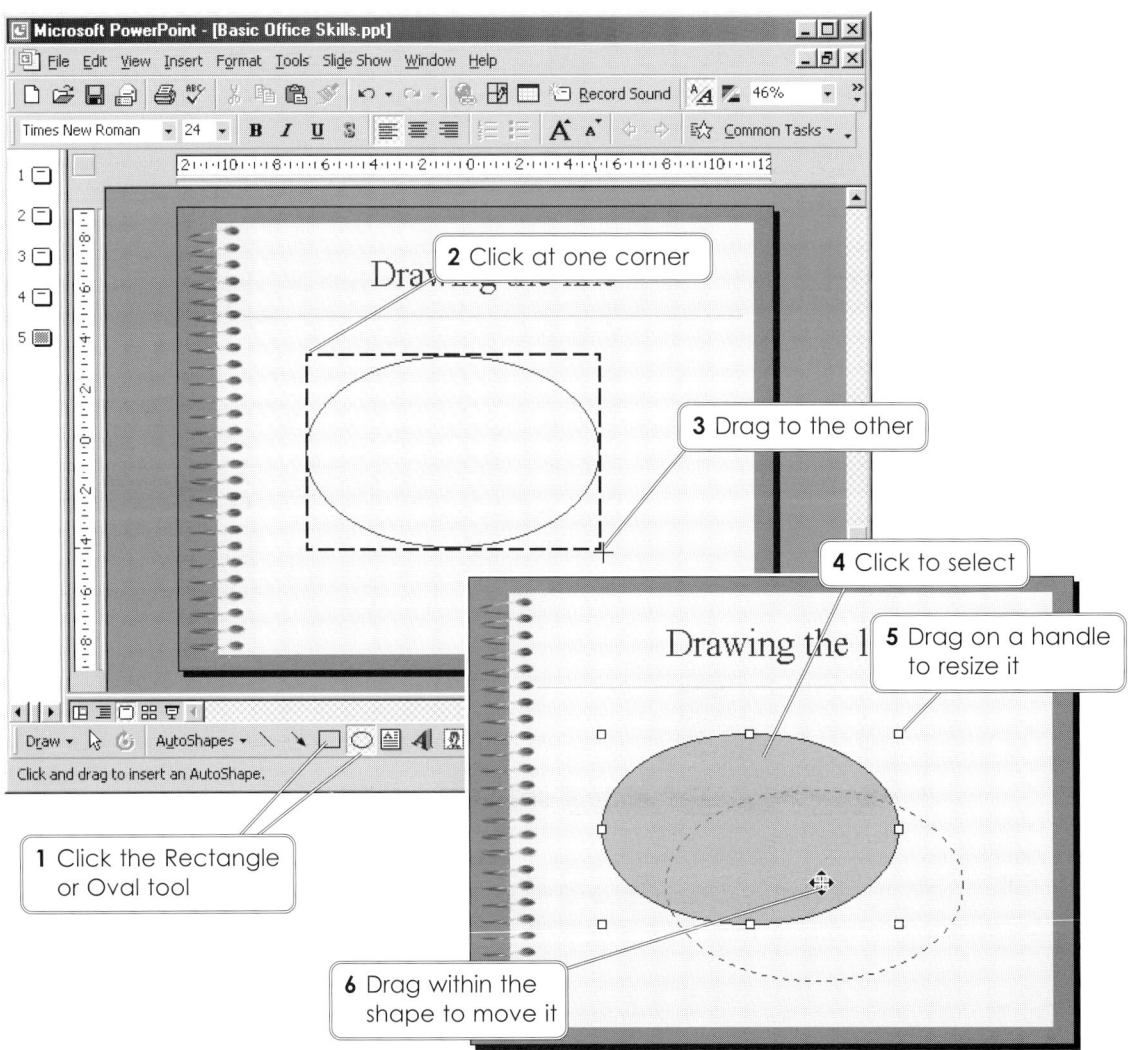

Skills builder 17: The drawing tools

This exercise gives practice in the use of the drawing tools. The aim is to illustrate the idea of fitting square pegs into round holes – it might be used in a career guidance presentation.

❶ Start a new presentation, selecting *Title only* for the first slide.

❷ For the title, enter 'Square pegs and round holes'.

❸ Use the drawing tools to draw one rectangle, one circle and one line.

❹ Set the circle's fill colour to black.

❺ Make the line 6pt, with a single arrowhead.

❻ Select the rectangle, and drop-down the 3-D options. Select a setting which makes the rectangle appear as a 3-D block.

❼ Move and resize the rectangle, circle and line as necessary, so that the rectangle is above and to one side of the circle, with the arrow pointing to the circle.

❽ Save the file as *guidance.ppt* in your IT Skills folder.

Your slide should look something like this

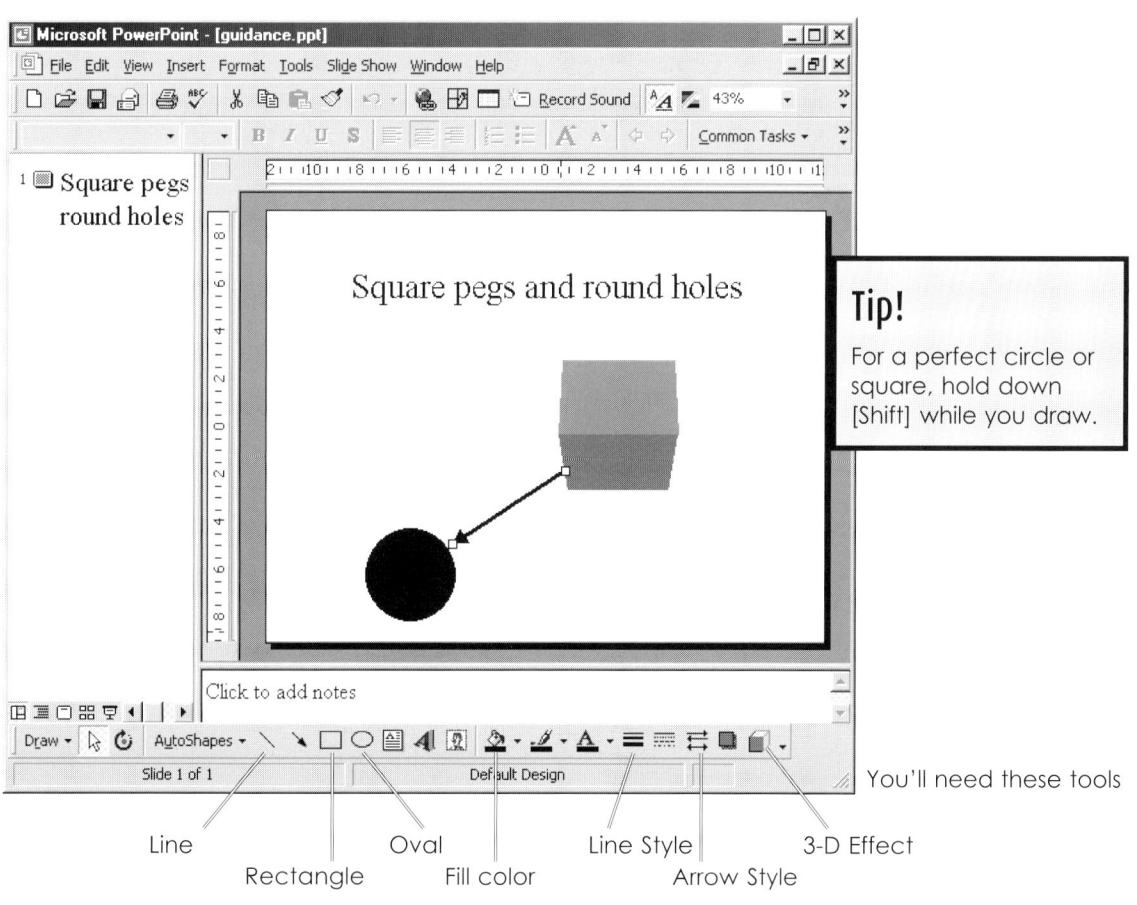

Tip!
For a perfect circle or square, hold down [Shift] while you draw.

You'll need these tools

Line · Rectangle · Oval · Fill color · Line Style · Arrow Style · 3-D Effect

Using the computer

Word processing

Spreadsheets

Databases

Electronic communications

Presentations

Objects on slides

The easiest way to add a picture, chart, media clip or other object to a slide is to start from an AutoLayout containing the right kind of object placeholder. Just double-click on the icon and you will be taken into a routine for creating or inserting the object.

To create an object from an AutoLayout:

❶ Click the **New Slide** button 🖼.

❷ Select an AutoLayout designed for the right kind of object.

❸ Click **OK**.

❹ Double-click on the object icon.

What happens next depends upon the type of object. Charts, organization charts, Clip Art and other objects are covered in the next few pages.

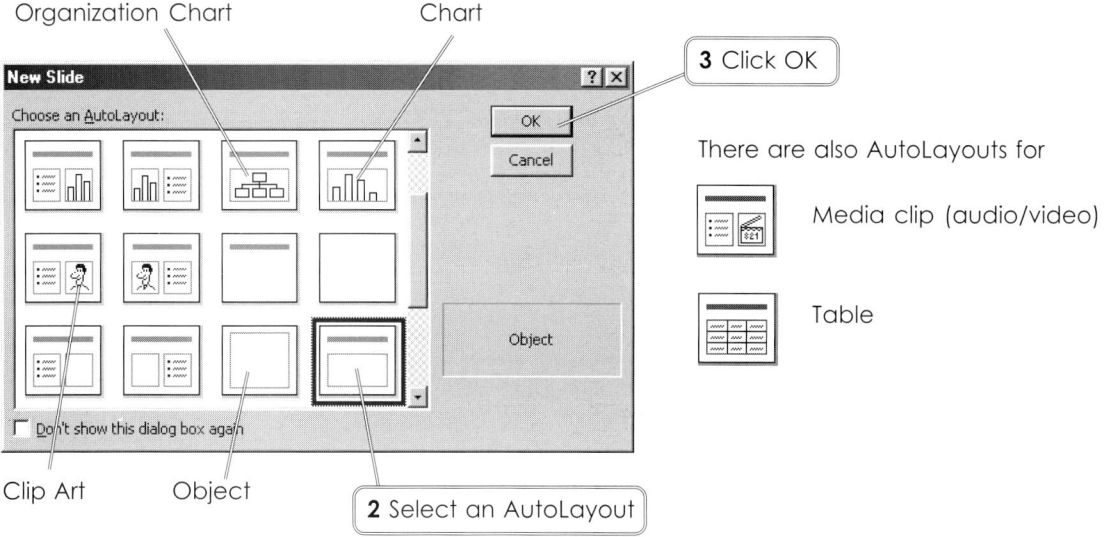

Organization Chart   Chart

3 Click OK

There are also AutoLayouts for

Media clip (audio/video)

Table

Clip Art   Object

2 Select an AutoLayout

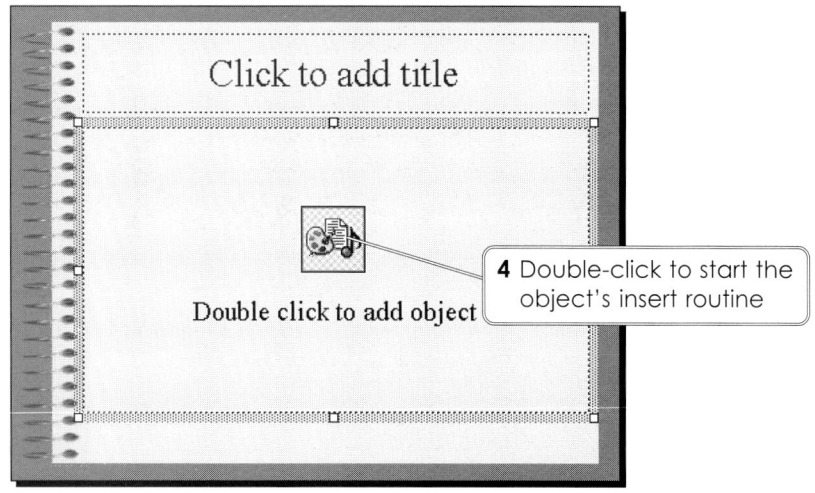

Click to add title

Double click to add object

4 Double-click to start the object's insert routine

Inserting objects

An object can be added to an existing slide using the **Insert** menu options. Pictures, movies and sounds, charts and tables are each handled by their own routines. For other types of objects, use the **Object…** option.

❶ Open the **Insert** menu and select **Object…**

To create a new object:

❷ Select the **Object type** from the list and click **OK**.

❸ The related application will start up, within PowerPoint. Create the document (or other object) as usual. At the end, look for an option on the **File** menu to save and exit and return to PowerPoint.

To use an existing object:

❹ Select **Create from file**.

❺ Enter the path and filename or browse for the file, then click **OK**.

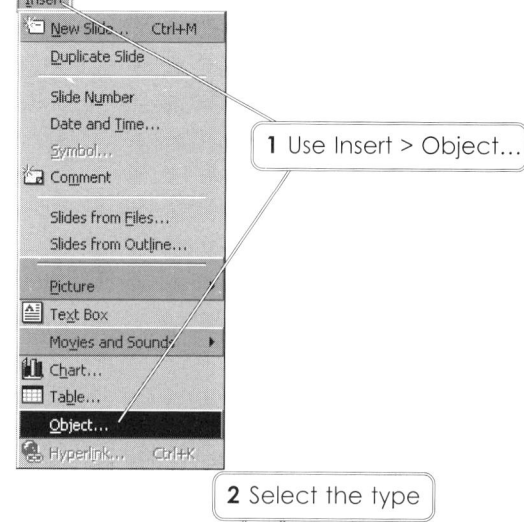

1 Use Insert > Object…

2 Select the type

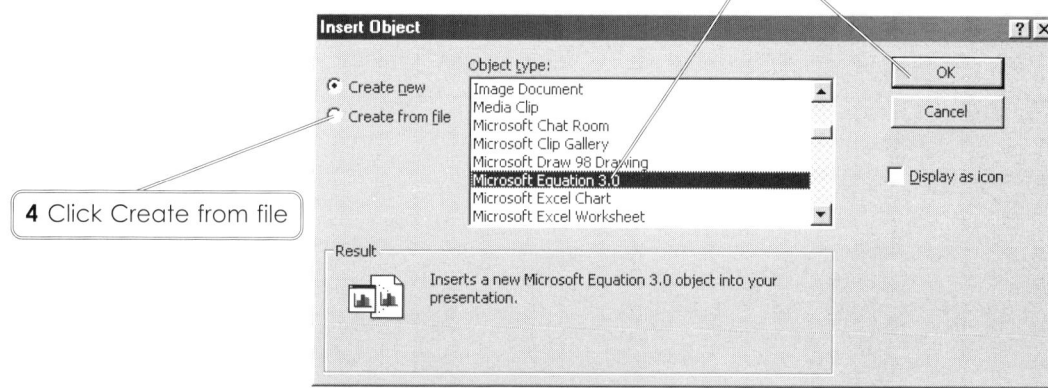

4 Click Create from file

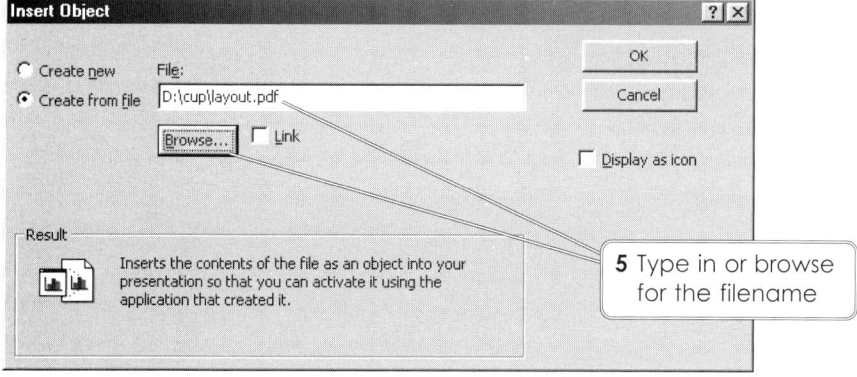

5 Type in or browse for the filename

Using the computer

Word processing

Spreadsheets

Databases

Electronic communications

Presentations

Charts

Excel charts and worksheets can be inserted into a slide – created either from new or from existing files – but if you have a small set of data to chart, it is simpler to use the Chart facility.

❶ Start from an AutoLayout containing a
    Chart object and double-click .

Or

❷ Use **Insert > Chart**.

❸ You will see a datasheet containing example data, and the chart produced from this. Replace the headings and data with your own, adding rows or columns as needed.

❹ Close the datasheet when it is no longer needed.

❺ To change the chart type, use the options on the **Chart** menu.

❻ To adjust the appearance of any element on the chart, right-click on it and select the **Format** option from the context menu.

❼ When you have finished work on the chart, click on the background of the slide.

❽ If you want to return to the chart for further editing, double-click on it.

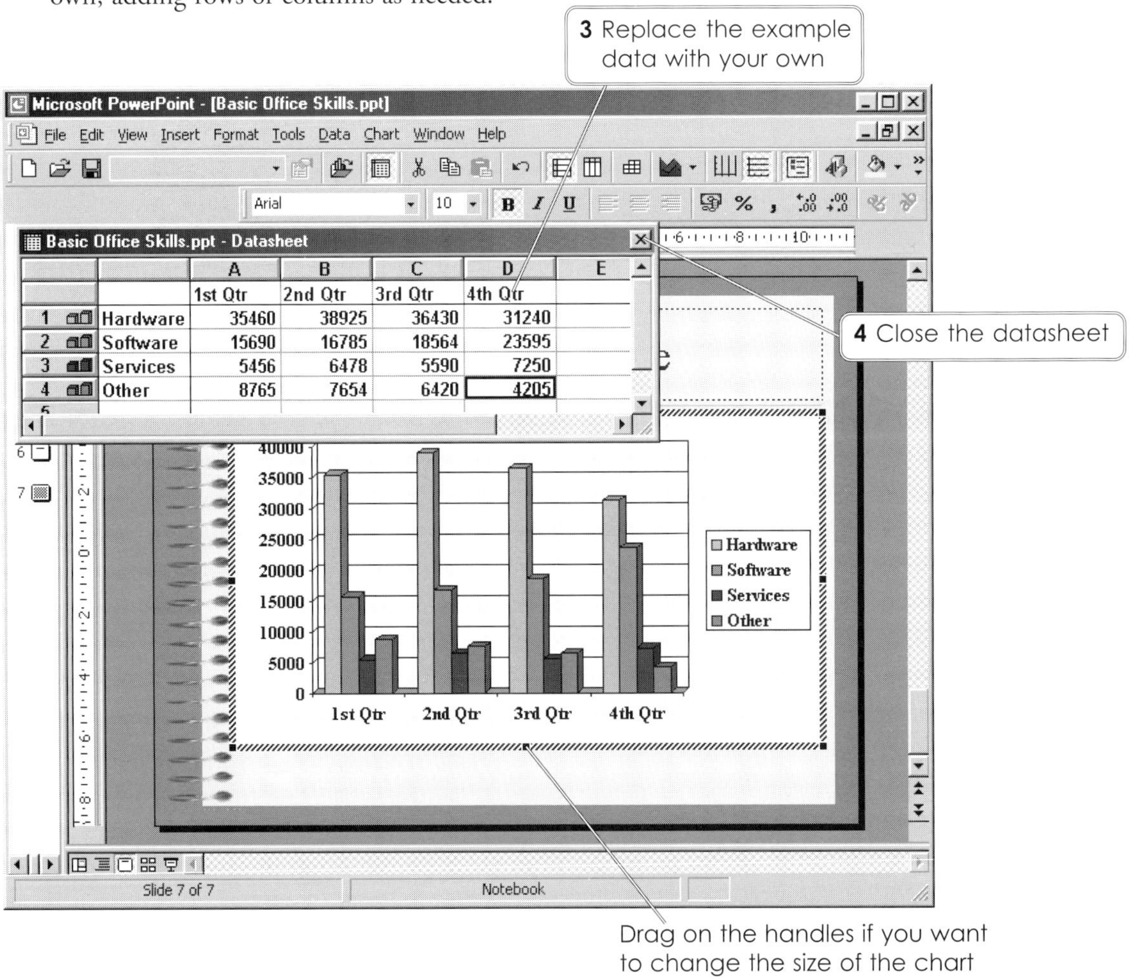

> **3** Replace the example data with your own

> **4** Close the datasheet

Microsoft PowerPoint - [Basic Office Skills.ppt]

File Edit View Insert Format Tools Data Chart Window Help

Arial   10   **B** *I* U

Basic Office Skills.ppt - Datasheet

			A	B	C	D	E
			1st Qtr	2nd Qtr	3rd Qtr	4th Qtr	
1		Hardware	35460	38925	36430	31240	
2		Software	15690	16785	18564	23595	
3		Services	5456	6478	5590	7250	
4		Other	8765	7654	6420	4205	

- Hardware
- Software
- Services
- Other

1st Qtr   2nd Qtr   3rd Qtr   4th Qtr

Slide 7 of 7   Notebook

Drag on the handles if you want to change the size of the chart

5 Change the chart type?

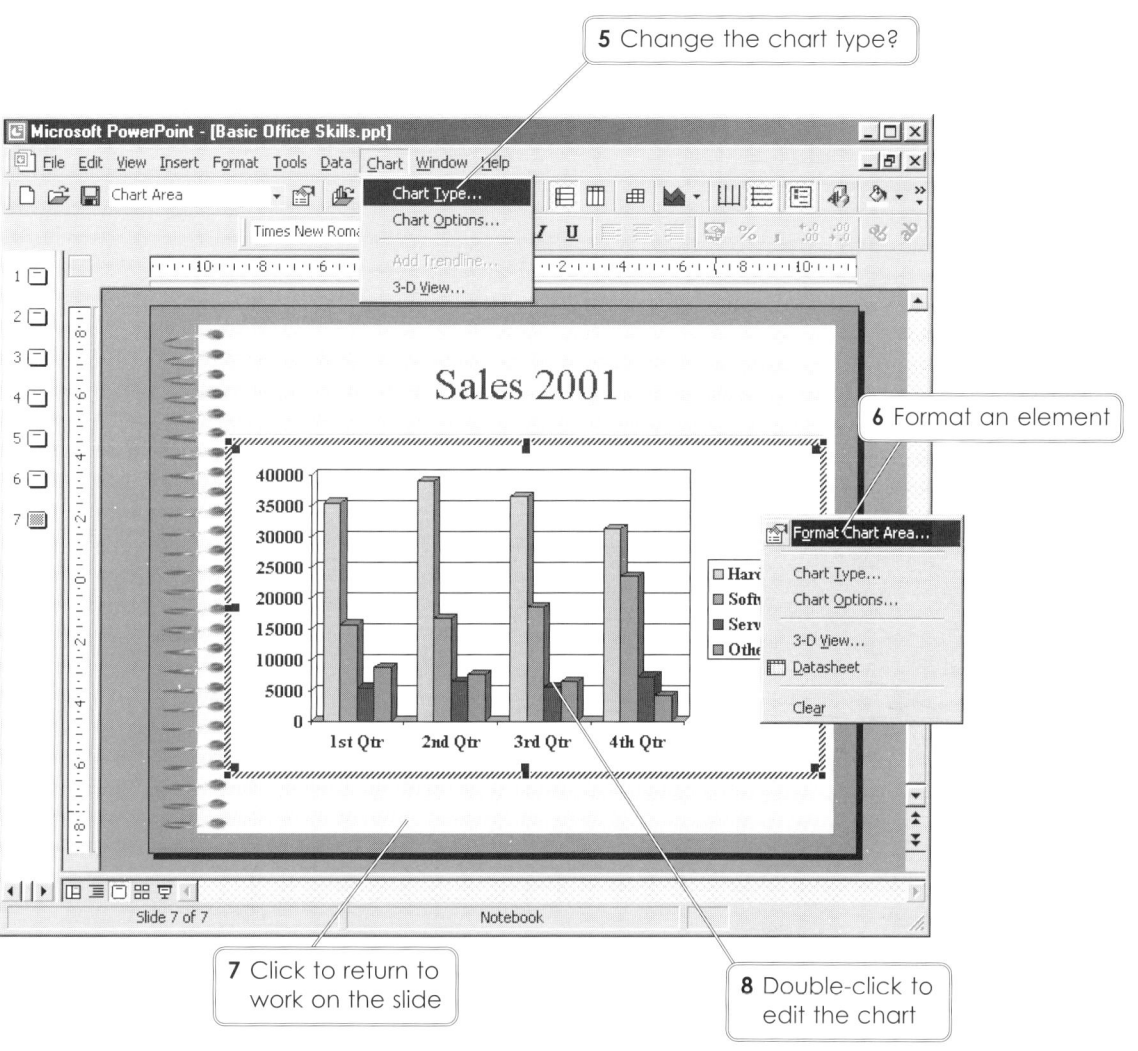

6 Format an element

7 Click to return to work on the slide

8 Double-click to edit the chart

Tip!

These charts can be formatted in exactly the same way as charts in Excel – see page 57.

Organization charts

These are typically used to illustrate the staffing structure of an organization. A chart consists of boxes containing the name, title and comments for each person. The boxes can be linked to each other to indicate the nature of the relationship. The starting shape has a boss plus three staff. You can change these or add more boxes for different types of relationships to build a chart for your organization.

❶ Start from an AutoLayout containing a

   Chart object and double-click 🔲.

Or

❷ Use **Insert > Picture > Organization Chart**.

❸ Replace the names and title, and type comments if wanted.

To **add a box**:

❹ Click the tool for the relationship.

❺ Click the box that the new one relates to, e.g. if you are adding a subordinate, click on that person's boss's box.

To **delete a box**:

❻ Click on it and press [**Delete**].

To **add an extra link line**:

❼ Click the **Auxiliary Line** tool.

❽ Click on the box to link from.

❾ Click on the box to link to.

When you have finished:

❿ Open the **File** menu and select the **Update** option, then open the menu again and select **Close and Return**.

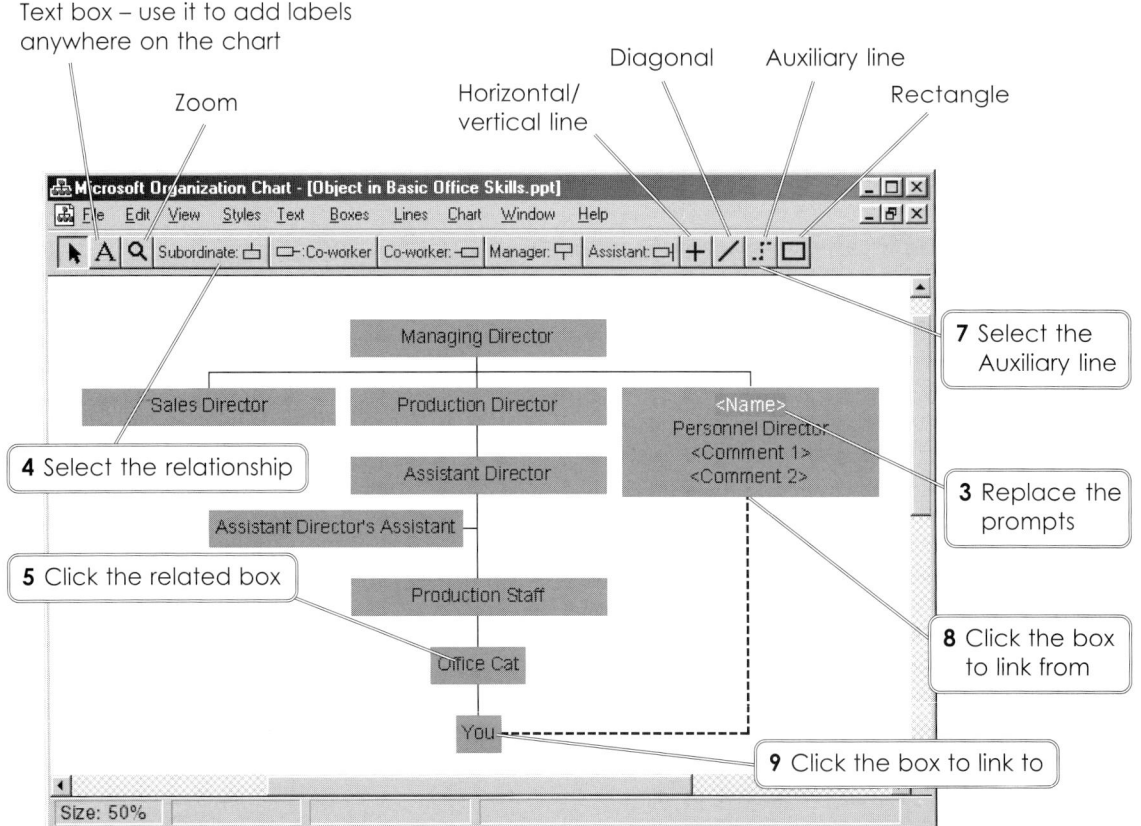

Text box – use it to add labels anywhere on the chart

Zoom

Diagonal   Auxiliary line

Horizontal/vertical line

Rectangle

7 Select the Auxiliary line

4 Select the relationship

3 Replace the prompts

5 Click the related box

8 Click the box to link from

9 Click the box to link to

Using the computer

Word processing

Spreadsheets

Databases

Electronic communications

Presentations

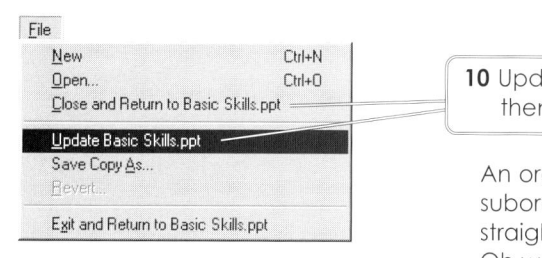

File

New	Ctrl+N
Open...	Ctrl+O
Close and Return to Basic Skills.ppt	
Update Basic Skills.ppt	
Save Copy As...	
Revert...	
Exit and Return to Basic Skills.ppt	

10 Update the chart, then close and return

An organization chart – in this case *You* appear to be subordinate to everyone from the *Managing Director* straight down, and subject to the *Personnel Director*. Oh well, the only way is up!

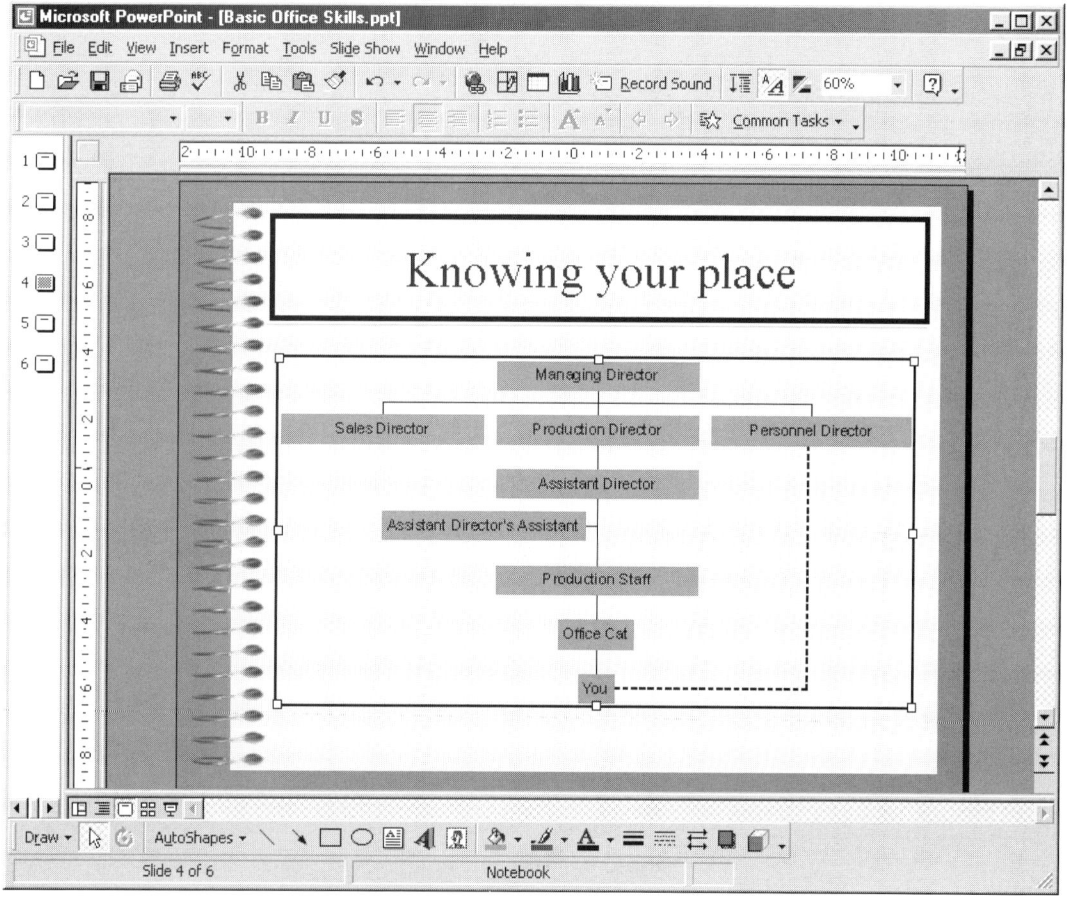

Microsoft PowerPoint - [Basic Office Skills.ppt]

File   Edit   View   Insert   Format   Tools   Slide Show   Window   Help

Record Sound   60%   Common Tasks

Knowing your place

Managing Director

Sales Director   Production Director   Personnel Director

Assistant Director

Assistant Director's Assistant

Production Staff

Office Cat

You

Draw   AutoShapes

Slide 4 of 6   Notebook

Tip!

The horizontal/vertical and diagonal line tools and the rectangle tool are there for decorative purposes and can be used anywhere in the chart area. To format any line, right-click on it (or use the **Lines** menu) and set its thickness, style and colour.

Clip Art

Images and Clip Art are inserted in almost exactly the same way as in Word.

❶ Start from an AutoLayout containing a Chart object and double-click ▣.

Or

❷ Use **Insert > Picture > Clip Art**.

❸ Select a picture from the Gallery (see page 26 for Office 97 or 27 for Office 2000).

❹ To format the picture, right-click on it and select **Show Picture Toolbar**. Use its tools to adjust the brightness, contrast, and other properties (see page 28).

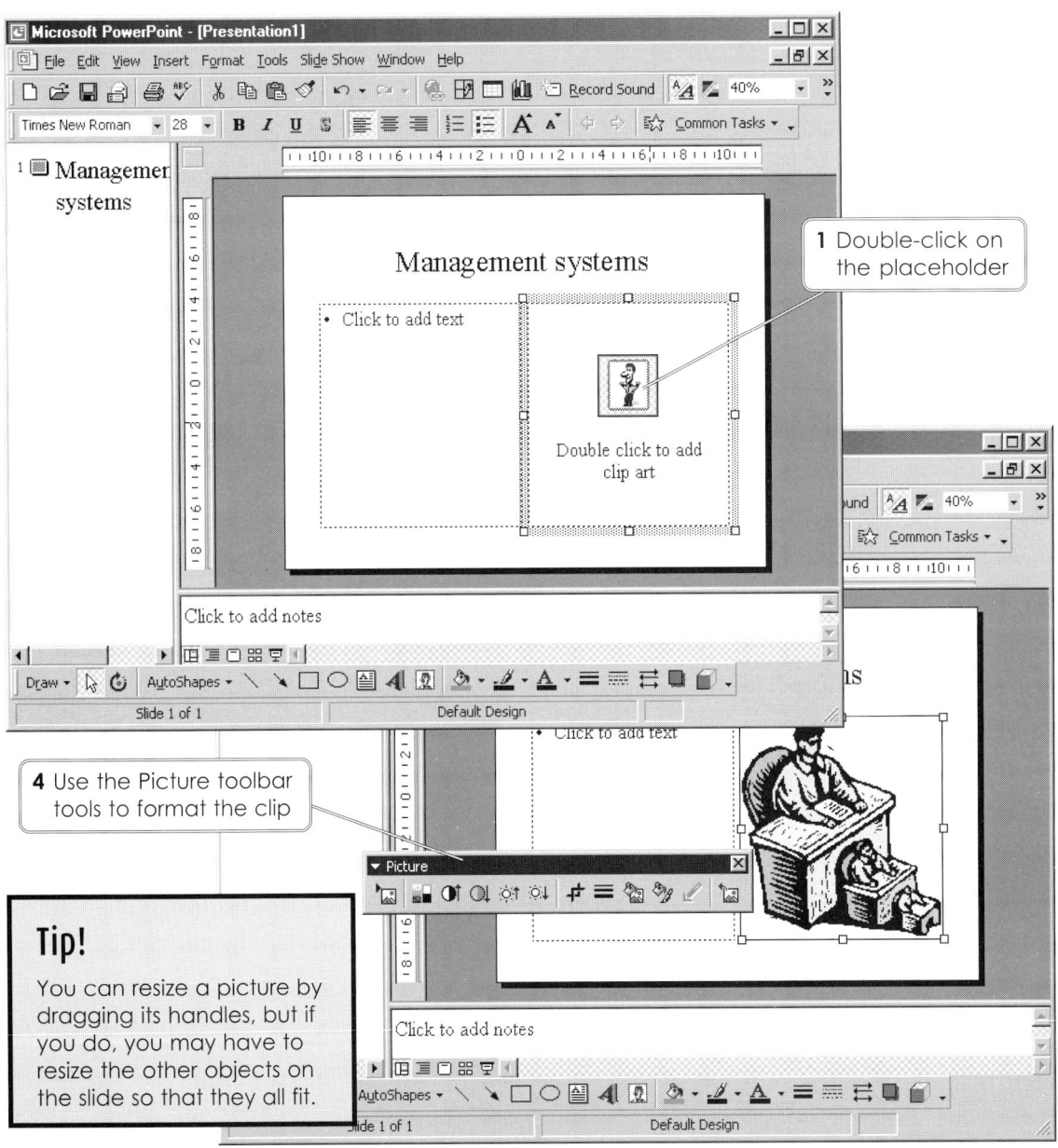

1 Double-click on the placeholder

4 Use the Picture toolbar tools to format the clip

Tip!

You can resize a picture by dragging its handles, but if you do, you may have to resize the other objects on the slide so that they all fit.

Borders

You can add a border to any item on a slide – title, bullet list, picture, chart or whatever. The technique is always the same, and that is because you are adding the border to the placeholder, not the text or object within it.

❶ Click on the object or text placeholder to select it.

❷ Use the **Line Style**, **Line Color** and/or **Dash Style** tools to format the line.

Or

❸ Right-click and select **Format Object…**

❹ At the **Format Object** dialog box, use the **Line** options in the **Colors and Lines** tab to specify the border.

❺ Click **OK**.

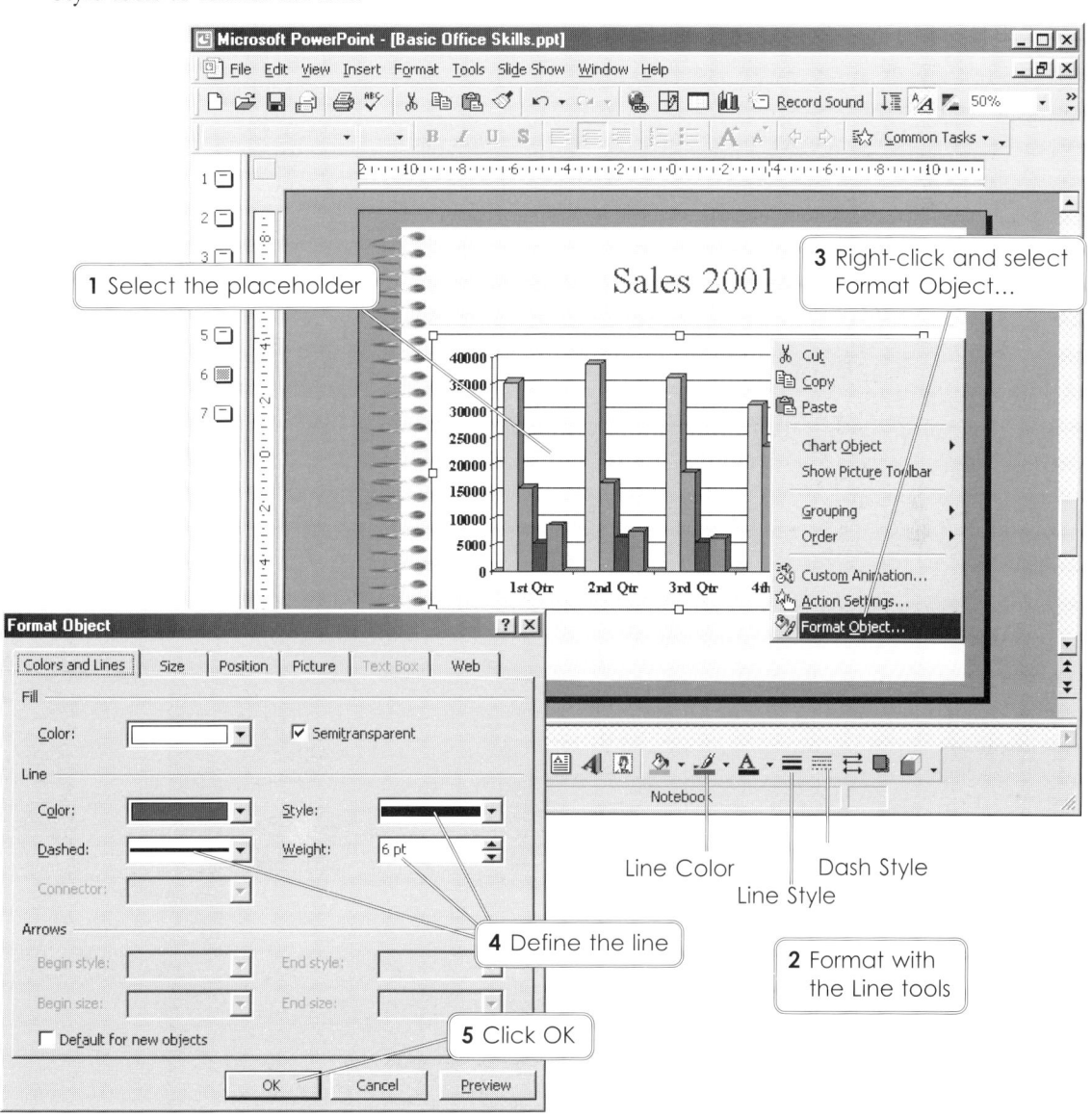

1 Select the placeholder

3 Right-click and select Format Object...

4 Define the line

5 Click OK

2 Format with the Line tools

Line Color

Line Style

Dash Style

Using the computer

Word processing

Spreadsheets

Databases

Electronic communications

Presentations

Skills builder 18: Objects on slides

In this exercise you will be asked to create an organization chart outlining the structure of your college or business. Work out a simplified structure on paper first, making up any parts that you do not know – in this exercise, factual accuracy is not important.

❶ Start a new file, selecting *Organization Chart* for the first slide.

❷ Go to the Slide Master view. Insert an image or Clip Art picture for a logo. Reduce it to a reasonable size and move it to the top right of the slide.

❸ Switch back to Normal view.

❹ Double-click on the Organization Chart icon to open it for editing.

❺ Delete the name prompt, and replace the titles in the boxes with the names of the divisions in the organization.

❻ Add more boxes, as needed, to increase the levels or expand the width of the structure.

❼ Update the chart, then return to the Slide view.

❽ Save the presentation in your IT Skills folder.

The organization chart slide, showing the image that was inserted on the Slide Master

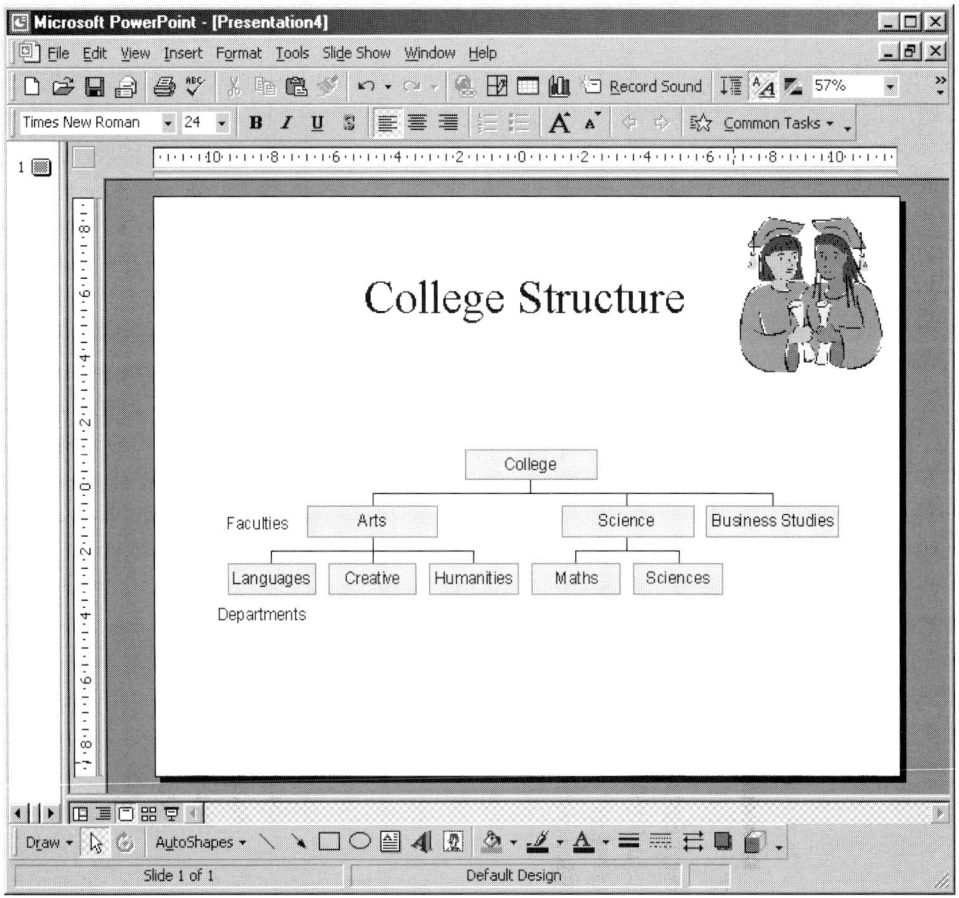

Animation

This controls how the elements of a slide are brought into view. At the simplest level, all the elements are in place when the slide is displayed. At the most complex, you can specify a different animation for each element of every slide. In between, you can apply one animation style to a slide, or to the whole set – here is how.

❶ Go to Slide Sorter view.

❷ Select the slides that you want to animate in the same way – hold down [**Control**] while you click on each one in turn.

❸ Open the **Slide Show** menu, point to **Preset Animation** and select a style.

❹ View the show, or use **Animation Preview** to see how it looks.

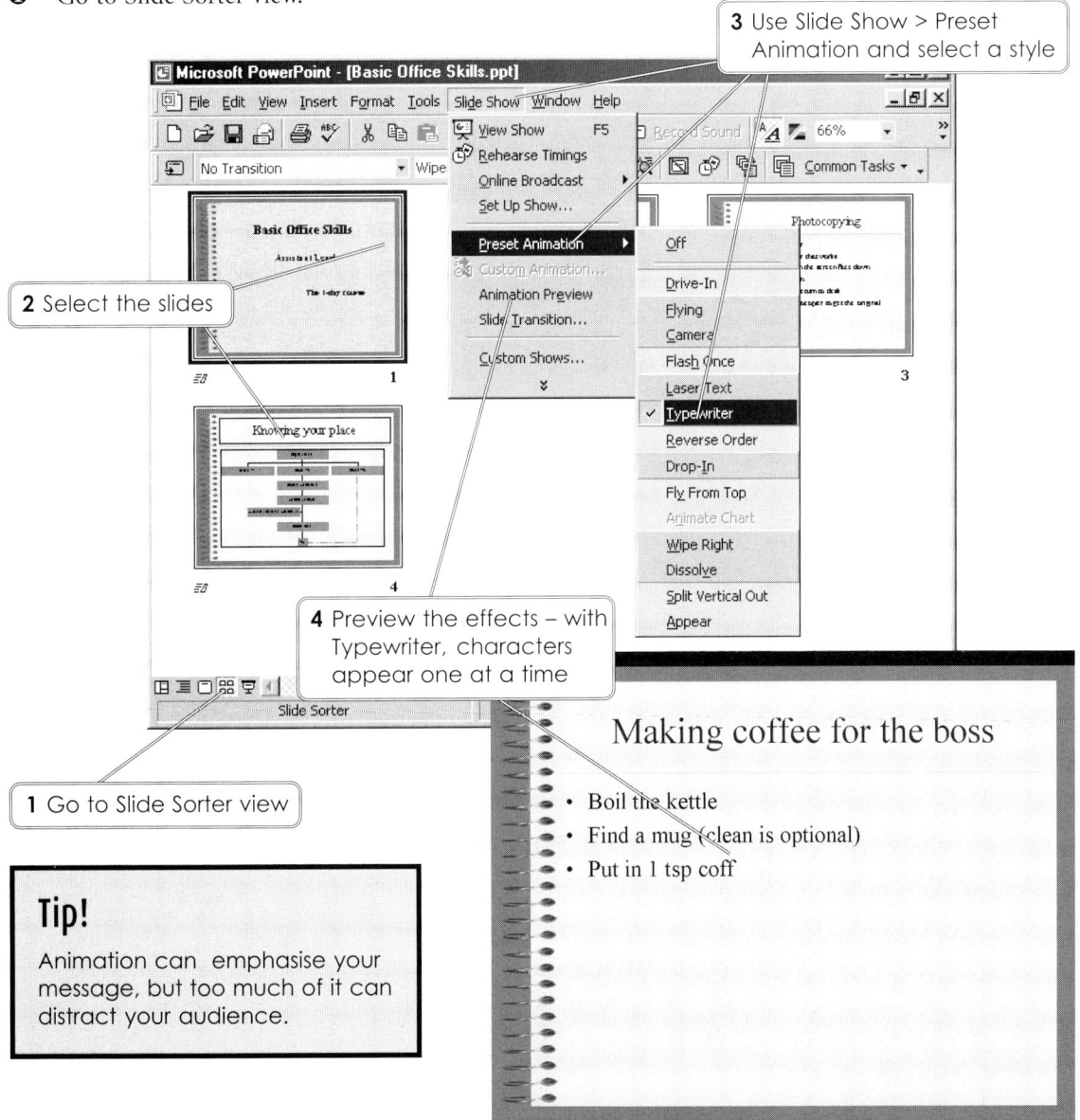

3 Use Slide Show > Preset Animation and select a style

2 Select the slides

4 Preview the effects – with Typewriter, characters appear one at a time

1 Go to Slide Sorter view

Tip!

Animation can emphasise your message, but too much of it can distract your audience.

Using the computer

Word processing

Spreadsheets

Databases

Electronic communications

Presentations

Transitions

Transitions control how the show progresses from one slide to another. You can specify:

➤ how a slide becomes visible – selecting from a wide range of cover, uncover, dissolve and other effects;

➤ the speed of the transition;

➤ accompanying sound effects;

➤ when the new slide should appear – after a set time or on a mouse click.

If none are set, slides will appear when the mouse is clicked or a key pressed, and they will simply replace the previous one.

To create a transition:

❶ Open the **Slide Show** menu and select **Slide Transition…**

❷ Select an **Effect**.

❸ Set the speed.

❹ Turn on **Automatically after** and set the timing, if wanted.

❺ Pick a **Sound** if useful.

❻ Click **Apply** to apply the transition to the current slide, or **Apply to All** to apply it to the whole show.

Tip!

Spell check your presentation before you finish – open the **Tools** menu and select **Spelling** to start the check.

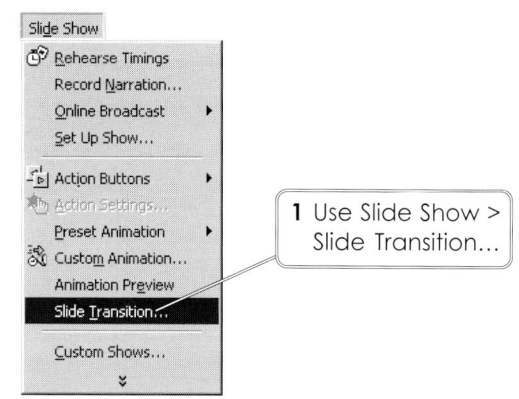

1 Use Slide Show > Slide Transition...

When you select an effect, you will get a preview of it at work

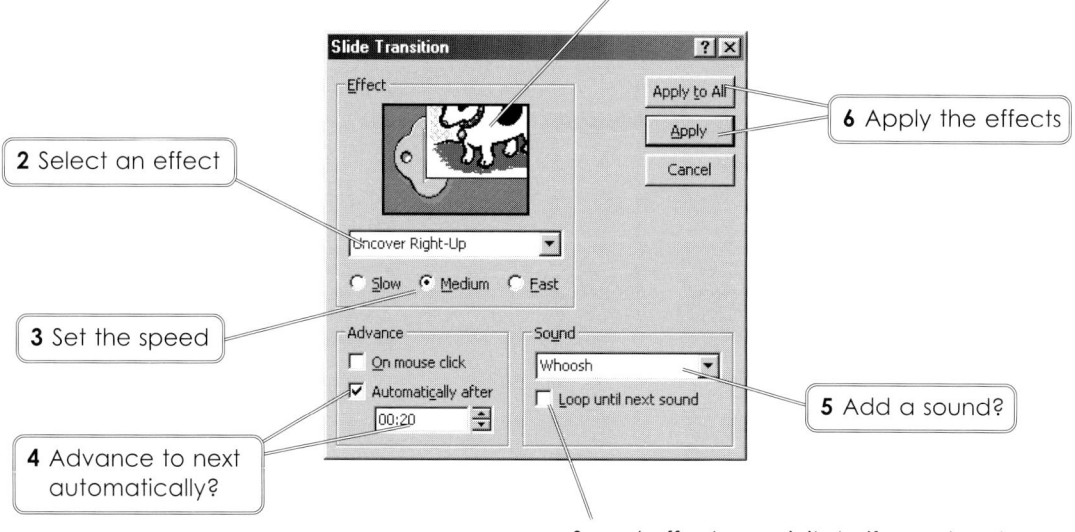

2 Select an effect

3 Set the speed

4 Advance to next automatically?

6 Apply the effects

5 Add a sound?

Sound effects can irritate if overdone!

Notes Page view

In Normal view, there is a small Notes pane at the bottom of the screen. You can write notes here – formatting the text, if you like. The notes can then be printed, with their slides for your own use when giving the presentation, or as handouts for your audience.

To enter notes:

❶ Go to Normal view.

❷ Select a slide.

❸ Click into the Notes pane and type the text.

❹ Format the text as required.

❺ Open the **View** menu and select **Notes Page** if you want to preview the page.

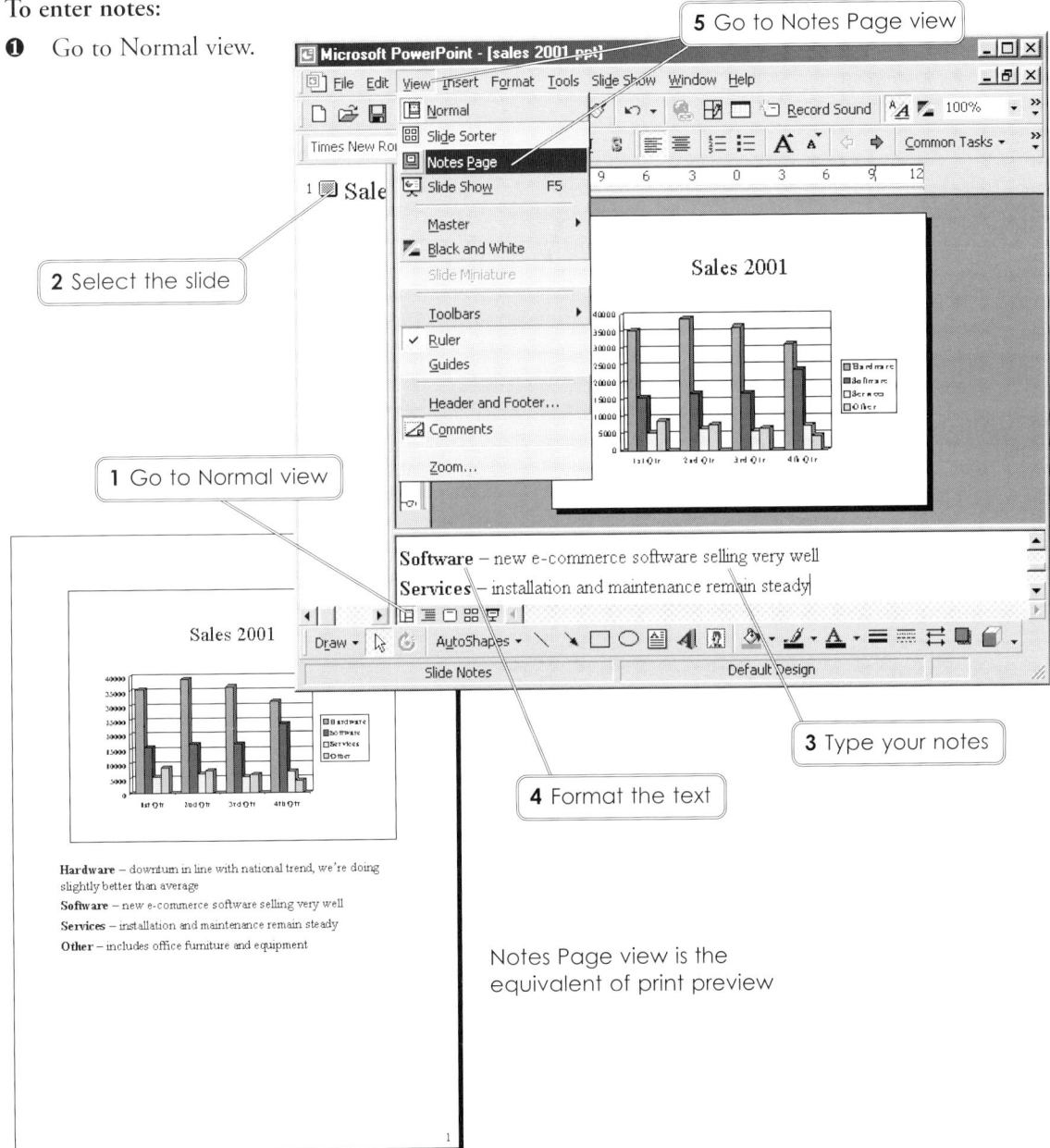

5 Go to Notes Page view

2 Select the slide

1 Go to Normal view

3 Type your notes

4 Format the text

Notes Page view is the equivalent of print preview

Using the computer

Word processing

Spreadsheets

Databases

Electronic communications

Presentations

Notes and handouts

If you want to give your audience some printed material, you could give them a straight printout of the slides, one to a page, but there are better alternatives.

➤ A Notes Pages printout will give the audience the slide and its accompanying notes, printed one per page.

➤ If there are no notes – or they are only for your use – a Handouts printout uses less paper. Handouts can be printed 2, 3, 4, 6 or 9 to a page.

To print for your audience:

❶ Open the **File** menu and select **Print…**

❷ Select the slides to be printed in the **Print range** area.

❸ Drop down the **Print what** list and select *Notes Pages*.

Or

❹ Select *Handouts* then set the number of **Slides per page**.

❺ Click **OK**.

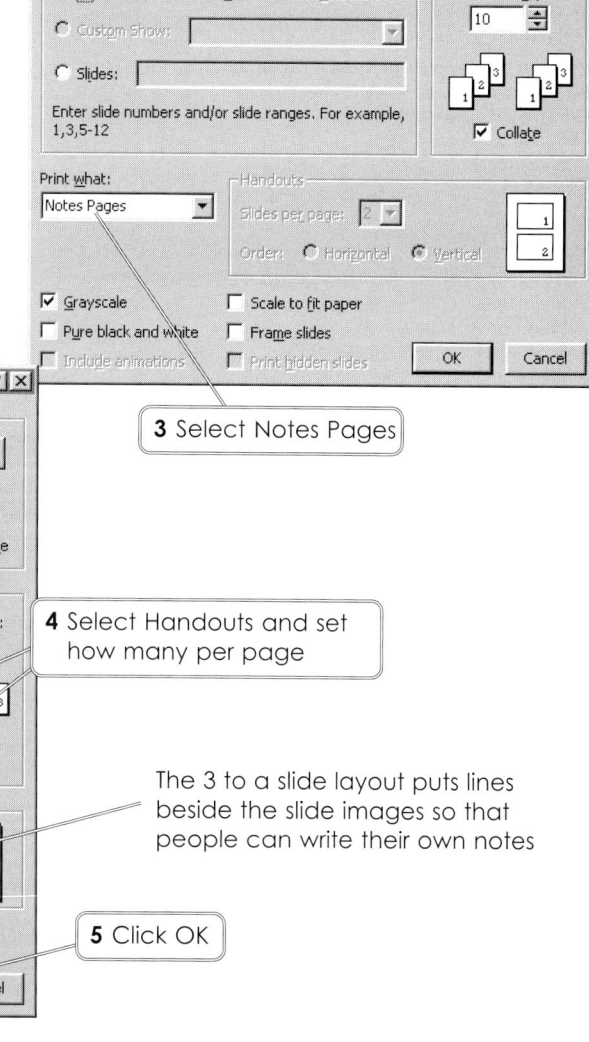

Remember to use the Print to file option when doing CIE assessments

2 Set the print range

3 Select Notes Pages

4 Select Handouts and set how many per page

The 3 to a slide layout puts lines beside the slide images so that people can write their own notes

5 Click OK

Custom shows

If you want to show only a selection of the slides, or present them in a different order – without actually moving or removing them from the presentation – you can set up a custom show.

To create a custom show:

❶ Open the **Slide Show** menu and select **Custom Shows…**

❷ At the **Custom Shows** dialog box, click **New**.

❸ Enter a name to identify the show.

❹ To include a slide in the show, select it and click **Add >>**.

❺ To change the order of a slide, select it and click the up or down arrows.

❻ Click **OK**.

To run a custom show:

❼ Open the **Slide Show** menu and select **Custom Shows…**

❽ Select the show and click **Show**.

1 Use Slide Show > Custom Shows…

Existing shows can be edited

2 Click New

8 Select the show and click Show

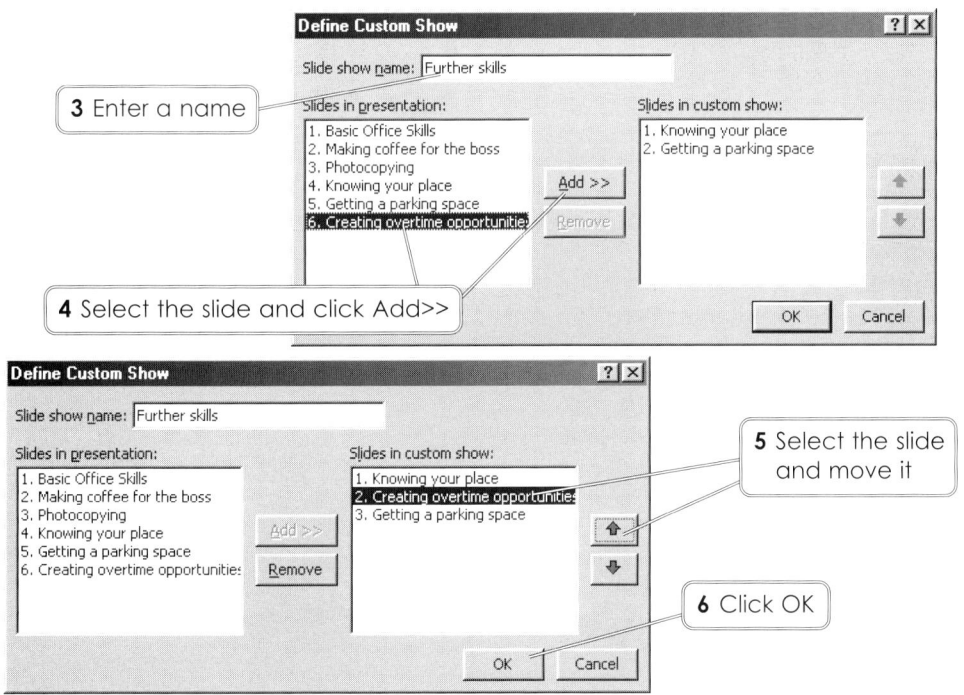

3 Enter a name

4 Select the slide and click Add>>

5 Select the slide and move it

6 Click OK

Using the computer

Word processing

Spreadsheets

Databases

Electronic communications

Presentations

Skills builder 19:
Printing and slide shows

This exercise gives practice in animating, adding notes, printing and running a short slide show.

❶ Open the file *Basic Office Skills.ppt* in the *Cambridge/Exercise files* folder.

❷ Set a different preset animation effect for each slide.

❸ Add transition effects between the slides. Use a *blind* between slides 1 and 2, a *checkboard* between 2 and 3, and a *dissolve* between 3 and 4.

❹ Add your own notes to the *Knowing your place* slide, then print it as a Notes Page.

❺ Set up a custom show containing two or three of the slides, calling it *My Show*.

❻ Save the edited presentation in your IT Skills folder.

❼ Run the slide show on your PC.

Are you ready?

Get your tutor to check your work.

If you have successfully completed the skills builder exercises in this section, and are confident in using those skills, you are ready for the *Presentations* test.

If you need a little more practice before taking the test, ask your tutor for the *Presentations* pre-test exercise.

Index

A

Access screen 66
Address Book 104
AND and OR queries 73
Animation, PowerPoint 125
Attachments to e-mail 102
Attributes of files and folders 6
AutoFit, Word 29
AutoFormats, Excel 52
AutoLayouts, PowerPoint 110
AutoSum, Excel 46
AVERAGE function, Excel 46

B

Backslash 4
Bcc: (Blind carbon copy) 99
Borders around slide objects 123
Bullets, Word 16

C

Cc: (Carbon copy) 99
Cell references, Excel 43
Charts
    Excel 54
    formatting 57
    PowerPoint 118
Clip Art
    PowerPoint 122
    Office 2000 27
    Office 97 26
Custom shows, PowerPoint 129

D

Data types, Access 67
Database window, Access 66
Databases
    modifying 67
    relational 69
Documents, Word 20
Drawing, PowerPoint
    lines 112
    rectangles 114
    ovals 114

Dynaset, Access 75

E

E-mail
    reply and forward 100
    sending 99
Excel tools 42
Explorer bar searches 90

F

Favorites, IE 95
Files
    attached to e-mail 102
    finding 8
    managing 2
    moving and copying 2
    selecting 2
    viewing 7
Find 8
Folders
    managing 5
    paths to 4
Formatting charts, Excel 57
Forms, Access 77
Formulae, Excel 43
    logical 50
Functions, Excel 46

H

Headers and footers
    Excel 60
    Word 19
Home page 87

I

IF function, Excel 50
Images, Excel 53
Indents, Word 17
Internet Explorer 86
Internet options 87

L

Line spacing, Word 14

M

Mail merge, Word 36
Margins
　Excel 59
　Word 22
Master Slides, PowerPoint 109

N

Notes and handouts, PowerPoint 128
Notes Page view, PowerPoint 127
Numbered lists, Word 16

O

Objects, PowerPoint 116
Operators
　Access queries 73
　Excel 43
Organization charts, PowerPoint 120
Outlook Express 97
　options 98

P

Page Setup
　Excel 59
　Word 22
Paper Size, Word 22
Paragraph formats, Word 14
Paths to folders 4
Pictures
　formatting 28
　show in IE 88
　Word 25
PowerPoint window 108
Print area, Excel 61
Print Preview, Excel 62
Properties of files and folders 6

Q

Queries, multi-table, Access 74

R

References, relative and absolute, Excel 45
Relational databases, Access 69
Relational operators, Access 73
Relationships, creating, Access 70
Reports, Access 80

S

Search engines 90
Search for files 8
　Windows Me 9
Searching the Web 90
Signatures 98
Slides
　modifying 110
　transitions between 126
Sorting, Access 75
Sound effects, PowerPoint 126
Subject: line, e-mail 99
SUM function, Excel 46

T

Tables
　formatting in Excel 52
　formatting in Word 31
　Word 29
Tabs, Word 18
Templates, Word 20
Text, Word
　formatting 13
　selecting 13
Toolbar buttons (IE5) 86
Transitions, PowerPoint 126

U

URLs 89

V

Views
　PowerPoint 108
　Windows Explorer 7
Viruses 103

W

Web page data 92
Web pages
　printing 94
　saving 92
Word tools 12
Worksheets
　multiple, Excel 48
　Word documents 33